PURSUE POSSIBILITIES

365 DAYS OF EXPLORING INTENTION, PURPOSE AND EXCELLENCE IN BUSINESS AND IN LIFE

SUSAN GOODMAN

Barringer Publishing, Naples, Florida
www.barringerpublishing.com
Cover art by Caroline Simas
Graphics, layout design by Lisa Camp
Editing by Carole Greene

ISBN: 978-0-9891694-5-5

Library of Congress Cataloging-in-Publication Data
Pursue Possibilites / Susan Goodman

Printed in U.S.A.

INTRODUCTION

Every business day for over three years, I have been blessed to write a morning message for a highly respected global company. No matter where we are or what time a flight is, my supportive, wonderful husband brews me uber bold coffee; and as I open my computer, I am as interested to learn what will emerge as a reader who is opening the email. I don't know what I will say until my fingers hit the keyboard. I wish I could tell you I have a master plan, but I don't. Like most of us, I am simply pushing through fears to contribute my purpose one day at a time. This book is the result of those early-morning appointments. I feel like I am given a gift every day, and I have a responsibility to give back.

They say we do what we have to learn the most. I think I write and speak about the negativity triplets—fear, pride and guilt—not only because I have to overcome them daily but because I have become an expert at them. I lived half my life with fear, pride and guilt, and we still hang out together at least once a day. I have learned to recognize them quicker and choose whether to run to my emotional closet or push through and keep going.

This book may be as much about my journey of pushing through fears as it is about you exploring what is possible in your life.

Like many of you, I experience thoughts like: "I want to make whatever difference I can, but I don't want notoriety." "I want to bring forth what is within me but 'what if' it's not valuable?"

We all have our pains, obstacles, mistakes and sad stories... and we all have a purpose we were born with. We can either let the triplets keep us going in circles or push through to pursue our possibilities. There are still days I wonder if I will have anything to say; then when it comes forth, I wonder why I ever doubted.

People often comment on my joy, I feel compelled to tell you there was a time in my life I didn't know if I would ever know real joy again because I let life happen to me instead of choosing it. And as a result, I would get to a certain point and fear would subtly remind me I wasn't worthy or good enough. I would then shrink and stop myself from going any further toward what I wanted or what I knew I could contribute. Many of you experience something similar or know someone who does—people who are squandering possibilities rather than pursuing them. If you are one of those people, I want you to know what is possible. We aren't going to get it right all the time and that's okay—we aren't supposed to. But we do want to keep moving toward our purpose instead of leaving it inside of us, unfulfilled and undone.

I am a believer in God, grace, people and not just second chances, but 5th, 8th, 27th, 62nd, 74th, 84th and 85th chances...we are all prodigals. I argue with my husband just like you, but we choose to be quick to recover, resolve and forgive. I have pains, struggles and problems, just like you and I mess up every day in some way. This book isn't about being perfect; it is about overcoming our imperfections to pursue our possibilities and fulfill our purpose. Let's do it together every day.

I am not a pyschologist (but I am related to one). My education is experiential—I have lived nearly every topic in this book for either three seconds or thirty years, and I have had great teachers along the way... some of them actually people, the rest sticky problems I had to persevere through. I don't have as many answers as questions (but I do always have an opinion) and maybe we can explore those together. Miss Amanda taught me that guilt separates us and Pam taught me not to feed the monster of co-dependency. I have learned and owe so much to more people than you care to see listed. Some of them are not currently part of my everyday living but their effects are. They may never know the impact they made on my journey.

My "healing" journey began when I realized that we pass things on to our kids—nieces and nephews and grandchildren. And I only wanted to pass the best on to these people I love most. I don't want to leave a legacy of fear or pride or bitterness. In order to pass on the best I can, I had to learn what that is. I still fall short, but I want them to use their gifts and be a contributor so I must try to do the same.

Like you, I also had people who impacted my life negatively, but I recognized I had a part in that, too. And it was my choice to step out of a victim-mentality and choose grace or stay in my personal pit and choose to keep myself stuck. If you find yourself unable to move through an obstacle or to unclog your emotional sink, get professional help. You have too many fabulous contributions inside of you to be stuck going in circles rather than stepping toward your goals and into "more wonderful than you can imagine."

I am annoyingly optimistic, high energy, high fun and very funny (*I think*)—

I tell you this because no matter how joyful or confident a person is or appears, each of us has to push through something to pursue possibilities. Nothing happens without faith and focus.

I want you to explore what's possible for you. Whether you do that by reading this book or through some other adventure, spend the time and energy necessary. We don't want to leave love ungiven because of pride...goals unmet because of fear...and possibilities unpursued because we didn't push through the obstacle of ourselves.

If you have a story, thought or possibility to share, email me at
susan@pursuepossibilities.com

Touch as many lives as you can, then come on home.
Cody Lane

JANUARY 1

BE COMMITTED

Happy New Year! Let's make this our best year yet. Our year of saying yes to our possibilities…opening wide the door and welcoming them in. That idea is scary to many of us because we have built walls of protection to keep from being hurt, embarrassed or criticized. Fear, pride and guilt have convinced us that is the safe way to go. And it is "safe". But safe doesn't equal security.

Many of us put part of our life on hold to complete something or because we get stuck—in a past moment, an unhealed wound or a multitude of mistakes. But when we do that, we miss the fullness of life and maybe what we are to contribute to the world. We compartmentalize and end up hitting the pause button on our desires. We are living, but we aren't engaging, growing and experiencing joy or genuine happiness. We are watching our possibilities pass by or happen for someone else. This is it. And it is time to hit the play button on our possibilities instead of keeping them on hold.

Let's make a decision to step out from behind our safety walls and make our decisions instead of allowing negative emotions to do it for us. If we aren't mindful, we can let life happen to us instead of making our own choices. The problem with this is that if we aren't doing the choosing, fear could be; and fear will leave us silent in shame, taking shortcuts to avoid embarrassment and making choices to avoid rejection. But that leaves us shrinking—not calling potential clients, withdrawing rather than talking honestly with our significant other, feeling inadequate and not experiencing the fullness of a contributing life that is there for each of us.

If you haven't already, write down your goals. Now pick one of them and make it your focused intention for the year. What do you want most? That is what you are going to give focus and attention to every day.

Go All-in with your possibilities rather than just going in circles with them. Hit the play button and unpause the joy to make this year a fun and productive one—your best year yet.

Success isn't a result of spontaneous combustion. You must set yourself on fire.
Arnold H. Glasow

JANUARY 2

BE AN INSTRUMENT OF INSPIRATION

I have come to the frightening conclusion that I am the decisive element. It is my personal approach that creates the climate. It is my daily mood that makes the weather. I possess tremendous power to make life miserable or joyous. I can be a tool of torture or an instrument of inspiration. I can humiliate or humor, hurt or heal. In all situations, it is my response that decides whether a crisis is escalated or de-escalated, and a person is humanized or de-humanized. If we treat people as they are, we make them worse. If we treat people as they ought to be, we help them become what they are capable of becoming.

Johann Wolfgang von Goethe

We are the decisive element in our lives. The problem with that is most of us do not want to be; we want someone else to be responsible for us emotionally, physically and financially. But the fact is, we decide if we will be happy or unhappy; a contributor or a taker; a healer or a punisher.

The first step in bringing your goals to fruition and having your best year yet is to take responsibility for yourself and what you are creating.

Make a decision to be an instrument of inspiration to yourself and others as you move forward toward your goals for the coming year. Your possibilities and your happiness could depend on it.

JANUARY 3
BE ON A TEAM

As we head into a new year full of possibilities, we need to reassess our team. To joyfully and successfully maneuver this life and business, we need a team: those people who give us guidance and support as we seek to be productive and happy.

When we are making changes to move forward with our goals, it is quite easy to slip back into old patterns and never get past "go." From getting physically fit to giving up a victim mentality, we will likely want to slip back to our old ways and will find many excuses against making the changes we say we want to make.

We need people around us who will help us achieve the excellence we desire to see in our lives, not just support our excuses.

If you don't want to make any changes in your life, then there is no need to assess anything. But if you want to change something, then likely you will need to turn previous ways of thinking inside out. We all need help to do that. If you don't already have those kinds of team members, hire them: a trainer, a counselor or a coach. Look at the changes you want to make this year and get the people on your team who will help you get there. Your possibilities are waiting.

Don't follow your dreams; chase them.
Richard Dumb

JANUARY 4
BE PREPARED

Possibilities are easier to see and pursue when we have an excellent team. Your team isn't just a cheerleading squad; your team is a subtle workforce sharing knowledge and ideas, pushing you through when you are stuck, and helping you remember you are awesome when you forget.

We also have team members that aren't part of our normal day, but that we want on our side when troubles arise. When your plumbing bursts, isn't it great to already have a plumber you trust and who knows you rather than having to find one, explain where you live, find out what he'll charge, and determine if he is credible...in the middle of the emergency?

When you have a problem with a client's account, it is much easier to call someone who you know has expertise in that area rather than calling and hoping you get someone who will turn over every rock to help you. Don't wait for the emergency. You know there are going to be problems ahead, so prepare for what is coming down the road as best you can.

Call a department you are starting to utilize or a company you are going to do business with and introduce yourself. Find out who your contact people are, get to know them, and put them on speed dial.

The world tries to tell us we are more powerful when we do it on our own. We are told that somehow our accomplishments are more meaningful if we struggled more for them than the guy down the hall. But when we do it on our own, our accomplishments aren't "bigger"; 100 million is 100 million. We are just lonelier, a little more worn out, and probably didn't have as much fun.

You are on your clients' teams. Who is on yours?

The main ingredient of stardom is the rest of the team.
John Wooden

JANUARY 5
BE DIFFERENT

To have our best year yet we might want to think of turning things upside down, for example: look at what the world says and try the opposite.

If the world says to fight, maybe talk it out.

If the world says to withdraw and sulk, try turning around and calmly expressing yourself.

If the world says to blame someone else, don't.

If the world says it's okay to lie to get what you want, try working on figuring out the truth.

If the world says you "deserve" something, consider that you probably really don't.

If the world says not to forgive someone, do.

Or take the advice of a reader who was depressed: she found a person who was happy and began to imitate her. Her life-long struggle with depression was changed.

Often it takes turning our world upside down and inside out to find new ways of living and new possibilities. We don't have to keep any new habits or behaviors we don't want to, but we might find we like the results.

We all mess up, but the more we can be deliberate about our lives instead of just going along with what we see around us, it's likely the happier we will be. It goes back to: do we want to be right or happy?

To have your best year yet, try the opposite of popular demand. You could be met with not only new possibilities, but a few miracles, too.

Observe the masses and do the opposite.
Walt Disney

JANUARY 6
BE POWERFUL

Without a doubt, to have our best year yet, an important component is to live in the present moment.

To live in this moment means we are completely engaged, not pre-occupied.

It means we are making decisions based on people as they are right now, not as they were three, five or ten years ago.

It means we are grateful for what we have now or did experience, not angry that we don't have it anymore.

It means we are more able to make the differences we are supposed to make now rather than be stuck in past ones.

It means we take the steps we are supposed to take today and let the path unfold rather than be afraid of it.

When our thoughts go to the past, they often involve pain. When they go to the future there is often fear. But when we act, live and love the best we can right now, without excuses, we are likely happier and more productive and probably allow others to be, too.

The point of power is always in the present moment.
Louise L. Hay

JANUARY 7
BE A WINNER

We have all heard the phrase pertaining to prizes: "You must be present to win." We decide whether the prize is important enough to us to choose to be there or if we will miss the opportunity. It is similar with our possibilities.

Possibilities live in the present moment. We must be present to win.

We decide whether the prize is important enough to show up for. We can be with a client but thinking about another client instead of hearing her needs. We can be home with our family but preoccupied with something else. We can be at a meeting but looking at our emails.

We can be alive right now but living in the past or the future.

Are you making decisions for the potential client sitting in front of you because of a past exchange or on the present situation? Are you making decisions about someone based on their past behavior or who they are now? (We all learn and grow.) Are you holding a grudge over something that happened yesterday or three years ago? (Are you perfect? Can you think of something you aren't proud of?)

The prize could be monetary or personal peace, but regardless, our relationships are stronger and our interactions more productive when we choose to be and live in the present.

Possibilities live in the present moment. If we choose to show up, we are pretty much guaranteed a prize.

*Life gives you plenty of time to do whatever you want
to do if you stay in the present moment.*
Deepak Chopra

JANUARY 8
BE FRESH

Learning to live in the present and *be* present will be a great contributor to having our best year yet. We must live in the now in order to continue to move toward our purpose instead of trying to relive an old one.

Do you keep reliving the highlight reel of your past? That can keep you in an illusion of something you are not. You are not a homecoming queen or a star athlete or your previous production level. Maybe you were, but you are not now.

Do you keep reliving the low-light reel of your past? That can keep you in an illusion of something you are not, too. You are not a victim and you are not your mistakes. Maybe you were, but you do not have to be now.

We want to use our lessons from the past to move forward to our next purpose, not try to keep reliving an old one.

One problem with gazing too frequently into the past is
that we may turn around to find the future has run out on us.
Michael Cibenko

JANUARY 9
BE PURPOSEFUL

What will make decisions for you today, your past or your purpose? Your circumstances or your intention?

Is it possible to live in the past and still fulfill our purpose for our future? It could be, but it seems tiresome rather than energizing.

What is your purpose?

What steps, activities or changes do you need to make to move toward it?

What is something you can do today?

If part of your purpose is to help people but you aren't doing business-building activities because you were told "No" by every person you talked to last month, you may be shying away from prospecting. Is your purpose to help people or to hide out in your emotional closet?

Living in past no's will keep us hiding out in our emotional closets, but living our purpose to help people will keep us talking to every person we can because we don't want to miss anyone who may need our support and service.

The commitment to our purpose must be fresh each day. People, problems and our own thoughts will attempt to deter us, but we must choose which direction we will go and with what kind of attitude. We can go back toward the past or forward toward our purpose.

Where are your better possibilities?

Learn from the past, set vivid, detailed goals for the future, and live in the only moment of time over which you have any control: now.

Denis Waitley

JANUARY 10
BE CONSCIOUS

As we talk about our purpose, we need to be aware that if a goal or our feeling of purpose involves something negative, we might want to ponder that. What does a negative purpose say about the state of a person's life/heart/happiness?

For example, consider whether a purpose or goal involves revenge instead of resolution: "He'll pay. I'll show her." Be aware if you enjoy tearing a person down rather than working to build a team: "She's an idiot. He stinks."

If you recognize your motives as negative, you might want to take a moment to ask yourself if that is what you really want. If it is, you can continue to choose that, but more often than not, it is one of those times that you are letting negative emotions make decisions for you rather than consciously making your choice. And if you stop and think about it, most likely that is what the person you are angry with did, too.

Where does the point of responsibility begin and where will the cycle of "revenge" end if not with us?

We seem to come to honest resolution and more productive outcomes when we are honest with ourselves. To have more productive interactions and more enjoyable relationships, try focusing on resolution (or forgiveness), rather than revenge, and building something positive, rather than tearing another person down.

It can take a while to process pain because we are human, but when we find ourselves stuck in anger, resentment or bitterness rather than moving through it, we probably want to stop and realize what we are choosing. Some possibilities depend on it.

How people treat you is their karma; how you react is yours.
Wayne Dyer

JANUARY 11
BE GIVING

To live our best year yet we must be conscious of what we give. Not money, but thoughts, words, attitudes, and actions.

What are you giving to the world or, on a smaller scale, to the people around you? Are you giving silence to someone you don't like or are you giving them the opportunity to be understood? (If we are giving silence, that is probably our own problem. We could be hiding behind it because we know we were wrong, too). Are you giving forgiveness or a grudge? Are you giving encouragement or criticism? Are you giving referrals or seeking only to get them? Rudeness or kindness?

You can call it karma, reaping what we sow, or something else, but often we get back what we have given—sometimes right then and, other times, years down the road.

We want our children to be affectionate with us, but we aren't willing to give affection to others. Or maybe we want someone to give us a break at work when we are having an off day, but we aren't willing to give the same break to a sales associate.

If we give to others what we want ourselves, we may not get "it" back right away, but we will be living more intentionally and probably happier regardless of whether we ever get the kindness back. In fact, contribution isn't about what we get back; it is about the pure joy that comes from giving goodness. Looking at what we give as coming back to us is just a good reminder for us to live and give our best.

If you get what you give, what are you going to be getting this year?

As I give, I get.
Mary McLeod Bethune

JANUARY 12
BE RESPONSIBLE

"If you get what you give," what are you going to be getting this year? Are you going to be getting grace or grudges? Resolution or revenge? Peace or guilt?

Stop and ask yourself if there is anyone you want to be unhappy, less popular or less successful than you. If you answered yes to any of those, that is a good indicator of jealousy. Jealousy has more to do with you than with the other person.

Stop and ask yourself if there is anyone you haven't forgiven. Unforgiveness has more to do with you than what anyone else did.

Stop and ask yourself how you may have been an obstacle in achieving previous goals. Sometimes it is just not yet a goal's time, but often your thoughts and choices keep a goal away instead of welcoming it in.

To have our best year yet, we want to focus on our goals instead of the "negative noise" that robs us of productivity by taking up our thoughts and energy.

The recognition that we have more control than anyone else over our attitude, goals and happiness is both irritating and exhilarating—irritating because we want to blame someone else rather than take responsibility ourselves and exhilarating because when we take that ownership of our lives, our possibilities become endless.

Freedom makes a huge requirement of every human being.
With freedom comes responsibility.
For the person who is unwilling to grow up, the person who does not
want to carry his own weight, this is a frightening prospect.
Arnold H. Glasow

JANUARY 13
BE FORGIVEN

Yesterday, we asked ourselves if there is anyone we haven't forgiven. Today, we want to make sure we have not forgotten to forgive an important person in our lives—ourselves.

As we prepare to have our best year yet and are clearing out emotional clutter, forgiveness is a great starting point. But we often miss the vital task of forgiving ourselves.

Many of us know at least a few things we need to forgive ourselves for, but if you still have unforgiveness for someone else, you will want to look there first. Well, you won't *want* to; that has likely been a problem all along. When we won't forgive someone, it could be because we don't want to look at our own contribution to the problem. Blaming and unforgiveness are ways to keep responsibility off of us and place it on someone else.

The problem with that behavior is we will be unhappy and not know why.

Are there any situations as adults that we do not have a part in—even if simply in our responses? When we blame, we are trying to make the other person completely responsible, so we get to continue playing a victim and using that role to control others. We can actually become addicted to victimization, angst and misery.

Could it be the more we blame, the more we need to forgive ourselves? Unforgiveness could be a way to keep the focus off our part in a situation. When we choose not to forgive, we move from being part of the original problem, to the whole of our current problem.

Remember, we all mess up pretty much every day, in some small way. So put aside pride and make a decision to forgive yourself and forgive others. If you need help, get it. You have way too much to do to waste another year playing chase with your goals and your happiness.

To forgive is to set a prisoner free and discover that the prisoner was you.
Louis B. Smedes

The weak can never forgive. Forgiveness is the attribute of the strong.
Mahatma Gandhi

JANUARY 14
BE LOSING CONTROL

Our energy, attitude and mood are contagious. Our happiness or unhappiness affects those around us. So if for no other reason, make a decision to forgive in order to not contaminate those around you.

When we look at it that way, we can see our responsibility to forgive, but here's where it can get sticky: you may find you have grown to like what being angry and holding a grudge gets you. It's hard to admit, but when we know our behavior is negatively affecting those around us (including those people we say we love) and we choose not to change, then we likely have found we enjoy what that behavior gets us.

It may not have started out that way, but now that you realize you can manipulate people with your anger, your judgment or your helplessness, you may not be willing to let it go so easily. You may wonder how you will get what you want if you make that change. *How would I control others and situations to be how I want them to be?*

Don't deny negative emotions. We all have to vent and process honestly in order to move through problems and hurts, but when we find we are enjoying them instead of experiencing them, it is probably time to let them go. Look at each thing and person you are still angry about and decide if you will hold onto it or let it go.

"Losing" control and letting go of the negative strongholds in our lives could be the first step to experiencing our best year yet. When we find we need help we want to ask for it because this year's possibilities are waiting.

I tried to manipulate and control people, and I harbored resentment.
I wanted to be forgiven, but I wouldn't forgive others.
Lauryn Hill

JANUARY 15
BE PROGRESSING

Having our best year yet includes moving forward. So what if we stopped blaming and started progressing?

As adults, very few situations occur that we do not have a part in, even if it was simply in our response (internal and external). We all need to process problems, but if we are still angrily blaming instead of moving on in life, we might also need to take a look at ourselves.

That old saying about when we point at another there are three fingers pointing back at us is a good reminder. In fact, try it out: when you blame another person, try to come up with three ways you contributed to the problem. It may be you can't come up with three, but your willingness to examine your part is the difference between blaming and owning—and may be the difference between misery and happiness.

Blaming wants to subtly deflect fault and create more pain. Owning wants to heal and move on. It doesn't mean we agree with the other person or that we like the situation; it just means we aren't willing to stay stuck in it.

If we are angrily blaming another instead of looking to understand/ resolve/discuss, then we are likely looking to hide an intention or behavior so that we can be "right." Make it a practice that when you angrily blame another, you also seek to own something you did to contribute to the problem. You may find yourself more willing to resolve the problem and move on instead of hold on to it.

Positive possibilities seem to multiply when we seek to understand rather than blame. Make this your best year yet!

The worst-tempered people I've ever met were
people who knew they were wrong.
Wilson Mizner

JANUARY 16
BE HOPEFUL

To have our best year yet, we must remember to dream. In some season of our lives, many of us forgot how to dream—we feel unworthy, we don't believe good stuff happens for us, or maybe we have become so pragmatic that we can't visualize anything more.

Dreaming lets us visualize a new way, decide if we really want that vision and if we do, motivates us to put our energy behind it. Our ability or inability to dream could be a reflection of our current state of hope. If we can't dream, we might have lost hope.

But thank goodness, hope doesn't have to be so hard to get back. Sometimes it just takes awareness, while at other times it may take a few books or a few visits with a friend, clergyman or therapist.

Whatever it takes, it's worth the work; because while we want to live in the present moment, we also want a strong hope that influences our actions in it. If we can't dream, we might not ever know all that is possible.

If you were to dream big, what would that dream be? Now, go beyond your self-imposed limits and take it two steps further. *That's* the dream we're going for.

If we don't dream and visualize, we could stay stuck in our fears. If you aren't dreaming, what are you afraid of?

It may be that those who do most, dream most.
Stephen Butler Leacock

JANUARY 17
BE A DREAMER

We can find ourselves dreaming for other people more than we dream for ourselves. Is that because we don't want to put the effort into our own? We would rather live through our children or friends than take chances ourselves.

Certainly, we can dream for others, but those persons will have to catch that dream if it is going to become reality. Others can dream for us, too, but they can't make it happen for us. Each of us must desire a vision for ourselves, believe in it and put the work in, to see it come to reality.

Ask people what their dream is for you. That dream will likely involve you pushing through a fear, facing pride in some way or owning your part in a problem. Sadly we aren't always willing to do those things, and thus a perfectly good dream is wasted.

The relationship remains broken, the destructive behavior continues, or maybe the fear keeps you from using your gifts and talents.

We don't have to choose others' dreams for us, but we do have to dream our own and do the work necessary to push through and make it come to life. Otherwise, we will have missed a really amazing part of living and, possibly, our purpose, too.

It is not folly to dream; big dreams are the seeds of great goals. What's your dream?

Capture your dreams and your life becomes full.
You can, because you think you can.
Nikita Koloff

Dreams are renewable. No matter what our age or condition, there are still
untapped possibilities within us and new beauty waiting to be born.
Dr. Dale E. Turner

JANUARY 18

BE CONNECTING THE DOTS

Did you ask those close to you what their dream is for you?

The question isn't because you should be taking on their dream (sometimes their dream is really just an agenda to get you to do what they want); it is because sometimes people see possibilities in us that we can't see for ourselves.

Many of us "under-dream." We don't give ourselves enough credit and can end up missing all that is possible for us. Rather than walking in the fullness of this life, we simply make it through without sticking out or risking much. We play it safe with our dreams so we won't be disappointed if they don't happen. Maybe worse, we play it safe with our dreams because we know they can happen.

We may know we can reach professional goals beyond our current ones, but we don't know how we would handle all the business and extra work.

We may know we can make a difference in the world, but we don't want the notoriety.

We may know we can continue to be promoted, but we don't want to listen to the critics.

If you have a dream you know will happen when you go All-in yet you are afraid of it, step back and, as Eleanor Roosevelt said, believe in its beauty. Don't worry about how it will happen; often all we need is waiting for us to simply uncover it... like a treasure hunt. We will look back one day to connect the dots, and find they were already connected for us.

What dreams did you shelve because they weren't happening for you? Get them back out, dust them off and decide if they are still a dream you desire. If they are, turn them into a solid vision.

Sometimes a dream is just a dream, but sometimes our dreams are a glimpse of our purpose.

$\mathcal{L}$❤

Be willing to be uncomfortable. Be comfortable being uncomfortable.
It may get tough, but it's a small price to pay for living a dream.
Peter McWilliams

The future belongs to those who believe in the beauty of their dreams.
Eleanor Roosevelt

JANUARY 19
BE READY

What is clouding your dream?

We forget that dreams come with problems, too. We might be living one of our dreams, but are experiencing difficulties we didn't see coming. We mustn't let those problems discourage us from dreaming new dreams. We all get worn down and worn out. We all want to give up. We think: *If this is living my dream, I don't want any more dreams.*

We get weary of mean-acting people, and of sometimes being unkind ourselves. We get tired of the obstacles that arise and lose hope…but we can't. We need that hope to dream a bigger dream…and to start taking action toward it.

Identify the obstacles that are clouding your dream. Push those things out of the way so you can get a clear vision for what you want and then make choices in thought and action that will move you closer to it. The dream may not come for a long time, but don't give up; possibilities come fresh every day. We want to be ready for them.

No matter how your heart is grieving, if you keep on believing,
the dreams that your wish will come true.
Walt Disney Company

JANUARY 20
BE SURRENDERED

Maybe one of the most important things you can do with your coming year's goals and accomplishments is to surrender them. I know that seems like a contradiction—why do all this work and preparation if you are only going to give up?

This surrender is not the waving of the white flag, "I give up" kind of surrender. This is the active, working, powerful kind.

Maybe think of it this way: *Resignation* is giving up and there is no power in it. *Surrender* is active and intentional and there is great power and peace in it.

When you work diligently toward your goal and surrender how it happens, you are able to stop worrying and fretting. (Take note, if you do not work toward your goal, no amount of surrender will help—you will still worry and fret.) To bring your goal to life, fully give yourself to it, deliberately working toward it with a focused intention.

Surrender does not mean you stop working, it means you stop struggling—and in doing so, you might start to have a little fun along the journey, too.

It is very difficult for us type-A personalities to walk the balancing act between making things happen and surrendering how they happen, but it is possible. True surrender helps you hear your manager when she has another idea for you to achieve your goal. It helps you tweak your plan midway when you find your current one isn't working; it allows you to ask for help and lets you make decisions. Because with surrender, you know your goal is coming—you aren't giving up on it; you are giving up fear and allowing it to happen.

Surrender helps you take "self" out of the situation and allows you to be flexible, relaxed and present as you deliberately move through this year toward your accomplishments and desires. Leave no possibility un-pursued.

A wise unselfishness is not a surrender of yourself to the wishes of anyone,
but only to the best discoverable course of action.
David Seabury

JANUARY 21
BE NOW

Today, tend to the one thing you have been putting off, the thing you have not wanted to do. Just do it or it will keep pulling you down until you use it to push you forward. The person you have wanted to avoid, the task you have been putting off, the blame you have been putting completely on someone else...

After you take action and do the one thing you have avoided, stop and experience how you feel. You will likely feel confident instead of hesitant, energized instead of weary.

What we avoid pushes us down, but if we will face it in the appropriate way, it will likely push us forward toward our goal. Sometimes "facing it" doesn't even involve an action; sometimes facing it is simply making a shift in our own belief system from blaming to taking responsibility. If your one thing you have been putting off does involve an action and you need help with determining what that is, get it. There are plenty of people who will give you guidance and support, but be conscious of whether they are people who will tell you the truth or only what you want to hear.

If your "avoidance" involves a person and they aren't willing to talk or work toward resolution, that's okay; we can't control others, but we can control ourselves. Our own willingness to talk things through (rather than avoid) is what is important. If we are willing and actually want to resolve an issue, then we aren't avoiding, we are waiting, which has its own set of difficulties. But the good news is we will still be confidently moving forward to our goals while we wait.

Whether it is building your business, doing your taxes or giving kindness, stop and ask yourself what you are avoiding and face it in the appropriate way—in action or attitude. You will be pushing yourself through to new possibilities.

We are so scared of being judged that we look for every excuse to procrastinate.
Erica Jong

JANUARY 22
BE PATIENT

Are you avoiding or are you waiting? What if you have faced your part in an issue and now you are waiting? Waiting has its own set of difficulties.

As we wait, we can grow impatient that we don't have what we want, and we all know what choices come with impatience: we can choose acceptance or frustration. If you are sitting in traffic and want to get somewhere, what do you do? Accept the situation or become angry? We control our emotions or we let them control us. When we let our emotions control us we can begin to make decisions based on anger and frustration rather than on what is the right thing for us to do.

Whether we are waiting for an answer or for the right relationship, we want to be aware of our emotions in our waiting. In our impatience, we can end up going down the "wrong" road because we settle for good enough when "right for us" is just around the corner.

We are human; when our dreams and desires are slow in coming, we can grow weary of waiting and become discouraged. When that happens, we have to find a way to push through the disappointment—surrender the timing, persevere or try something new. Only we can know what is right for us. But we do know that ongoing anger, bitterness and blame aren't our best choices.

Be aware that waiting can be difficult and determine what you need to help you get through without blaming or taking shortcuts. Because impatience can make you angry, bitter or something else you don't want to be.

Impatience can cause wise people to do foolish things.
Janette Oke

JANUARY 23
BE TACTICAL

Where do we get our attitudes? Well, we get a bit from genetics, part from experiences, a lot from thoughts, or our own choices and some...we catch.

Have you ever walked into a room with a bad attitude and walked out of it with a great one because of the people, or music or colors that were in it?

Of course the opposite can occur, too. We can walk in feeling great and walk out feeling inadequate. The point is we want to be aware of what improves our mood and attitudes so that we can utilize those tools when we find ourselves in need of a lift. People who seem in a good mood all the time aren't just that way; they have developed their own personal tactics for catching a good attitude. Whether it is reframing a thought, stretching for ten minutes a day, dancing or hitting a punching bag—they have put in the work to figure out what punches their "productive button."

Are there any mornings you pop up and exuberantly want to take on the day? What are you doing that day that you are looking forward to?

How can you incorporate something similar in other days?

What elevates your mood? ...music, giving, talking to a particular person, finding the truth? What inspires you? What sets you on fire?

You have goals to accomplish and purposes to fulfill. If you don't know your personal tactics to lift your mood or create a personal buzz around your goal, contact someone on your team to help you identify your tools to set you on fire. When you want to quit in the middle of your goal or just in the middle of a day, you will be prepared to push through and persevere.

You will be surprised how much more you will accomplish and how you will positively affect those around you when you create and implement your personal tactics to catch a good attitude.

Our attitude toward life determines life's attitude towards us.
John N. Mitchell

JANUARY 24
BE AWESOME

There is a t-shirt that reads, "I was born Awesome." You were born Awesome. You still are. Do you feel it?

If you don't, what happened to your Awesome? You are probably thinking about the argument with your daughter this morning and don't feel so awesome. Or about the fifteen pounds weighing you down. Or about wanting something unfortunate to happen for someone who hurt you so you can "get them back." Or those things you did that were not nice or the ones that were just flat-out wrong. Or the times you hurt people or were rude or when you wanted to make yourself look better in a situation. And when you lied or were greedy or resentful. All those thoughts and more come flooding in to remind you that you are not so awesome.

We can look and be confident and ready to reach any goal we have, but as we move closer to some of them, we might silently pull ourselves back because we have lost some of our "Awesome." I assure you, you still have your Awesome. We just cover it up sometimes. No matter what we have done, said or thought, we can get our Awesome back.

What choices in action, thought, intention and word have you made that you think took some of your Awesome? Write them down and own them. If you need to apologize, seek understanding, let go of your selfishness, stop blaming someone else, own your part, or forgive, do it.

We have all fallen short. We have all had times or even seasons that our behavior was not Awesome or even close. But do not let those past times of < (less than) choices keep you from fulfilling your purpose and pursuing every possibility. Remember, if we will own those times we fell short, we can make a difference for someone else and help others avoid the pains and problems we experienced. And in fact, you might have even *more Awesome* and wisdom because you turned things around.

Live in the present moment. In this moment, do you feel Awesome? If not, why not?

It's time to get our Awesome back.

Self-confidence is the first requisite to great undertakings.
Dr. Samuel Johnson

JANUARY 25

BE YOUR OWN AWESOME

One way we let insecurities creep into our confidence and sabotage our goals and possibilities is that we let others' opinions of us decide our Awesomeness. Do not let anyone else decide your Awesome but you.

Yes, it is wonderful to hear praise about ourselves or our work, but there will be a time when there is no praise and we will need to be able to keep living happily and keep working toward goals. Remembering (or Finding) our Awesomeness will help us do that. People say don't listen too much to the critics or the praise. That is so true for healthy self-confidence and motivation.

Listen to the criticism, make adjustments you think are needed, forget about the rest and move on. And do the same with the praise. Listen to praise, realize what you are doing well, note what you need to work on, forget about it and move on. Sometimes people's praise or criticism is accurate, but there are just as many times that praise or criticism is based on their own agenda, jealousy, or insecurities. We do not want our accomplishments and emotions dictated by the words of others instead of by our purpose. Otherwise we can end up with more regrets than we would like.

Remembering "too much" of criticism and praise can have you living in the accomplishments or "failures" of the past rather than being the best you can and making a difference in the present. If you need praise to feel Awesome, you want to take a step back and ask yourself why that is.

More possibilities are pursued on the strength of our own Awesomeness than on a thousand other people's opinions.

The tragedy is that so many people look for self-confidence and self-respect everywhere except within themselves, and so they fail in their search.
Dr. Nathaniel Branden

JANUARY 26
BE ESTEEMED

Feeling valued and amazing isn't a feel-good thing to help you keep a smile on your face and a happy front for the world. It is the deeper sense of knowing you are valued and worthy. If we do not have a healthy self-esteem we may stop ourselves from doing all we are capable of.

Simply put, our self-esteem is how we treat or view ourselves. Self-esteem levels can be revealed in how we allow others to treat us and in how we treat others. It seems the more authentically healthy our self-esteem, the kinder and more honest we are with ourselves and those around us. Life is dynamic and ever changing. We are going to have areas and seasons of low self-esteem; look at those as signals showing you where you need to heal something or learn a lesson. And then seek to heal or learn that lesson.

We do not want to look back on our lives and say, I could have done more. I could have done better.

This is it.

To reach our endless potential and make the difference we are supposed to make for our clients and community, we must recognize our value and the value of those around us. Our possibilities depend on it.

Having a low opinion of yourself is not "modesty." It's self-destruction.
Holding your uniqueness in high regard is not "egotism."
It's a necessary precondition to happiness and success.
Bobbe Sommer

JANUARY 27
BE IM-PERFECT

Healthy self-esteem is important in pursuing our possibilities and completing our goals.

Understanding that healthy self-esteem is not perfection is just as important. Your work brings high responsibility and things must be right, but none of us is perfect and a belief that we should be will certainly wear us down.

Working for excellence is energizing. But working for perfection is frustrating and oftentimes counterproductive because we won't let something go until it is "perfect."

We can't schedule a client event because we can't find the perfect venue. A great place is important, but which is more important, the perfect spot or your clients and future clients being informed and connecting with you?

We won't put a communication process in place until every letter is just right and the time cycles are perfect. But which is more important, deciding between letter A and letter B (both of which are appropriate) or serving your clients through communication and connecting?

What have you been putting off because it is not "perfect" yet? Move on it today, and if you need help evaluating its usability, talk to your manager or someone you respect to help you push through and either let it go, or go for it. Stop and recognize the difference between which of your job responsibilities need to be "perfect" and which ones just need to be done.

More possibilities are born from an attitude of excellence than an expectation of perfection.

Healthy self-esteem is important in pursuing our possibilities and completing our goals.

Striving for excellence motivates you; striving for perfection is demoralizing.
Harriet Braiker

JANUARY 28
BE LIGHTER

When we refresh, we feel lighter, more creative and more productive. We want productive interactions and moments, so sometimes we need to look at signals in our lives to find hidden things that could be pulling us down.

One signal of a negative emotion hiding out in our lives is choosing silence. If you won't talk to your friend, associate, or family member (whether for ten minutes or for ten years), there is likely a problem you need to deal with.

In the short term, if you are angry and leave the room and won't talk, you need to hit "refresh" and deal with your negative emotions. Over the longer term, if you find there is a relationship you have chosen to be silent and not communicate in, you probably need to hit "refresh" and deal with your emotions. The silent treatment is a form of punishment, but while we intend that punishment for the other person, we are also hurting ourselves, too.

When we don't like someone or choose silence, it is likely about us and not the other person. Maybe we are jealous, angry, selfish or we just don't need them anymore.

Negative emotions weigh us down. So if you find a negative emotion is the cause of your silence, hit the refresh button and get to the truth. You will feel lighter.

For example: A person received a phone call out of nowhere from a former colleague who had treated her coolly and didn't communicate with her for years. The former colleague called to say that she had been jealous and wanted to apologize for her behavior. When she got to the source of her silence, she found jealousy and she dealt with it. Both parties were refreshed and lightened with that call.

Sometimes it takes courage to deal with our truths. Sometimes it takes a while to figure out what the truth is, but when we do, it helps to bring it out. If not to the person involved, then to your friend, therapist or your journal. And as always, if you need help, get it.

The silent treatment is often a signal of our own negative emotions. Get to the truth and we will likely be hitting the refresh button for the moment, for our lifetime and, certainly, for our possibilities.

You never find yourself until you face the truth.
Pearl Bailey

JANUARY 29
BE ENERGETIC

To really enjoy this New Year and experience all the possibilities it has to offer, we may need to move "self" out of the focus of our lives. Have you ever noticed that we are happiest when we are "others"-focused rather than self-focused?

Now it goes without saying we have to take care of ourselves mentally and physically, and have healthy boundaries. But when we are unhappy in a moment, often it is because we are more concerned about us, what we will get and what people think of us.

One of the biggest possibilities busters is self-pity. "How could you?" "Why did this happen to me?" "Why me?"

Those are great questions to ask, but with an intention of seeking to understand and own your part in the situation rather than the pity-seeking, finger-pointing intention many of us tend to have when we ask those questions.

Which gives more energy and perspective to you and the situation? A response of—"Here it is, what am I going to do about it?" Or a response of—"Poor me?"

When we get caught in self-pity, we want others to be responsible for us. We want to get others on our side. We want someone to blame and we won't accept our responsibility.

We know blaming doesn't open up new possibilities and we know pity doesn't do any good in the long run. We may be able to gather sympathy and play the victim, which feels good to us now, but we will still be unhappy and not know why.

We are either pitiful or powerful. Wallow in the pity for a little while, then bust out of it, because we aren't going to find new possibilities or happiness until we do.

Self-pity is easily the most destructive of the non-pharmaceutical narcotics; it is addictive, gives momentary pleasure and separates the victim from reality.
John W. Gardner

JANUARY 30

BE UNCOMFORTABLE

Seize this day to recognize blame and look for objective balance. The problem may involve someone else, but the source likely involves us. The source and solution starts with "I" not "they."

One of the reasons for this is our choice of response. Maybe our child drives the car and leaves it on empty. We forget to check the gauge and end up running out of gas. We can be angry, annoyed or we can be grateful to have AAA to bring us some help.

We choose our reaction to things and we can choose drama or blame, or something else that escalates an issue. (We can choose this if we want; we just need to know we are choosing it.) Or we can choose objectivity, an intention to work things through and find a workable solution so the problem doesn't arise again.

There is rarely a time that we do not have a responsibility in a problem. And of course, at some point, we may want to have a conversation about the other person's responsibility, too. But starting a conversation with blaming someone else, rather than seeking a solution, is a signal we may want to check our perspective.

Blaming may be comfortable, but it tends to take focus and energy away from a solution and leaves everyone with the problem.

We habitually erect a barrier called blame that keeps us from communicating genuinely with others, and we fortify it with our concepts of who's right and who's wrong. We do that with the people who are closest to us and we do it with political systems, with all kinds of things that we don't like about our associates or our society. It is a very common, ancient, well-perfected device for trying to feel better. Blame others.... Blaming is a way to protect your heart, trying to protect what is soft and open and tender in yourself. Rather than own that pain, we scramble to find some comfortable ground.

Pema Chodron

JANUARY 31
BE MINDFUL

Take thirty seconds to count your blessings…just thirty seconds to be grateful for the things we can easily take for granted. Things like electricity, heat, safety, the market opening when it is supposed to, a home, waking up to family, our friends, the garbage truck coming, games to watch, music to listen to, phone service, a job, a car that works, freedom, insurance, roads.

Gratitude is miracle working. The effect it has on our lives, happiness and outcomes is immeasurable and indescribable. So while someone can tell you about the power in gratitude, you likely need to experience it yourself to believe it.

Try taking thirty seconds a day for one week and writing down at least three things you are grateful for. You will likely find a shift for the better in relationships, attitudes and outcomes because a grateful awareness seems to bring more positive possibilities than an unappreciative mindlessness.

A grateful mind is a great mind,
which eventually attracts to itself great things.
Plato

FEBRUARY 1
BE LOVING

It's February...the "love" month. But what if we simply looked at it as the "No Fear" month? If we really focus on "love" instead of fear, we will push out fears and not only take action on what we have avoided, but maybe even begin to enjoy our lives and jobs more.

Fear avoids. Love doesn't.

If we focus on ourselves and fear, we won't call our clients when they have lost money or when we've lost the shipping order. But if we focus on "loving" and serving our clients, we will make the uncomfortable calls when the market goes down or when the shipping date has changed.

If we focus on us and our fears, we won't go to our manager when we didn't get the paperwork in on time. But if we focus on doing a great job for the client, we will go immediately to ask for help to get the overdue paperwork through.

When you find yourself avoiding, stop and ask yourself: "Am I making this decision based on serving my customer and company or on serving my fears?"

Decisions made in the best interest of everyone are likely better decisions than those based on avoiding being yelled at or avoiding admitting a mistake. "Love" doesn't avoid. Possibilities show up when we address an issue instead of trying to hide it in the back of the closet.

Avoiding the topic doesn't help it go away.
Unknown

FEBRUARY 2
BE NOT BEHIND

Others get ahead of us when we avoid.

Other people get "ahead" in relationships we want to have because they will have the difficult conversations we won't.

Other people get ahead in jobs we want because they will do the marketing and extra activities we won't.

Others get ahead in fitness because they will do the physical work we won't.

We don't want to compare ourselves to others, but when we find we are looking at someone's back who is ahead of us, we might want to reassess our plan and its execution. Instead of being mad at others, we need to take a look at ourselves and see if we avoided responsibility instead of "loved" (our job, a person, business-building or being fit).

So when you find yourself jealous of another person, just try doing some of the necessary tasks you avoided in the past and see if perhaps you move forward to a point that you lose your jealousy and anger. The person you lose the anger for will likely be yourself, because when we are jealous, isn't that just a signal that we aren't happy with ourselves? It is easier to put the anger on someone else than on us and that's when it becomes jealousy.

When you find you are not progressing the way you want to be, stop and examine whether you are avoiding the tasks and processes involved in your goals or "loving" them. Fear avoids, love doesn't. Sometimes we have to fall in love with the process in order to be in love with the outcome.

Don't be afraid of your fears. They're not there to scare you.
They're there to let you know that something is worth it.
C. Joybell C

FEBRUARY 3
BE A TREASURE HUNTER

What are you afraid of?

Our fears often dictate our actions, and unless we are intentional, we don't realize it.

Do you want to make your life's decisions or have fear do it for you? You and fear may agree sometimes, but don't you want to make sure you are making a decision based on what is right for you rather than on avoiding what you fear?

I read that "fear crushes the treasures." What treasure is fear crushing in your life?

Is there a prospective client you aren't contacting because fear says, "They won't do business with you"?

Is there a personal relationship, you aren't engaging in because fear says, "You don't have to forgive that person" or "She's better than you"?

Is there a hobby you would like to try but you aren't because pride says, "You won't be good enough at it anyway"?

Not everything is good or right for us and we want healthy boundaries. The point is to stop and be intentional about what we want and where we want to go rather than allow fear to decide for us.

Make a list of things you are afraid of—from spiders to losing control over someone. When we find out what we are afraid of, we may find possibilities, too.

Find out what you're afraid of and go live there.
Chuck Palahniuk

FEBRUARY 4
BE LIVING YOUR PURPOSE

I read a heading: "Don't live beneath your calling."

How many of us can honestly say we are not living beneath our purpose, our gifts, and our potential? Probably very few of us, because we allow other things to get our attention—like our fears.

We have been given the gifts we need to fulfill our purpose. All of us have the talents and abilities we need to live our purpose—some talents we aren't aware of yet because we have been afraid to try something new. When we don't allow fear to stop us from moving in a new direction, we could begin to live our purpose instead of beneath it.

For example, maybe you feel you are supposed to share information you have—your stories, knowledge—perhaps to educate others, but you won't speak in public because you are afraid. If helping people through educating them about their financial or health issues is part of your purpose but you will not push through a fear to do that, you are likely living beneath your purpose.

Keep in mind that none of us knows the whole plan or has all the knowledge we need up front. The plan unfolds as we go. With every step we take forward, we get what we need (the knowledge, resources, etc.), but if we stay in the same spot, we are going to mark time with the same information and the same story. When you first started at your job, did you have all the knowledge you have today? No, none of us did. But you sought it out and it was given as you needed it.

We don't have to know up front how things are going to turn out; we simply have to be willing to say yes to our possibilities, and that means saying no to fear. We don't have to do anything we don't want to do and we certainly do not want to do anything that isn't good for us. However, if we are not moving in a direction we know is right for us because it's unfamiliar or because we are afraid, we might need to use "no fear" month to push through and see what's on the other side.

Sometimes we find our purpose isn't in the obtaining of the dream but simply in the pursuit of it.

Curiosity will conquer fear even more than bravery will.
James Stephens

FEBRUARY 5
BE SUCCEEDING

We have all experienced fear of failure, but what about fear of success? Most of us would deny ever being afraid of succeeding, but we probably have been at some point.

What if I get that big account and then something goes awry?

What if I succeed at getting a large turnout at the seminar but then I don't lead it well?

What if I achieve this goal but encounter problems?

What if I "make it" and people criticize me?

There are always going to be problems and there are always going to be people who don't like us. It helps to expect both—not fearfully expect them—but preparedly expect them. For example, there will be problems, but there will also be solutions, and problem solving can actually strengthen a relationship if done well. There will always be people who don't like us, often because they haven't taken the time to seek to understand us yet. (So we probably want to remember to like people where they are rather than waiting for them to be who we want them to be, because we would like that same courtesy.)

We all have fears of success, so maybe our question becomes: am I moving toward my purpose? We KNOW we can achieve our purpose. If we are moving in the direction of our purpose but we choose to shrink back in fear instead of step forward in curiosity, we are likely afraid of succeeding at exactly what we are supposed to become. We don't know the plan up front, but we do know that if we are seeking to serve our clients and to do the right thing, the plan will unfold and likely be better than we could have imagined. We don't want to miss our purpose simply because we are afraid of it.

What one step can you take today to move toward your purpose and serving those you are supposed to serve?

Procrastination is the fear of success. People procrastinate because they are afraid of the success that they know will result if they move ahead now. Because success is heavy, carries a responsibility with it, it is much easier to procrastinate and live on the "someday I'll..." philosophy.
Denis Waitley

FEBRUARY 6
BE EXCELLENT

We can be fearful of success for many reasons. One is that the "bigger" we get, the more of a "target" we become and most of us don't want to be target practice for critics. Many of us would rather not be famous—whether in the world or just in our community—we would much rather fly under the radar. But if we shrink back instead of moving forward, we could end up shrinking back from our purpose.

We have a responsibility to our purpose in this life. So if you are one of those people who have a fear of success, try taking it all one step at a time and let the plan unfold. Shoot for excellence, not perfection, as you serve your clients and family, and you will also end up serving your purpose. If you still have anxiety and find yourself fearful instead of enjoying the journey, talk with people who have already excelled in the area you are working in and ask how they handle the things you are concerned about.

We can't be afraid of where excellence may take us or we will end up desiring to be mediocre.

Many of our fears are tissue-paper-thin,
and a single courageous step would carry us clear through them.
Brendan Francis

FEBRUARY 7
BE DETERMINED

Our fears can dictate our actions and we not be aware of it. Therefore, a good exercise for us is to list our fears.

Make a list of the things or situations you are afraid of and as the opportunity presents itself, face a fear. You may have done this exercise before and, if so, you know the benefits—so you will probably be excited about doing it again. Old fears linger and new fears pop up and you do not want them deciding your direction in life.

From being afraid of the water to being afraid to run into someone, our fears affect us and those around us. After you make your list, be creative about how you might face the fear. For example: If you are afraid of the water, sign up for a mini triathlon.

It is not always fun to push through a fear and we don't have to do so, but we want to know we are making the choice and that it is no longer being made for us by fear.

Confront your fears, list them, get to know them,
and only then will you be able to put them aside and move ahead.
Jerry Gille

FEBRUARY 8

BE CREATIVE

When you made your list of fears yesterday, did you have any thoughts on creative ways to face them?

You have heard it said that we create our lives. When you look at the list, can you recognize any ways your fears have shaped your life?

…Situations or people you have avoided?…Opportunities you were presented with when you said "No" rather than "Yes!" "No" is healthy and we need boundaries, but when we are saying no to things that would make our lives and our contributions richer, we may need to reconsider.

If you are afraid of spiders, you may have said no to really cool things you wanted to say yes to—like a trip to Africa or South America.

If you are afraid of flying, you may have said no to a trip with your family or to business opportunities.

If you are afraid of speaking, you may have said no to business-building opportunities.

Ask yourself: Is this serving me, my clients or the people around me? If not, reconsider.

You can definitely say no, but make sure it is you saying no, not your fears declining possibilities for you.

Do not let your fears choose your destiny.
Unknown

FEBRUARY 9
BE OPPOSITE

When fear and pride are involved, oftentimes our best choice is the opposite of what we "want" to do. When we are prideful and want to be churlish and silent, the opposite (communication) is likely better. When we are afraid and want to avoid calling the client or potential client, the opposite (making the call) is likely better.

Fear paralyzes us and stops us from acting (What will they think of me? Who am I to... ?, I can't go talk to him.) So what if when we want to freeze, we use it as a signal to act? When we don't want to give a kindness, we give it. When we don't want to reach out to someone, we do. When we don't want to praise someone for a job well done, we speak the praise anyway.

Timing is important. Sometimes we have to wait on the right time to act. But we know the difference between waiting on the right time to act and avoiding to act because of fear or pride. One waits patiently for its possibilities to come together while the other tells your possibilities to go away.

Inaction breeds doubt and fear. Action breeds confidence and courage.
If you want to conquer fear, do not sit home and think about it. Go out and get busy.
Dale Carnegie

FEBRUARY 10
BE LIVING YOUR DREAMS

When you look back on life, the times you will want to change are likely not the times you acted in love (kindness, encouragement, forgiveness, praise), but the times you acted on fear or pride (avoiding, withholding kindness, not saying the encouraging words, shrinking back in fear instead of stepping forward, seeking to be right instead of to resolve).

I saw an advertisement saying thousands of men will die this year because of stubbornness. That could be applied to many situations. Thousands of marriages and relationships will dissolve this year because of stubbornness. Thousands of people will miss out on happiness because of pride. Thousands of potential clients will not be helped this year because of fear of rejection. Thousands of people will wish they had…

Are you embarrassed to walk into an event or excited? Are you fearful to find new clients to make a positive difference for or are you excited? Are you seeking to stay angry after an argument or elated to forgive and move on? The tiny shift from fear, pride or guilt to "love" can make all the difference in your attitude.

Don't miss your possibilities because of fear or pride. Many are exchangeable, but some have a shelf life.

Do not let your fears choose your destiny.
Unknown

Too many of us are not living our
dreams because we are living our fears.
Les Brown

FEBRUARY 11
BE EMBRACING POSSIBILITIES

What is one thing you are afraid of today? Afraid to see someone who holds you to past mistakes? Afraid to admit you were wrong? Afraid people will find out you don't know all the answers?

Once you know what it is, embrace it. Embrace (willingly accept instead of avoid) seeing that person, admitting you were wrong or that you don't know all the answers.

When we embrace something we are afraid of, our fear begins to dissipate and we can gradually move through it rather than being stuck in it.

Our attitudes and perspectives are important to our possibilities. We want to make sure we are helping them rather than hiding from them.

Panic at the thought of doing a thing is a challenge to do it.
Henry S. Haskins

FEBRUARY 12
BE LIMITLESS

Our fears limit us. Certainly, our skill sets limit us, along with our attitude and our physical situation, but what limits us the most could be our own fears and doubts.

A young teenager takes his younger brother on junior triathlons with special equipment (I can't do that). A spouse forgives the other—and him or herself—and the relationship becomes stronger (I won't do that). A person pushes through fear of succeeding (what if I fail...?).

The fullness of life is there for all of us for the taking. It is the choices we make along the way that determine if we live all the life we were meant to. Are we giving up? Are we quitting on our goals because of pride or fear? Are we lying to ourselves and others? Are we choosing love, grace and forgiveness or anger, resentment and bitterness? Because I am thinking that the second choices are not going to be the key to a limitless life.

Perhaps one of the best things we can do to live unlimited is to stop blaming and take personal responsibility for ourselves and where we are, not look to others for our happiness, finances, security or to fix what we don't like in our lives or ourselves. When we do that, not only do we stand a better chance of fulfilling our purpose but we also begin to push through fears that have limited us previously.

Taking personal responsibility is a great first step to unlimited possibilities. Look at it as blame and entitlement are cement bricks attached to our feet and acceptance and gratitude are big balloons that help us soar. Do you want to be stuck in the cement or soar to more than you imagine?

Somebody should tell us...right at the start of our lives...that we are dying. Then we might live to the limit, every minute of every day. Do it! I say. Whatever you want to do, do it now! There are only so many tomorrows.
Michael Landon

FEBRUARY 13
BE IMPROVING

Everyone has had "bad" experiences: clients leaving, accidents happening, broken relationships at work or homes.

If we haven't dealt with them honestly, then we could have grown bitter rather than better. Better is excellent; bitter is a signal we need to hit the refresh button.

We are always growing either crooked or straight. Bitter or better. Crooked keeps us going in circles, but straight is a more direct path to our goals and a happier life. Sadly, our biggest times of growth seem to be through pain, and when we get angry about that pain and fearful of the future, bitter can set in. So not only are we angry, but we have missed the lesson and maybe a purpose for the pain.

On the other hand, when we step back and look for the lessons (which most of us don't want to do because we have to look at our contributions to the problem), healing begins and better overcomes bitter.

If you want to refresh, look at memories of situations that "leave a bad taste" (the memory of what an associate said, the memory of something you did, the memory of a "failure"), you will likely find something you are bitter about that needs converting so you can be more productive and engaged for your clients, future clients, family and yourself. We all have problems, we all make mistakes, we all have pains. The attitude of "what can I learn?" rather than "why me?" will give us a more curious perspective as we move through the problem, so we are more likely to come out better on the other side.

Hit the refresh button on old hurts and you will experience fresh, new possibilities.

Affliction comes to all not to make us sad, but sober; not to make us sorry, but wise; not to make us despondent, but it's darkness to refresh us, as the night refreshes the day; not to impoverish, but to enrich us, as the plow enriches the field;...
Henry Ward Beecher

FEBRUARY 14
BE UNHURT

It seems appropriate to talk about love and possibilities since it is Valentine's Day, but not the romantic kind—the love that is kindness, patience, honoring those around you and treating others as you would like to be treated. You have heard that it is giving not receiving that makes us happy. Why does happy matter? Because possibilities are easier to pursue when we are "happy"—we are more open, confident and hopeful.

Now back to the love part. Most of us believe others cause our hurts, that our pain is created when someone is unkind or rude to us; but what if we are the cause of our pain—what if the real source of our pain isn't from not *receiving* love but rather *from choosing not to give it?*

For example:

1. When someone is rude to you, if you respond internally with, "Who are you to be rude to *me?*" and you have an internal response of prideful indignation at her behavior. You will be "hurt" and likely angry.

2. But if that person is rude and you respond internally with, "Ohhhh, who hurt you?" or "What is happening in your day?" You are not going to be negatively affected by the interaction—you will be like emotional Teflon.

The person is rude in both examples, but in the first you are choosing to *withhold* love and be unkind, too, whereas in the second, you are choosing to give love. What if it is when we choose to hold back love that we "hurt"? Boundaries are important, and sometimes we may need to have a talk with people about how they treat us. But if we internally keep "loving" them instead of taking offense, that talk will be easier to have and the possibilities multiplied because we are seeking resolution.

We also get to the heart of a problem quicker when we are not "hurt." When we are hurting (even a little bit), if we stop and think about it, the verb we are really craving may be giving rather than receiving. Give love rather than take offense and possibilities will multiply.

If we give love, we get love. And even in...the most difficult of times,
we find there is always a way to get through.
Harold Klemp

FEBRUARY 15
BE CIRCULAR

We all want to be loved, appreciated and respected. We want our clients to love us; we want our spouse to appreciate us; we want our kids to respect us. But if we try to get that "want" from the people we desire it from, we can end up choking the relationship because our intention becomes about getting rather than giving. You know what I am saying—we aggravate our children when we are too clingy. We annoy our spouse when we are whiny, and we can distance clients when we are desperate.

Don't underestimate the importance of knowing your needs and stating them. That along with consciously *giving what you want to get* begins a change in your perspective that somehow changes the situation. When you want something (love, respect, appreciation), turn around and give it. In other words, give respect to the person rather than looking to just receive it from him or her. Seek to give love rather than only get it and give appreciation rather than seeking to receive it. Think of it as a circle—that when you are genuinely giving, it starts flowing back—and you are full again rather than standing alone and empty waiting to be filled up by someone else.

When we seek to give rather than to get, our intentions change from what are you doing for me, to what good can I do for you? Sometimes the tiniest shift in our intentions makes the biggest difference in our possibilities.

We need people, appreciation, respect and love, but what if we assumed our relationships were healthiest when we are giving those things we want as deeply as we are desiring them? How would that change your behavior?

If you wish to experience peace, provide peace for another.
Tenzin Gyatso

FEBRUARY 16

BE SELF-ASSURED

Other languages have different words for different types of love and kindness. Because we don't have that, we have to use the word "love" for all types, and that can be uncomfortable for people, particularly when we talk about business. But it might be important.

So what about this love thing? How does it help us in our business? Well, it can make you act on things you have been avoiding, or it can make you more engaged in activities you do not want to do.

For example, what are you afraid of? Not the shaking-in-your-boots kind of afraid, but the subtle fear that makes you procrastinate and avoid rather than act and engage. Are you "afraid" of prospecting, of going to a function, or of a co-worker?

When we fully choose love, we don't fear. Maybe it is because when we fully choose to love, the focus is not on "us" it is on *"What can I do for you?"* Whether in prospecting or walking into a party we don't want to attend, our thoughts become, *"How can I help you?"* instead of *"Please don't reject me."* Or *"Who needs attention?"* rather than *"This dress is out of place here and everyone is noticing that."*

You become genuinely interested and engaged in the present moment when you choose "love" and may end up with a new client or a new friend at the event you once dreaded. And about that co-worker you avoid—you may not want to be around them, but walking around the whole building in order to avoid their office area is exhausting physically and emotionally. Your fear is dictating your actions. Change your thinking about them; if you see them, look them in the eye and say hello.

When we let fear dictate our actions, we gradually become more insecure. When we choose "love" we are somehow stronger and more confident. Fear seems to crush possibilities while "love" seems to create them.

Create more possibilities.

Each time we face our fear, we gain strength, courage, and confidence in the doing.
Unknown

FEBRUARY 17
BE KIND

When you encounter people who are aloof or withdrawn, your first reaction might be that they believe they are better than others, particularly if they are beautiful or wealthy or have some cool car or any of the stuff society values. But if you would seek to understand, you would probably find they are simply afraid.

…Afraid you are going to corner them at the party and they are shy and have nothing to say. …Afraid you are going to talk about them because they are perspiring and it is showing. …Afraid you are going to look down on them or think they are inept in some way. …Afraid they are going to run into a particular person at the party, so they hide out in the corner and won't speak to anyone.

Aloofness and not engaging come from fear. Remember we can "catch" attitudes, so be aware because we do not want to catch someone else's attitude of fear.

Sometimes people may really think they are better than you, but regardless of whether their behavior is from an attitude of superiority or a reaction to over-sweating, if you choose a kind internal reaction to them you will not be hurt or negatively affected by their behavior.

Mediocrity requires aloofness to preserve its dignity.
Charles G. Dawes

FEBRUARY 18
BE CARING

We can be drawn into the idea that being kind and loving is not ever saying no and giving people everything they want.

But "no" can be very loving because sometimes we need protecting from ourselves.

It doesn't always feel good, but if someone in our life is unhealthily overweight, saying no to giving him or her a banana split might be very loving. If a friend is unhealthily obsessed with something, saying no to encouraging that obsession might be very kind. If someone is about to do something wrong or illegal, telling them no is the most kind and loving thing you can do.

Love says no as well as yes, sets boundaries and doesn't get and give everything that is asked for. Life would be easier if no, as well as yes, was chosen from loving care, not anger, manipulation or selfishness. We won't always get it right, but our possibilities will be prolific when we do.

Half of the troubles of this life can be traced to
saying yes too quickly and not saying no soon enough.
Josh Billings

FEBRUARY 19
BE IN LOVE

From very *unscientific* observations, I have determined that decisions made out of fear are ultimately not going to be successful. Decisions made in love may not always be either, but they sure seem to stand a better chance.

In small things like shopping, if I love it and can afford it, then I buy it; but if I don't (unless I am desperate), I am better off leaving it in the store for the right person to love because, otherwise, I will probably wear it twice and then it will just take up space in my closet and life.

When we have a disagreement with someone, if one party will not apologize and the other receive it, or neither party will seek to understand, then the relationship may not be successful—because at least one person is choosing fear, pride or unforgiveness. When that happens, an emotional separation begins. The cycle of distrust, emotional wounds, withdrawing and blaming becomes harder to get out of with every little fear decision.

When we find ourselves in those decision moments, a good self-monitoring question is, "Are my actions in-line with my goals?" If your goal is to make your friend feel bad and deteriorate your relationship, then absolutely hold the grudge. If your goal is to have an awesome, trusting relationship, then seek to understand the other person's position and resolve the conflict.

Intention is a big part of our possibilities. Do you want to be "right" or happy?

I believe that every single event in life
happens in an opportunity to choose love over fear.
Oprah Winfrey

FEBRUARY 20
BE POSITIVELY

What if your first internal response was Yes?

Yes, I can do that!

Yes, I will try that new sales idea!

Yes, I will wear a pink tie for the first time in my life!

Many of us have an initial internal reaction of "no."

No, I have already tried that.

No, I want the same toe nail polish I have worn for twenty years.

No, that can't be done.

No is sometimes fear... *I am afraid if I wear that pink tie, people will laugh at me.* If you really look bad in pink and don't like it, don't wear it. But if you won't wear it because you think your co-workers will tease you, then reconsider. A pink tie might open a whole new world of possibilities for you as your manager sees you as thinking outside the box and fearless (or admires how you handle the teasing).

If you say to your manager..."Yes, I will try that marketing idea again. Let me tell you what I did before and maybe you can help me come up with new concepts to make it successful and less time-consuming." Your manager is probably going to be supportive and want to help you make your marketing effort a success.

Of course, don't overextend and don't over-indulge yourself. Don't say yes to the $60,000 car when you only have budgeted for $30,000. Do say yes to one bite of dessert and savor it, then say no to more.

It is easy to say yes to desserts and things that satisfy our desires; these things we likely need to monitor more closely. The point is that consistent internal no's keep us in a box we may not realize we are in, the same as consistent yes's can keep us on a hamster wheel trying to catch up or correct situations we didn't think through. Our yes's and no's can develop into habit and that can become a problem in situations and relationships.

If you are a "no" person, try an internal "Yes, that might work" response. But before you say it aloud, ask yourself: Is it safe? Is it right and legal? Then, make a conscious, deliberate decision for action. No one will get every decision right all the time, so give yourself and others grace. Be aware of your yes's and no's and open new opportunities for growth and knowledge.

Yes and No are very short words to say,
but we should think for some length of time before saying them.
Unknown

FEBRUARY 21
BE PROGRESSIVE

We sometimes say no to new possibilities simply out of habit. "No" can start as fear and turn into a habit.

I would only wear black, brown, blue or gray for a long time—colors that didn't call attention to me. It started out of fear and then just became a habit. Then, one day, I bought red. It was a weighty decision for me to say yes to red, yet somehow it became my new favorite color.

I would turn up my nose to sushi as if it was beneath me, when actually I was just scared of it. I finally faced the fear and said yes, and now I am thrilled when I find a good spot for sushi.

We are limiting ourselves and our possibilities when we say no to new experiences, whether they be food, colors or prospecting ideas. Say no because it is not right for you, not because you are afraid or out of habit.

When we step outside our comfort zones and try new things, we enter into new possibilities.

Progress always involves risks.
You can't steal second base and keep your foot on first.
Frederick B. Wilcox

FEBRUARY 22
BE BIGGER

As we close out "no fear" month this week, it is important to look not only at our fears that hold us back but also at our fears that can hold others back.

If we find we are attacking others in our thoughts or words, we are likely afraid and putting our fears on them. If we gossip or belittle another, we are attempting to make that person look bad in others' eyes.

If you have a problem with someone, when possible, talk to him or her about it instead of to others. Of course we need to process, but we know when our processing and venting are turning to gossip and complaining. (What is your intention, to belittle the person or to seek a solution?)

Different personalities can have difficulties naturally getting along. Don't let yourself be sucked into a negative attitude toward someone just because others have one or out of habit. You wouldn't want people doing that to you. If you have trouble respecting someone or getting along with them, seek to see their good qualities and the ways they positively contribute and focus on those things. We don't know what someone else is going through or why they are in our lives, but more likely than not, it has more to do with us than with them.

If you find yourself "building a case against someone," step back and ask what you are afraid of then talk to the person (Are you insecure? Are you judging them unworthy of their job? Are they being unreasonable because of their own fears? Are they being dishonest? Have you decided you are better than they are?). Maybe you are being easily offended, fearful or maybe you have a valid complaint. If the person will talk with you, do so.

When someone is willing to talk with us and we won't—we talk *about* them instead—we become the problem.

When we belittle others, it says more about us and our insecurities and attitude than it does about them. Be aware of when you use your fears to hold others back and decide if that is the person you want to be.

When we seek to build others up, we are built up, too. When we seek to tear others down, we eventually tear ourselves down instead.

To belittle is to be little.
Unknown

FEBRUARY 23
BE BETTER

If we don't want someone to be happy, we need to step back and ask ourselves what we are afraid of.

Why would we not want someone to be successful?

Why would we not want someone to change for the better?

Why would we not want someone to be liked?

...maybe because we are afraid we will find out we are not as important and needed as we thought? Or that we don't have as much power and control over others as we want? Or because we want to be #1? Or because we want to be right?

The conscious or subconscious desire for someone not to be his or her best and happiest is likely a signal we are unhappy with ourselves. The simple act of choosing to be happy for that person and their success will shift your focus from lack to abundance, and you may become happy and successful, too. Choose a different perspective and you will be choosing new and likely happier possibilities.

It can be difficult to desire good for those we don't like or are jealous of, but when we genuinely do, we will find the one we ultimately make a difference for is ourselves. When we let our fears hold another back from being their best whether with our words, actions or just in our thoughts—we hold ourselves back, too.

Seek to help others be better rather than to tear them down and you will be better, too.

One man cannot hold another man down in the ditch
without remaining down in the ditch with him.
Booker T. Washington

FEBRUARY 24
BE SECURE

Life can be hard enough. Why do we want to make it harder on each other?

When we continually make snide comments about someone instead of discussing our problem with them, we are likely afraid.

When our intention is to put another person down rather than help them to learn/change and move up, we are likely afraid.

Many of you are thinking, "I'm not afraid, he's just an idiot" or "She is stupid." Maybe you aren't afraid of that person, but you are likely afraid of something or you wouldn't feel the need to talk the other person down to people who will listen. Maybe you are afraid you will lose control of "your group." Maybe you think "the group" will start liking the other person and you are threatened by that.

We can be factual without being degrading. It is all in our intention. Do you want to help and support the other person, or do you want to put them down to build yourself up?

If a colleague doesn't know how to do a task, do you help them then talk poorly about them? Or do you help them and move on without having a need to tell others about it? If we have a need to tell others about how John or Susie didn't know how to _____, then we are likely afraid and insecure.

Granted, there are going to be situations where we must discuss people's skill sets and abilities. The difference is in our intention, and we know when it is to help or hurt. The thing is, when we want to hurt another, we end up hurting ourselves—maybe not right now, but eventually.

Our fears get in the way of our own lives enough. When we feel a need to put another person down instead of being helpful or neutral, we are letting our fears get in the way of other people's lives, too.

When we feel the need to degrade another person, it is a signal we need to stop and check our insecurities. We can hide our feelings of inadequacy behind false bravado, cutting remarks and a sense of superiority, but only for so long. Pushing another down to elevate yourself is one of those actions that makes you feel better for a bit, but you still won't be happy and you won't know why.

Our fears get in the way of our possibilities. Do we really want to let our fears get in the way of other people's possibilities, too?

Insecure people need to make excuses and put others down to feel confident.
Unknown

FEBRUARY 25
BE HONEST

When you feel the need to speak poorly about another person, stop and ask yourself what you are afraid of.

It could just be habit: you have been beating up that person with others so long that it has become a habit.

It could be you enjoy it, but that is sad, isn't it? How would you feel if someone enjoyed belittling you in their thoughts or verbally with others? (and again, if you enjoy it, isn't that because of your own insecurities?)

It is likely fear. Granted, various personality types are going to have conflicts, but to put people down instead of discussing the problem is likely your insecurities coming to the surface.

Instead, try building that person up whom you have been tearing down. Just the simple act of changing your words about them will change your attitude toward them. Or as one woman said: "I used to think it was him. But as I started to change my need to be critical, I realized the problem was me!" The couple enjoys a great relationship now with honest words rather than snide comments and biting criticisms voiced to others.

Building others up doesn't mean we aren't honest about our feelings. It means that we *are* honest about our feelings. We can say, "I think you need to improve..." or "This is bothering me" *to* the person instead of *about* them. And if we are honest, we can see really great characteristics in that person as well as the aspects we are being critical of.

When we have the need to tear others down we likely aren't being truthful about our feelings—to others or to ourselves. It is easier to gang up on someone and get a following against him or her than it is to have an honest conversation with them. But if we reap what we sow, which is going to be the better option for our peace and possibilities down the road?

I think anybody with an insecurity, which is everyone,
appreciates the fact that it's much easier to be a predator than it is to be prey.
James Van Der Beek

FEBRUARY 26
BE ON TRACK

Today, review your goals for the year.

Are you on track?

If your goal is to have monthly client gatherings, have you done that or do things keep coming up?

If your goal is to have processes in place, are you moving toward that or has there just not been time?

If your goal is xx number of calls/visits per week to build new business, are you doing that or have you been busy?

You get the picture. We all get busy and things will always come up. Sometimes our goals just happen, but more often than not, we have to be deliberate about taking the initial steps and getting them started. If "things keep coming up" or you "just don't have time" then likely there is another source for the lack of progress. Are you procrastinating? Are you putting it off because you are not prepared or perhaps because you are fearful?

There are seasons in life where our goals go on the back burner, but in regular day-to-day living, we are often the ones who put them there.

If you are having trouble with this year's goals, try time-blocking or prioritizing. If you still find you are having trouble, talk to your manager, in-house specialist or a coach.

If we aren't deliberate, we can leave our goals on paper instead of bringing them to life.

Procrastination is opportunity's natural assassin.
Victor Kiam

FEBRUARY 27

BE IN SYNC WITH YOURSELF

Everything seems a little easier when we work with ourselves rather than against ourselves.

This seems obvious, but obvious to see doesn't make it easy to do.

We can let pride, fear, drama, resentment, jealousy, others' opinions, gossip, entitlement, laziness and other "stuff" make our decisions for us and get in the way of our ultimate intentions, goals and desires. (Of course, if your intention is revenge or to be right, then that negative stuff would likely be working for you.)

Many of us know what to do to get our businesses, relationships and lives heading in the direction we want, but we often don't do it. We tend to get in our own way; we become our biggest obstacle to success and happiness.

Possibilities seem to become realities easier when we work for ourselves rather than against—in sync rather than in conflict.

If you need help spotting where you could be the problem, talk to your manager or friend or a professional. You have too much to do to be wasting time and energy going in circles with a goal instead of moving toward it.

You are the only real obstacle in your path to a fulfilling life.
Les Brown

FEBRUARY 28
BE GRATEFUL

I heard of the question: "What if you woke up today with only what you were grateful for yesterday?"

We ask how your marketing plan is coming. How is prospecting going? How is your family and health? But we don't often ask: How is your gratitude?

When we are unhappy it could just be we are being ungrateful. Stop and be grateful for what you do have and look for—as I heard it said—the treasure in the trial. It won't always be easy, but you can find at least three things to be grateful for that can make a difference in your attitude.

Consider gratitude as a business practice. We tend to utilize it around the holidays, but what if we made it a point to practice gratitude all year long? Since gratitude can improve attitudes, energy levels and relationships, why would we not be conscious of "giving gratitude" all year long? Being consciously grateful for our jobs, our skills and resources, our clients, our arms and legs, our hair, our opportunities, our families, our cars, our homes, a morning cup of coffee—the little things… and even the unpleasant things, too. When we can be grateful for even one thing around the unpleasant, somehow that situation loses its power. If for nothing else, be grateful for the opportunity to learn a new lesson.

When we practice gratitude, our problems seem to dissipate while our possibilities and the number of things to be grateful for seem to multiply.

Live this day giving thanks for what you want to wake up with tomorrow. It puts a whole new perspective on gratitude, doesn't it?

Feeling grateful to or appreciative for someone or something in your life actually attracts more of the things that you appreciate and value into your life.
Christine Northrup

MARCH 1
BE POSITIVE

I read that our brains are thirty-one percent more productive when we are positive and that we are thirty-seven percent better at sales when we are positive rather than neutral, negative or stressed.

People tend to think the whole "happy" thing is just fluff, but actually it could be not only a key element to improving relationships, but your business, too. We are more productive, creative and energetic when we are positive instead of neutral, negative or stressed. So laying a positive foundation by making the "happy" choice could be a key to new possibilities for yourself and with others.

If you aren't joyful today, stop and ask yourself why not. Then take a step toward improving the cause. Is it simply a choice of attitude or do you need to take action? It doesn't have to be much; sometimes the internal choice to go All-in with something is all it takes to improve where you are right now.

Do you need to hire someone to help you push through a task or problem?

Do you need to make a choice to not be offended?

Do you need to be grateful instead of feeling entitled?

Do you need to eat healthier and exercise? Make the decision of what you will do today.

Do you need to schedule a business-building activity you have been putting off?

Take one small step toward your new commitment, and you will be taking a giant step toward new possibilities.

How wonderful it is that nobody need wait a single
moment before starting to improve the world.
Anne Frank

MARCH 2

BE MOST PRODUCTIVE

W e are more productive when we are positive rather than neutral, negative or stressed. Unfortunately, many of us subconsciously believe that we must be stressed to be successful.

For example:

If I am not worrying, something bad might happen.

I have to hold on to my feelings of guilt.

If we aren't deliberate, our success equations involve a negative and look something like this:

Work + consistency + resourcefulness + ambition + determination + passion + stress = Success

Consistency + love + dedication + desire + commitment + communication + being in control and not vulnerable + pride = Relationship

Encouragement + discipline + love + guidance + time + constant worry = Parenting

I can't relax and enjoy my business or my relationship or my children because I have to be in complete control. It might be more fun to enjoy life, but I would lose control.

We grip tightly to what we know, even if we aren't enjoying it, because we don't know who we would be otherwise. We don't want to be reckless, but we do want to examine our life equations and be aware of beliefs we may want to change.

If we are more productive and better at sales when we are positive rather than stressed, it stands to reason that by consciously de-stressing we may not only enjoy our work more, but be better at it, too.

Look at the ways fear has worked its way into your life equations (stress, control, constant worry) and decide if you want to let fear go. Test it out. If it doesn't work for you, you can take the stress and angst back. But your possibilities and the people around you likely hope you won't.

Your ability to generate power is directly proportional to your ability to relax.
David Allen

MARCH 3
BE WILLING TO FAIL

As we are seeking to be more productive (without more time or effort) we must be willing to fail. If we are unwilling to risk failure, we could be contributing to our stress and not realize it. Perfectionism puts us in a little box that doesn't allow for expansion; we won't try new things unless we are certain we will succeed.

But that ideology keeps us from doing client events because what if "not enough" people come?

> If this worry is keeping you from moving forward with an activity that will make a difference for others, then start small. Invite ten people and have a few friends on standby to fill in for last-minute cancellations. When you do your part, you can trust that exactly who is supposed to be there will be—regardless of the number.

Or what if we don't talk to prospective clients because we may not have the "right answer"?

> If you aren't hearing new objections or questions you don't know the answer to, then chances are you aren't stretching yourself enough and are still in that little box stressing yourself out. Even the person in business twenty years doesn't have all the answers.

Perfectionism is about pride and fear. Yes, we want to be excellent and prepared in our endeavors—and there are some things that must be perfect—but we know the difference between what needs to be perfect and what needs to simply "be." It is in our attempts that we gain the knowledge and experience needed to "perfect" the imperfect.

When you find you are shrinking back from possibilities because you are afraid of appearing substandard to others, immediately step forward with a new attitude of exploration and you may be stepping into a world of new opportunities.

While one person hesitates because he feels inferior, the other is busy making mistakes and becoming superior.
Henry C. Link

MARCH 4
BE AN EXPLORER

Sometimes we need a modified relationship with failure to be willing to fail. In other words, we have to be willing to risk appearing imperfect. Some of us have become unwilling to try new things because it might not work and we could look stupid. But that attitude leaves us in the little box and we miss out on great possibilities.

So what if we became curious? What if we decided to explore possibilities with the anticipation of finding great treasures? The old explorers didn't know what was on the other side of the mountain; they were simply eager to discover what was waiting for them. Sometimes it was just more trees, but other times it was something astounding. The point is, when we are explorers instead of perfectionists we are excited about the journey rather than worried about the outcome.

It takes confidence to "fail." Don't let others' opinions of you determine whether you will risk failing to try something new. A simple shift of perspective from fear to curious exploration can make all the difference in our attitude and our possibilities.

What do you want to do but haven't attempted yet because you are afraid of failing or not being good at it? Whether the project is personal or professional, adopt a curious attitude, take on the role of explorer and take an action toward it today.

We do not want to miss possibilities we could be enjoying.

There is no failure except in no longer trying.
Elbert Hubbard

Curiosity will conquer fear even more than bravery will.
James Stephens

MARCH 5
BE UNPLUGGED

Do you let your technology dictate your day or do you determine how you spend it? If you find you don't have enough time, and are busy and stressed, try limiting how often you check your email. That small change can make a large impact on your productivity.

If you are in a position where you must be immediately reactive to a group of people or work with time-sensitive material, of course, you must consistently monitor emails. But if you are someone who can, consider limiting how many times a day you check your inbox. You will find you accomplish more and are less stressed when you have uninterrupted blocks of time to complete tasks. You may already realize this, but checking email can be a way to waste time. Yes, you must be responsive, but must you respond as soon as you receive it? Most people don't expect you to answer immediately, simply within the day. The important thing is to prioritize your activities and know what is essential.

Alert the people you need to that if they must connect with you immediately, call the office. Otherwise you will get back to them in an acceptable amount of time.

For some of you, "limiting" may be three times a day; for others, it may be ten. Try it out. If you don't like it, you can always go back to email on demand.

Productivity is never an accident. It is always the result of a commitment to excellence, intelligent planning, and focused effort.
Paul J. Meyer

MARCH 6
BE NOT ANXIOUS

Stress doesn't help our productivity or sales abilities and it doesn't help our bodies. The Mayo Clinic says that stress can affect your body with headaches, muscle tension, chest pain, fatigue, sleep problems and stomach issues, among others. The clinic adds that our mood effects can be anxiety, restlessness, lack of motivation or focus, irritability, anger, sadness or depression. We can also see stress in our behavior in the form of overeating or under eating, angry outbursts, drug or alcohol abuse and social withdrawal.

And it wasn't mentioned in this article, but stress can cause heart disease and, in extreme cases, our hair to fall out. So if we won't work on de-stressing for our brains, we might want to work on it for our bodies.

We will experience stressful times in our lives—and our bodies can handle that—but if you are a chronic stresser, get help to shift perspectives, learn to prioritize, exercise or activate some other solution. While we can accomplish much while stressed, it is certainly not as much fun, and we may be creating problems in our bodies and relationships that aren't easily fixed.

If you recognize any symptoms in yourself from the list above as stress-induced, get help. You will be more productive in your job and relationships and generally happier all around.

I promise you nothing is as chaotic as it seems. Nothing is worth your health.
Nothing is worth poisoning yourself into stress, anxiety, and fear.
Steve Maraboli

MARCH 7

BE SO GRATEFUL

There is going to be situational stress in our lives when we hit overload or become over-worried. But if our stress and anxiety are habitual—a natural part of our daily living—then we must address it. There are many ways to do that: reframe the situation, organize, prepare, exercise or massage are a few. Research shows that a more powerful option is gratitude.

Stress is basically fear. Researchers say our brains operate in such a way that we cannot be grateful and fearful at the same time. So when we recognize we are stressed, if we stop and choose to be grateful, we will find a new perspective about the situation. With that fresh perspective comes a renewed energy and a more positive outlook for the situation or task.

Genuine gratitude changes everything.

Take a step back, recognize the thoughts of resentment, frustration or any other thought you would like to be different. Then find the gratitude spot in each.

Stop. Savor the moment—and look at who you can make a difference for rather than who should be making a difference for you. It will take the fearful focus off you and put a contributing focus on the situation. When we do that, we are the one who ends up with the blessing.

Gratitude doesn't mean we don't identify what we need and ask for help; it means we are able to do just that. When we are stressed, we tend to keep piling on to ourselves (like punishment) and are often unable to identify our real needs for the situation in order to take action on them.

Stop. Find what to be grateful for in the situation; focus and act on that change. You will experience a perceivable change in your stress level and your possibilities, too.

How we perceive a situation and how we react to it is the basis of our stress. If you focus on the negative in any situation, you can expect high stress levels. However, if you try and see the good in the situation, your stress levels will greatly diminish.
Catherine Pulsifer

MARCH 8
BE AHEAD

Procrastination creates stress. Some of us work well under last-minute pressure; that practice could be a habit, or it could be when we feel we do our best work. But if we would like to feel less stress, then we can test out working ahead of the schedule.

For example, if we know we have a task to complete in three weeks, then by scheduling thirty minutes each day (or ten minutes or two hours, whatever time is needed), we can likely accomplish our goal without much stress. But if we wait until the deadline is drawing near, we can end up scrambling to complete what could already be done.

We all struggle with this. As we prioritize tasks, we are going to have those that are less important now, but we find them at the top of the list next week and are trying to catch-up.

Our human nature is such that whether we have a year or two weeks to complete a task, we tend to spend the same time on it and at the last minute. But we don't have to. We can begin to schedule time into each day to work on our processes, our home projects or our knowledge. If we schedule a little time each day, we will likely find lower stress levels and higher rates of completion and confidence.

What do you need to complete that you are willing to give twenty minutes to today?

If you want to make an easy job seem mighty hard,
just keep putting off doing it.
Olin Miller

MARCH 9
BE EFFICIENT

In response to a message about procrastination and productivity, a reader emailed:

"I have gotten so much better at not putting off. I always thought the energy level of the pressure helped me succeed. But now I see by planning further ahead, I'm providing even better service to my clients as I am thinking out situations over weeks, instead of hours."

Those of us who think we work better under pressure might find it is true about some activities and not true about others. This week, test out doing a task "now" or spending twenty minutes a day on something that you know must be accomplished. That kind of commitment to a task can help us work more effectively, expending less energy and experiencing less stress than when we "put it off." When we put off that task, we could be putting off possibilities.

A year from now you may wish you had started today.
Karen Lamb

MARCH 10
BE ACCEPTING

We can increase our productivity simply by decreasing our stress. As a reader shared yesterday, she believed the energy level of the pressure helped her succeed. But really, it just makes us frantic.

Take five minutes today to assess where you are. Be still and identify what stresses you. We will usually find those things involve "not being where we want to be." We are stressed that an event is coming up and we aren't fifteen pounds lighter. We are stressed that another year has gone by and we don't have clear processes and strategies in place. We are stressed that we don't have the work done or the success we thought we would have achieved at this point.

Now that you know what is taking your energy, accept where you are right now and either do something to move toward where you want to be or let it go and realize it just isn't important to you right now (and that could be a problem, too). The simple act of taking five minutes to assess our stressors can get us off the hamster wheel—and not only alleviate stress in our bodies, but give us clarity to move forward toward where we want to be.

When we find ourselves continually operating under pressure, we may find that we have developed a habit we want to change. Occasional pressure and a sense of urgency is exciting and motivating, but a constant state of tension becomes a demotivating life of fire drills.

Tension is who you think you should be. Relaxation is who you are.
Chinese Proverb

MARCH 11
BE HAPPIER

To be happier and less stressed, don't gossip.

We all fall short on this one. We listen to or contribute to gossip about others. It seems harmless in the moment, but it is damaging not only to the subject but also to our pursuit of possibilities. When we don't participate in gossip, it will not occur to us that anyone would be talking badly about us. But the minute we participate (even just listening to unnecessary or diminishing stories), we will start to consider what others think of us or that someone is talking badly about us.

One powerful block to our pursuing of possibilities is what others think of us. So when we start spending our time and brain power worrying about what others are saying then, very simply, we are not going to be as productive or as happy as we could be.

Avoid gossip and you will eliminate one source of stress and strife in your life. Most of it isn't true anyway; it is just a tale told to make the teller feel better about him or herself. And we all know where dealing in half-truths will get us…nowhere. Just going in more circles with old possibilities.

Where no wood is, the fire goes out;
so where there is no tale bearer, the strife ceaseth.
Unknown

MARCH 12
BE HELPING

If we want to be happier and more productive, spending less time being critical of others (even in our thoughts) is an excellent option.

The more time we spend being critical of others, the less time we spend building something good, making a difference, and being productive.

You don't need any more hours in the day and don't have to put forth any more energy; you just have to decide to accept others' differences and move on. Spend your energy helping people to learn and change instead of putting them down in your thoughts or to others with your words. Use your thoughts to find reasons to praise rather than pick a co-worker apart. Those simple choices can increase your productivity with no more added time.

Remember, our need to be critical says more about us than it does the object of our criticism. We can evaluate a person's skills or assess a situation without adding the element of criticism, which is really just the element of our own desire to build ourselves up (in other words, the element of our insecurities).

A better option is that when you see an area that can be improved, either be willing to help or let it go. If we are willing to help, we aren't being critical…just honest with how we feel. The willingness to be honest and the attitude of helpfulness make all the difference.

And really, are any of us perfect? If we will keep in mind that what we are criticizing others for we have done in the past or we do now, perhaps we wouldn't be as deprecating. Maybe that is exactly why our insecurities come out and we have a need to be critical of the other guy because it is easier than being honest with ourselves.

Spend your energy on building up rather than tearing down and you will find time, happiness and possibilities you didn't know you had.

Any fool can criticize, condemn, and complain—and most fools do.
Dale Carnegie

MARCH 13
BE PLAYING

Do you want to feel less stress automatically? Find ways to play and have fun with those around you.

In our busy worlds with deadlines, goals and expectations to meet, we can forget the importance of play. Playing with others builds bonds, decreases stress, involves laughter and could make us risk being vulnerable.

It's the vulnerable part that makes most of us shy from playing, but it could be the willingness to be vulnerable that makes the difference: Willing to risk "losing," willing to laugh at ourselves, willing to connect with others instead of living behind a wall.

Note that playing to avoid responsibilities or problems is not helpful and will eventually increase stress levels. Everything has its time. Incorporate play and fun into your life and relationships and you will likely notice a decrease in stress and increase in possibilities.

Play energizes us and enlivens us. It eases our burdens.
It renews our natural sense of optimism and opens us up to new possibilities.
Stuart Brown, MD

MARCH 14
BE RE-THINKING

We can be more productive without putting forth additional time or effort. If that deal were offered to most of us, we would take it—until we found out it involved being positive and optimistic. Then that proposition would suddenly become worthless or "fluffy."

Sadly, there is the belief that positive people aren't going anywhere professionally. One has to be overly critical of others and severe to be respected and to "make it." (This is not true, just an impression many get.)

We do have to be serious about our work, but we can be critical thinkers without being overly critical of others. We can assess others' abilities or situations with an intention of helping rather than one of diminishing.

To succeed, we don't have to be consistently harsh or constantly complaining. But somehow, actually enjoying what we do and passing that joy onto others can be seen as "fluff." *Somehow those happy people must not be as smart.* Spending our time and thoughts on putting others down rather than on business-building activities doesn't seem so smart either.

What if it is the extremes we need to pay attention to? If we have the need to be overly critical of certain people, then we are likely just covering up our own fears. When someone is different, we don't understand them and, rather than be curious, we can end up criticizing. On the flip side, we don't want to be overly optimistic to the point of ignoring realities, either.

We don't have to agree with others; we also don't need to be critical, harsh and disrespectful. We all get there sometimes; we just don't want "sometimes" to become too often.

Test out a positive perspective for a day and see if you find yourself more productive and perhaps even encounter more possibilities.

It is easier to be critical than correct.
Benjamin Disraeli

MARCH 15
BE HEALTHY

The dictionary describes ego in a neutral manner as self-image or self-esteem, as well as in a negative way as conceit or self-importance.

We all desire a healthy self-esteem and positive self-image; these are necessary to pursue our possibilities. But what about conceit and self-importance? Do they help or hinder our pursuit? At first thought, the answer could be help, but do they really, or are they the insecure partner to self-esteem? Could ego actually get in our way of excellence and enjoying the journey?

A "big ego" could be confidence with an insecurity, and the insecurity could keep us from trying new things and exploring any idea we didn't come up with. It doesn't like to be challenged; it makes us think we are better than others and it may buck authority or anyone who it thinks is trying to control him. This process works fine for the big ego but is not so enjoyable for those around him or for his possibilities that are waiting.

We all let our ego get in the way sometimes, but if we are letting it lead our life instead of just occasionally get in our way, we are likely missing possibilities that are only seen by taking the focus off of "me."

Ego is the biggest enemy of humans.
Rig Veda

MARCH 16

BE OF HEALTHY SELF-ESTEEM

We have all heard the expression: "His ego got in the way."

Got in the way of what? Likely something good. Rarely does someone say, "Her big ego is what saved her relationship."

If something "gets in the way" it is not getting in the way of a disaster. It is likely going to be in the way of things like happiness, resolution, peace. So while our ego relating to self-importance may be helpful for a while, it is eventually going to disappoint us. At some point, we aren't going to get what we want just because we demand it, and people around us will eventually stop responding to our fire drills when we take offense.

More likely the bigger reason behind our eventual disillusion with big ego is that we find we really don't like being a person who puts up a shield of ego to cover up our spots of insecurities.

Honest conversation and healthy self-esteem might take us further and be better company than over-inflated ego. We can equate ego to pride, and if pride eventually destroys possibilities, big ego may, too.

The ego is the false self—born out of fear and defensiveness.
John O'Donohue

MARCH 17
BE COOPERATING

Our egos get in our way, but they also get in other people's way, too.

If we want to be an obstacle to ourselves, that's one thing, but we want to be aware of when we are an obstacle to another, usually by being obstinate.

We take a position and, once we dig in, we are unlikely to be moved. We can stay dug in to the point of loss yet still not admit we could be wrong: loss of relationship, loss of respect, loss of a client, loss of a job.

Life is hard enough. Why do we want to make it harder on each other and ourselves with our pride and insecurities?

When you find yourself "dug in," take a step back and ask yourself, "What is my intention?" Is it resolution or to be right? *A* solution or *my* solution? To respect others or inflate myself?

Once ego starts to gain control of a situation, it is tough for our cool head to regain control. But it is worth the struggle, because with big ego there is eventually loss, but with fair play everyone can win.

Big egos are big shields for lots of empty space.
Diana Black

MARCH 18

BE AUTHENTIC

Do you know who I am?!

How dare you!

You'll pay for this!

I deserve…!

I'm entitled to…!

I have a right!

We all slip, and when we find words like these coming from our mouths, we have likely slipped. A quick recovery can be made with a shift in intention. Stop. De-escalate and start over with the truth rather than pride and ego talk.

If these phrases and attitudes have become normal for you and are consistent with your beliefs, the "recovery" may not be so quick. You may like what this attitude gets you. Our egos can give us permission to be mean-spirited when we are offended or have been wronged. But isn't this victim-mentality really for the purpose of hiding something? Such as our inabilities, our part in a problem, our lack of knowledge, position or ability? Power trips are fun—for a moment—then they just become sad.

Truth doesn't need ego. Blame, insecurity and inauthenticity do.

If we find ourselves saying words like the above, (and we all will) we may want to reevaluate our perspective. We might not make any changes, and that's our choice, but when ego is making decisions for us, it could be our insecurities in disguise.

We all know there isn't much happiness there.

It is the nature of the ego to take, and the nature of the spirit to share.
Proverb

MARCH 19

BE MORE WILLING

Confident people have ego, but they control it. What does that look like? They can hear others out. They are willing to listen and are open to others' ideas, willing to change their minds. They can admit when they are wrong. They are willing to learn. They are not rigid or closed to new ideas and perspectives. They are willing.

If we want to be less ego-directed, it doesn't mean we must give up our position or that we allow others to manipulate us. Being less ego-driven means we are willing to work with others to help them catch our vision and to consider their point of view—and who knows, we may find we actually like the view from another angle.

Being passionately determined when we believe in something is fantastic. It is when we become determined because of revenge, anger or pride that more problems seem to appear than possibilities.

We want to make sure *we* are making decisions about our lives and businesses, not our big ego.

How to get rid of ego as dictator and turn it into messenger
and servant and scout, to be in your service, is the trick.
Joseph Campbell

MARCH 20
BE CHEERFUL

Complaining can become a habit that we are not aware we are doing. And since our habits can either deter or multiply possibilities, we want to become aware of them and choose whether we keep them or quit them. If you want to quit the complaining, a shift in attitude is a good place to start.

Think about what you have rather than what you don't have. There are people in the world who are being held against their will. Not just in jobs they don't like or relationships they don't want to be in, but actually held against their will—children and adults. There are places in the world where they pull your tooth (and do other procedures) without any numbing medication. Ouch! There are places without running water.

The list goes on and on, with the point being that many of the things we complain about are situations we can do something about.

Today, when you complain, stop and ask yourself: Is it really that bad? If it isn't, stop talking. If it is, ask yourself: What can I do about it? Whether it is a change in action or attitude, do it! Sometimes happiness is a choice. We all have bad habits, and awareness is a first step to changing them.

You can overcome anything if you don't bellyache.
Bernard M. Baruch

MARCH 21

BE PART OF THE SOLUTION

The next time you find yourself wanting to complain about something, stop and identify three solid solutions to the problem you want to complain about.

There are many reasons this is helpful, but one of the best could be that it puts some responsibility and ownership back on us rather than on everyone else. Granted, there are issues that we are not in a position to make decisions about, but in most cases, we can take initiative to make a difference in our personal situation rather than expecting others to do it for us.

How much more productive would your relationship and interactions with your child be if he came to you with three solutions to a problem rather than just complaining about it? Dialogue opens up, and both sides are allowed to see into the other's perspective.

Life is give-and-take, and sometimes our best seasons in life are born when we look for the opportunities to make a difference for our own situation rather than expecting someone else to do it for us. How much more peaceful and productive would all our interactions be if we sought three win-win solutions rather than seeking only our own personal comfort and satisfaction?

If you have time to whine and complain about something
then you have the time to do something about it.
Anthony J. D'Angelo

MARCH 22
BE MORE INTENTIONAL

As much as I enjoy sharing my shortcomings and laughing at my shortsightedness, this isn't the book for that, but I am doing so today.

Yesterday, I made a no-complaining pledge for one week...and broke it in one day. I was venting/processing a problem with a trusted team member. I laughed out loud at myself when just a few minutes after my venting ended, I realized I had thrown a complaint or two in that venting somewhere and that I had just blown the no-complaining pledge on day one! I told on myself for complaining and went joyfully on with my day...only to later walk into a situation where there was complaining. As the complaining continued, it subtly turned to gossip and not only did I listen, I wanted to hear more! I am embarrassed to admit that I actually wanted to hear about these persons' difficulties. My intention had subtly become a little bit of revenge. I was frustrated with the people being discussed because of their lies and gossip. Guess who had just enjoyed participating in the same behavior I found fault in them for! When my intention moved to the slightest hint of revenge, I became responsible for my pain, not the people who first created it. Intention is the difference-maker. And while we can lie to ourselves, we are best advised not to, because we will just be unhappy and not realize why.

So I am confessing that I blew the no-complaining pledge twice in the first day. I got caught up in the moment and not only enjoyed listening to the gossip and complaining, I added one myself! It is easy to do, but not necessarily the right thing to do. We must choose our intentions carefully, for our silent intentions choose the direction and joy of our lives. I woke up this morning feeling wrong instead of joyful, lethargic rather than energized and drained rather than excited. And I am the one responsible for those negative feelings. When we are getting carried away in a moment, we and those around us are better served to stop and be deliberate about words and intentions. Our positive possibilities depend on it.

Any fool can criticize, condemn, and complain,
but it takes character and self control to be understanding and forgiving.
Dale Carnegie

MARCH 23
BE GLAD

We complain about the mechanic's bill, but what if we shopped around to see if the fees were fair? And if we found they are, but are still unhappy, tried looking at their side...they have a family to feed and bills, too. Would we really want them to walk away with less than what they earned for those four hours repairing our car? Just because we don't like that our car broke down doesn't mean we should make others suffer. Your being afraid doesn't mean you can complain about/to others when they are really not part of your problem—but they could be part of your solution. You could ask if you could pay the bill over the next three months or if you could come in to answer phones for ten evenings to pay it off. Often we complain when we haven't earned it, but feel entitled in some way...we have a "right" or we "deserve" something. Who says? When we catch ourselves saying those words, we need to step back and examine why we feel entitled or deserving. Often those words and feelings are at the root of our problems. One way to explore why we feel entitled is to know what we believe and why. After we identify our belief, we can then explore if that belief is just and right.

When you want to understand a situation or another person's perspective, ask people you respect what they think of the issue until you find someone who agrees with the *opposite* side you do. Ask this person to explain their perspective to you.

If you still aren't satisfied, take the perspective of "the other side" for a day (or for a conversation). You may see new angles in the problem you hadn't thought about before and be more likely to come up with a win-win solution rather than a selfish, one-dimensional one. You may actually find you feel better about the outcome, see many more possibilities, and are much happier in the long run when you become responsible for your problem and solutions.

Don't complain that you are not getting what you want.
Just be glad you are not getting what you deserve!
Unknown

MARCH 24
BE THANKFUL

Things we complain about: Our jobs. How others do their jobs. Our significant others. Our children. The government. Our surroundings. Our bodies (height, weight, wrinkles). Our hair (or lack of). Service. Having to get up. The weather. I'm tired. I'm cold (I'm hot). The list goes on and on. The stuff we can do something about, let's do something about. The stuff we can't, let's find a way to be grateful.

For example: A gentleman had a serious illness that had multiple effects on his body and health. Besides being constantly cold and weary, his legs often swelled to three or four times their normal size. He didn't take the attitude of victim and he never complained. He just quietly took care of his needs. He always wore a jacket and if there was a heat source, he was by it. This went on for years during which he and his wife continued to work and live joyfully through it all—without complaint. Their attitude made all the difference in their happiness. What would your attitude be?

When you can't do anything about it, find a way to be grateful for it. Be grateful you have legs and arms that work and a home to live in. Be grateful you have hair and a job. Jump up and greet the day with an expectation of good. If you don't like your hair, get a new stylist and different products. If you don't like something your significant other is doing, talk to him or her. You could be part of the problem.

Complaining drains the energy out of us and those around us, and we don't even realize we are doing it. What if there were a direct correlation between our gratitude and our positive possibilities? How many possibilities would present themselves in your day today? Gratitude is a happiness habit...be grateful in this day.

Gratitude is riches. Complaint is poverty.
Doris Day

MARCH 25
BE ACCOUNTABLE

Remember that we are always creating our lives. When we complain, what do we create?

Venting and discussion with the intention of finding solutions is productive.

Complaining with a self-focused intention is non-productive and feeds the issue.

Why do you complain? Are you looking for sympathy? Then be direct and say, "I want sympathy...I want you to feel sorry for me." Do you want someone to do something for you or fix something that is actually yours to fix? Then say, "I want you to give me this without me doing anything more to earn it or contribute."

Once we get to the heart of an issue (truth), it is easier to see our part in a problem and take responsibility. Most of us don't want to do that because we won't be able to complain and blame someone else any longer. But until we own our part and take responsibility, we will continue to be dissatisfied and probably not know why.

Seek solutions to your complaints by asking, "What can I do about it?" rather than, "What can someone else do for me?" You will probably see a whole new perspective to your complaint as well as possibilities for solutions you hadn't thought of before. Personal accountability creates positive possibilities.

Good solutions seek to build everyone up. Complaining seeks its own way and often wants to push someone down, and when we seek to push someone down, we are pulled with them. Make this a no-complaining week and you will probably find you want to create a no-complaint life.

Say and do something positive that will help the situation;
it doesn't take any brains to complain.
Robert A. Cook

MARCH 26
BE JUST RIGHT

How can you make yourself feel good today?

You work hard for others, but you don't always take time for yourself.

Because we are often conditioned to be self-sacrificing, we can view the time we take for ourselves as self-indulgent when it can actually be more of self-sustainment.

Balance is the word of the day. Taking time for yourself in ways that energize you will make you fresher and more astute for your clients and colleagues. But just as overworking can deplete your energy, over-indulging can too.

Most anything can be energizing to a point; but over-indulging in anything from work to chocolate can quickly move from energizing to de-energizing. That "too much" threshold is different for different people. It is an awareness of our "full" gauge—when we have hit the satisfaction threshold—that helps us be most productive and enjoy our life.

When you love dessert, but eat three of them, you quickly go from feeling ecstatic to feeling lousy. You missed your "full" threshold.

When you overwork (even the work you love) for two months, and suddenly you are exhausted rather than energized, you missed your "full" threshold.

When you over-pamper or over-play, thinking that *if a little of something is good, then a lot of it must be better,* you will probably find yourself feeling unproductive rather than re-energized. And again, you might have missed your "full" threshold.

Only you know what yours is. Successful people learn their thresholds and when to say "when." From how much of the dessert they eat to how many hours at work they spend. Know your thresholds and feel your possibilities expand.

Be moderate in order to taste the joys of life in abundance.
Epicurus

MARCH 27
BE THE SOLUTION

Successful people know their thresholds and when to say "when."

There is a point where we are doing something because it is energizing and good for us and others; then there comes a point where we "over-indulge" and that same energizing action or activity becomes de-energizing. If you find yourself consistently going over your threshold with something particular that could be a Band-Aid for you—an activity you do hoping it will make you feel better or give you a desired outcome when it really doesn't—you know it's a temporary fix, not a long-term solution.

I may be working all the time, but a relationship is what I really want to be working toward, and I am embarrassed to admit it.

I am eating too much, but what I really want to do is spend time with my spouse, who doesn't want to spend time with me, and I don't know how to address it.

I am finding busy work when actually I am being lazy rather than working out or working on my marketing project, and I don't know why.

Successful people know their thresholds, and they know when something is a Band-Aid rather than a solution.

To excel in business, relationships, hobbies or projects, learn to recognize Band-Aids and diligently seek real solutions. If you spot a Band-Aid in your life and want a long-term solution, the truth is a good place to start.

There will always be Band-Aids in our lives. The key is to recognize them when they reveal themselves and to make the changes that will create the life, business and possibilities we desire. When we seek solutions, possibilities appear.

To the question of your life you are the answer,
and to the problems of your life you are the solution.
Joe Cordare

MARCH 28
BE LIGHT-HEARTED

Genuine laughter builds bonds. Somehow when people laugh and have fun together, they make connections and build trust more easily. Genuine laughter is energizing and healing. Even if we can't see the possibilities yet, it helps us believe they might exist. Humor can help de-escalate a situation and re-frame a problem.

So if laughter is so good, why do we tend to take ourselves and situations so seriously? Could it be we just get busy and forget to laugh at ourselves or a situation?

Of course, there are inappropriate times for laughter and there are some things that are not ever funny, but overall, laughing at ourselves and finding humor in difficult circumstances somehow makes us feel more optimistic and less stressed.

Supposedly we are better at problem-solving and more resilient when we involve our sense of humor and laughter in our lives. If this is true, why do we all not lighten up a little? Some of us feel we need permission to have fun. Sometimes we think if we don't look serious and busy, we won't be taken seriously. And sometimes we just don't have time to think about fun; we have too much to do.

But what if we got more done with a little humor, a little fun...a little laughter?

What if taking a little time to play and laugh with your kids made it easier in the long run to communicate with them? (It does.)

What if not taking everything so seriously freed you up to be ready to handle the serious stuff? (It can, because you aren't so stressed out over the little things that you have some energy and ability left for the big ones.)

Fun and laughter don't always just happen. And when they don't happen, we need to be deliberate about making it happen. Pursuing your possibilities is serious business, so make sure to incorporate fun and laughter into your life.

How can you add some laughter to this day?

At the height of laughter, the universe is flung into a
kaleidoscope of new possibilities.
Jean Houston

MARCH 29
BE FUNNY

If laughter is so great for our physical and emotional wellbeing, how do we incorporate more laughter into our day? Well, there are props, like the "extendable fork" and sitcoms and comedians that make us laugh, but you don't always have funny gear with you and you can't walk around all day with a Seinfeld DVD playing. But there is one potential source of laughter-inducing material that we are with all day long: ourselves.

There are many reasons why genuinely laughing at ourselves could be good, a few from helpguide.org are: Laughter eases anxiety and fear. It relieves stress and improves moods. Laughter enhances resilience.

There are also many reasons why we might not laugh at ourselves, a few could be:

1. We might have a pride problem in that area we need to look at.
2. We could have low self-esteem, maybe not in general, but in a particular area.
3. We haven't yet recognized how funny we are, or we might not like ourselves a whole lot.

Remember, we are talking about genuine laughter, not laughter used to avoid an issue, laughter meant to make someone feel small or humor used to express a dislike that should be addressed directly. Those kinds of laughter are empty. Genuine laughter feels good.

It is said that laughter is good for our mental and physical health. Sometimes humor is inappropriate, but in areas that are appropriate and you are having trouble re-framing so the load is lighter, talk to someone—a friend, your manager, a therapist—and laugh while you are working through the issue, not in order to avoid it. When we can see the humor in a situation, we can often see more possibilities, too.

Laugh at yourself and at life. Not in the spirit of derision or whining self-pity, but as a remedy, a miracle drug, that will ease your pain, cure your depression, and help you to put in perspective that seemingly terrible defeat and worry with laughter at your predicaments, thus freeing your mind to think clearly toward the solution that is certain to come. Never take yourself too seriously.

Og Mandino

MARCH 30
BE YOU

How do you think of yourself? We often think of ourselves through the perspective of others. And we can let others' opinions of us dictate our own opinion of ourselves. If others think we are great and are complimenting us, then we too start thinking we are great. But if someone is criticizing us, complaining about us or putting us down in some way, then we often think we are not so good or competent.

Reflecting on what others think of us can be good, because sometimes it can help us see a behavior or intention we are not aware of, but it is probably not a good idea to let what others think of us dictate our feelings and opinions about ourselves.

When we do that, our emotions can bounce all over the place, and we can spend our days catching up to our emotions rather than actively and intentionally moving toward our goals.

So how do we stay consistent in our thinking of ourselves? There are many ways, but one is to know who you are as well as who you want to be and line up your thoughts, words, intentions and actions to that. Revisit your personal mission statement. Is that still who you want to be? Have you been living it?

When you get off track and become someone else, (we are human, we will get off track) rewind and correct what needs correcting, and get back to being you.

To not let others dictate our opinion of ourselves, we need to know the truth about who we are and who we want to be. How do you really think of yourself? Is it the truth or someone else's opinion?

Risk! Risk anything! Care no more for the opinion of others, for those voices.
Do the hardest thing on earth for you. Act for yourself. Face the truth.
Katherine Mansfield

MARCH 31
BE LISTENING

Not letting others' opinions put us on an emotional roller coaster of how we feel about ourselves is not easy. We have to listen yet not let the judgment affect us.

Here is an easier way to look at it: My husband and I can be in an argument with completely different views and we still love each other. The argument doesn't change that. My love and respect for him does not go up and down depending on if we agree or disagree.

Similarly, someone may tell you a criticism (or a praise) of you and you can examine if it is true. Then you can decide if you want to change anything and do so without losing your love and your respect for yourself.

We can't let other people's opinions of us decide our opinion of ourselves, but we do have to listen to others' thoughts so that we can spot things we need to change as well as to understand others' perspectives of us.

Look at the opinion, examine it for truth and either make a decision to change or to stay the same, all the while still "loving" yourself. It is not easy, but it is possible. Pursue that possibility and watch a new world of peace and productivity evolve in your life.

Let others' opinions be a good source of information and guidance, not the final word and certainly not the source of your opinion of yourself.

You must have control of the authorship of your own destiny.
The pen that writes your life story must be held in your own hand.
Irene C. Kassorla

APRIL 1

BE INCREDIBLE

"I don't have time to work out."

You do have time to work out; you simply choose to sleep instead.

It's okay to choose sleep—just don't lie to yourself about not having time.

We all have time and we all choose how we spend it.

How often do you find yourself making an excuse when you have done the right thing? Probably very rarely.

We often make excuses when we don't do what we believe we should. It is not always possible to choose rightly, but it is possible to start recognizing our habitual excuses, own up to our shortcomings and make a decision to be better next time.

Instead of going into all the reasons you have not called a prospect, get to the truth. "I feel unprepared" or "I feel inadequate" or "I am afraid of..." or simply "I did not feel like it today."

Excuses are damaging to those of us who give them because we begin to believe them. Excuses are lies to ourselves. They may be little white lies, but they are still lies that block possibilities. And if we keep telling them, we could start living them.

The next time you make an excuse, stop and pay attention to how you feel. You will probably notice that you are a little defensive and feel powerless. Excuses and lies entangle us and are damaging to our confidence. Honest language is freeing and empowering.

Work to change any "excusing" to what you are "choosing" and watch the natural positive changes that occur in your life.

Don't make excuses; make something incredible happen in your life right now.
Greg Hickman

No one ever excused his way to success.
Dave Del Dotto

APRIL 2
BE STRONG

Excuses bring an overall sense of being a victim:

I don't have time to work out (I am a victim of my schedule, my family, my boss…).

I don't have anyone to go with (I am a victim of my singleness or my spouse's schedule…).

Blaming others or a situation for how you feel and what is happening may make you feel "right," but it isn't going to make you feel better. When we take the role of victim without realizing it, we also take on an attitude of defeat and powerlessness.

Blaming makes us feel right when often we are not. There are few situations where we do not have some responsibility for the outcome—even if it is an outcome we did not want. The sooner we own our part in a negative situation, the sooner we are released from its negative hold (resentment, bitterness, blame…) and can move on to the life and business we want.

Blaming without owning your contributions to a negative situation can make you feel "right" but robs you of self-esteem and creativity. Don't sacrifice the life you want in order to be "right."

You cannot hold on to a negative past situation and pursue all positive possibilities available to you.

As you turn the negatives into neutrals, you will experience a new peace and world of possibilities.

When you blame others, you give up your power to change.
Dr. Robert Anthony

APRIL 3
BE CREATING

We constantly create our lives.

Are your choices (in thought, intention and action) in line with the life you want or do you catch yourself getting off course because of pride or fear? Or maybe because something is just easier or because you want to spare someone's feelings?

We get off track for many reasons, and that is going to happen. The important thing is to correct a situation when we realize we have strayed from what we want to create in our lives.

Recently, an office manager shared the following story: an employee came into her office with an issue and she reacted defensively. The conversation quickly escalated, with agitated tones. When the manager realized this was not serving anyone, she de-escalated the situation by starting over.

After they lowered their tones and voices, she changed her intention from "wanting to be right" to "wanting to find a solution."

In the middle of the tense discussion, the manager realized she was creating an office environment and a relationship contradictory to what she actually desired. So she stopped…and made a different choice in order to create the life and business she wants.

No Excuses. When you find yourself in a situation that is not serving you:

1. Stop and rewind.

2. Acknowledge in some way that you want to start the conversation over.

3. Be intentional about what you want with your tone, words and actions.

We constantly create our lives. Be aware today of the life, business and relationships you are creating.

Some seek happiness, others create it.
Unknown

APRIL 4

BE AWARE

How do you feel?

A simple way to avoid disagreements and improve problem situations is to know how you feel.

Stop and identify your emotions.

When our emotions take over a situation, we may generate problems instead of possibilities. To consistently pursue positive possibilities, we must be deliberate about our words and actions, and to do that, we must know what drives our words and actions.

All day today, identify your emotions:

I am embarrassed I said that.

I am afraid they will think I am not intelligent.

I am frustrated I can't get my point across.

I am happy they heard me.

I am satisfied with the outcome.

I am confident.

I am nervous my information is not right.

I do not feel appreciated.

I feel good.

When you are in a tense situation, stop and ask yourself why. You may find that doubt, fear, guilt or frustration is the source. You could be creating the "tense" in the situation by reacting to a negative feeling subconsciously rather than *choosing* your actions.

When you find you are acting on negative emotion rather than truth, stop and start over. The issue will be resolved quicker and easier. Then you can be pursuing possibilities rather than fixing problems.

Let's not forget that the little emotions are the great
captains of our lives and we obey them without realizing it.
Vincent Van Gogh

APRIL 5

BE THOUGHT-FUL

Our thoughts, feelings and actions are all intertwined. Living all our positive possibilities begins with thinking positive thoughts.

Thoughts → Feelings → Actions

We are more likely to actively pursue possibilities and work toward goals when we get rid of what is not serving us. If you have a difficult time letting go of a negative thought or mindset, then consider this: If it is not serving you, then it is not serving your clients, family or friends, either.

Are you kind to yourself?

"You look great!" "You rock!"

Or do you beat yourself up?

"You are such a loser." "You are stupid."

Are you uplifting of others?

"She is sharp." "That is a great idea."

Or critical of others?

"He is an idiot." "That hairstyle is horrible."

Be aware of your thoughts today.

Are you kind, critical or neutral to yourself and others?

What is the tape that plays in your head?

Is it positive, neutral or negative self-talk?

Changing a self-talk recording of "I am unworthy and not good enough" to "I am more than enough and worthy" can be as simple as being aware of the negative thought and replacing it with a positive one or it can be a few visits to a therapist. Whatever it takes, do it. You are worth it.

Do not waste another day of your life or bit of energy thinking negative thoughts of yourself. Don't waste energy not liking something or someone—particularly yourself.

Watch your thoughts, for they become words.
Watch your words, for they become actions.
Unknown

APRIL 6
BE MORE UNDERSTANDING

In your active, busy life, you encounter many people in a day. Some of those people you connect with right away, others you may not be so fond of. We are not going to like everyone (and not everyone is going to like us), but remember, we don't want to waste energy or time not liking someone. If there is someone you consistently have negative thoughts about, it could be you really don't like that person or it could be you simply don't understand them yet.

Oftentimes, when we "seek to understand" a person we don't like, we will find we can think better thoughts of him or her. For example, the woman who is disinterested in you and appears rude and arrogant may really just be exhausted and sad. You might discover that her one-month old doesn't sleep at night and her uncle just died.

OR

That person at work who is dismissive of people might really just be afraid. He is insecure and doesn't want anyone to see what is really going on.

You might not like him any better, but understanding the situation can help you to be unaffected by his behavior.

You don't have to like their actions or behaviors. You don't have to socialize with them. But don't waste time and energy being negative in your thoughts and words about them.

You have too many possibilities to pursue to waste time and energy not liking someone.

It's a waste of energy to be angry with a man who behaves badly,
just as it is to be angry with a car that won't go.
Bertrand Russell

APRIL 7

BE ON A MISSION

We become what we think. Having your own positive words or phrases to replace negative thoughts can help you control what you think. A personal mission statement is helpful for a couple of reasons. First, when you become aware of negative thoughts, you can use it to replace them. Second, it can work as a personal compass to make sure your thoughts and actions are in line with what you believe.

A personal mission statement is helpful to have when the client is angry, or your kids are disobedient, or the advisor down the hall is pushing your buttons or your husband is not seeing things the way you want him to. In the middle of the emotion, a solid personal mission statement is an excellent default setting. Why? Because you want to choose your reaction rather than let a negative emotion do it for you.

What is your personal mission statement? If you do not have a personal mission statement, adopt one today.

Examples:

Leave people better than you found them...directs your thought and behavior toward people.

Be Excellent...can be an "excellent" guide for thoughts and actions.

Love Wins...can help you to decide what actions to take in relationships, including the one with yourself.

Seek the Truth...once we get to truth, we can usually get to peace.

Everything works out for the best...can help you to have peace in the midst of difficult situations.

Treat people as you want to be treated...gives you a concrete guide for living.

These are just some examples.

To make up your own, think about:

1. What you believe.

2. What you want your life to look and feel like.

3. What you want to contribute to this world.

Create your personal mission statement and live it.

What do you believe?

A man is but the product of his thoughts; what he thinks, he becomes.
Mahatma Gandhi

APRIL 8

BE MOST GRATEFUL

We have talked about different ways to have more positive and productive interaction with others. Another "thought" we are going to talk about is the belief we are entitled to something.

It is fantastic to deeply desire and work toward goals and to attain them. The problems can begin when we think we are entitled to have what we want rather than needing to work toward it. When we begin to believe we are entitled, we end up often frustrated and unhappy because we are not getting what we are "owed."

Symptoms: Believing we are owed something: health, big house, respect, best table at the restaurant, big job, marriage, money. Becoming angry because we didn't get what we wanted. Feeling robbed and cheated out of what I "deserve." Being controlling of others. Feeling that we have a "right."

Diagnosis: Feeling entitled.

Solution: Gratitude and a new perspective.

We can waste considerable time and energy being angry, believing we got robbed of that award or better office or the life we wanted.

We can waste a lot of possibilities and happy moments thinking we are entitled to what other people have rather than working toward what we want ourselves.

Choosing to be grateful doesn't mean you should not work toward solutions; it simply means you can be productive and factual, rather than angry and frustrated, as you work toward the solution. For example, ask your manager what you need to do to get the office you want or the extra sales support, and then work toward that goal he or she sets for you.

The bottom line is this: when we feel entitled to something rather than grateful for it, we end up with just more frustration, wondering why things are not happening the way we are "entitled" for them to work. Shifting our thinking to realizing we are not entitled to good health, a bigger house or a relationship just because we want it helps us to be happier now as we work toward the goal—and it helps us to find the possibilities where we are.

Being grateful where we are helps us to get what we want more than believing someone is obligated to give it to us.

Persistence and hard work with an attitude of gratitude rather than entitlement will reveal possibilities you didn't think were possible.

Don't feel entitled to anything you didn't sweat and struggle for.
Marian Wright Edelman

APRIL 9
BE ADJUSTING

Our thoughts, feelings and actions are so entwined that we must work to be intentional in order to make the changes we want in our lives. Remember:

Thoughts → Feelings → Actions

We have talked about habitual thought patterns. Responses can be habits, too. We can become conditioned to respond automatically to situations we don't like.

For instance, you might act out of anger and tell your child you are taking away something he values every time he does something you don't like. If someone doesn't return your call or solve your problem or get your tire repaired quickly enough, do you act out of anger and frustration by hanging up on her, thinking bad thoughts of the person or giving him the cold shoulder?

If these types of "anger actions" are working for you and you like the results they create in relationships and opportunities, then it is your choice to continue.

But you will probably find opportunities come along more often, problems are solved easier, interactions are more productive and relationships are stronger and more satisfying when you act on accurate information and intention rather than on negative emotion. You might even find those problems you choose to react more positively to stop occurring so frequently in your life: your child seems to do more things you like instead of things you don't, your tire gets repaired quicker than you thought, people actually like to return your call...

Positive possibilities seem to just appear when we take a step back, seek to understand and act on information and intention rather than negative emotion.

Live every act fully, as if it were your last.
Buddha

APRIL 10
BE SMART

In anger or frustration, we can make a decision that isn't the best for us or the other party. And sadly, when we realize that there are better options, instead of going back and correcting ourselves, we often stay silent and continue with a decision we really don't want. Pride doesn't let us go back and correct it.

Good rule of thumb: do not make a decision while you are angry.

Instead, take a step back and say, "I need to think about that." Then give an appropriate time frame of when the other party can expect you to come back with your response. This gives you time to find the true source of your anger, process it and make the best decision for everyone. You may also find this helps you let go of your anger more quickly.

If you do make a decision in anger that you later realize isn't the best option, don't let pride or fear keep you from going back to the other party and saying, "I was wrong. I think we should..."

Bonus Tip of the Day: it is also a good idea to refrain from making big decisions when you are tired or hungry. So sleep, eat and be merry!

If you are patient in one moment of anger,
you will escape a hundred days of sorrow.
Unknown

APRIL 11

BE WORRY-FREE (OR AT LEAST WORRY LESS)

Worry is fear that something "bad" will happen or that something "good" will not happen. Worry wears us out and leaves us with less brainpower to be productive.

Some worries we have no control over, such as the plane will crash or our bags will not arrive at the same destination we do. We have no control over the outcome of those worries.

There are, however, worries we do have control over—like the worries that come when we don't do the right thing.

For instance, we worry if the application will be approved in time because we left it sitting on our desk instead of processing it.

We worry if we are going to get in trouble because we are late again.

We worry that we aren't bringing in enough new business.

We worry that a friend is going to be hurt because we gossiped.

We worry we haven't had enough contact with clients.

These are all worries we have control over with our own actions. We can replace the negative energy of worry with positive, productive feelings by doing the right thing.

We can leave in plenty of time for the meeting.

We can build a prospecting campaign and give our focus to it or simply commit to making two calls a day to people who might need our services.

We can make a personal decision to not say anything *about* someone we wouldn't say *to* them.

We can create a consistent client communication process.

Worry robs us of productive time and energy. Surrender the things you can't control, take appropriate action on the things you can control and you will drastically reduce your worry levels.

What are you worrying about that you can act on today?

It takes less time to do a thing right than it does to explain why you did it wrong.
Henry Wadsworth Longfellow

APRIL 12
BE PASSIONATE

P ossibilities earnestly present themselves when we are passionate about what we are doing.

When we are passionate about our purpose, we are:

Bold rather than fearful

Focused and investing our intention and energy fully into the act

Completely giving ourselves to what we are doing

If at any point you find yourself a little anxious about your activities, whether it is prospecting or speaking in front of a group or learning something new, remind yourself of your purpose and find your passion in the situation.

If you are passionate about helping people understand investing, you will not be anxious about speaking because you will be focused on what the audience learns instead of what they think of you and how you perform. If you believe people need your services, you can actually be excited, rather than anxious, about making the prospecting call. If you believe your clients need a particular service or product, you will give the energy to understanding it.

And another great benefit of passion is that when we are passionate about our purpose, we have less of a need for something to be perfect as for it simply to be. Don't get me wrong; you must prepare fully for your talk or your prospecting call—passion without preparation is not effective. But once you are prepared, you can let go of perfection and let passion do its thing.

What are you passionate about?

What is your purpose?

What do you believe?

The more intensely we feel about an idea or a goal, the more assuredly the idea, buried deep in our subconscious, will direct us along the path to its fulfillment.
Earl Nightingale

APRIL 13
BE FOCUSED

Yesterday's message addressed passion and how it can help you succeed. One of the big reasons for this is that passion pushes out fear. When we are passionately focused on a goal, we are bold rather than fearful.

Look at it like this...while we have the possibility of abundance in our lives, we have only so much space in our brain. When we focus on a goal passionately, there is no room left in our brain for fear or laziness or procrastination; passion pushes out those negative thoughts and tendencies. And once we get rid of our fears and laziness, we have removed ninety-nine percent of the barriers between us and our goals.

If you knew you could cure cancer by earning a certain amount of money in three months, you would get creative and likely make it happen. If someone said, "I will put every child in your county through college if you earn one million dollars this year," you would work to make that happen.

When we become passionately focused about a goal, we lose all barriers and work to make it happen. You have the skills, resources and talents to do whatever you want. There is little you cannot accomplish if you really want to do it.

Put your passions to work for you.

A strong passion for any object will ensure success,
for the desire of the end will point out the means.
William Hazlitt

APRIL 14
BE RISK TAKER

To pursue your possibilities means that sometimes we have to get out of our normal routine and try something new.

When something is working for you and your clients, don't change it. But for those areas of your life and business that aren't working so well, try something new. There are many reasons we don't like to try something new: one is perfectionism.

If we struggle with the need to be perfect and are afraid to "fail," we don't like to try new things.

So what if you changed your view about failure?

Not everything you try is going to work. Not everything you do is going to "succeed." But everything you do will improve you and your business if you view an "un-success" as a lesson, not a failure. Use the un-success as a stepping-stone to the business and life you want.

A way to shift your perspective about un-successes is to:

    1. Own them.

    2. Review the lessons you learned from them.

    3. Then move on.

The key is to acknowledge the un-success and be grateful for what you learned.

To be open to all your possibilities means to be able to take a risk sometimes.

There are no failures – just experiences and your reactions to them.
Tom Krause

APRIL 15

BE RESPECTFUL

We all want respect. When we receive it, we have higher self-esteem, which makes it easier for us to pursue possibilities. Hard work, good output and performance are ways to get respect, but don't forget a simple key: when we want something, we need to give it.

If you want appreciation, turn around and intentionally give it.

If you want help, give it.

If you want respect, give it.

We give respect and appreciation with our words, actions, thoughts and intentions. If you want people to respect you, intentionally respect others with your thoughts and words. If you want to be appreciated, do something that says how much you appreciate someone today.

Make it a habit to give respect. When we intentionally and consistently give respect, a funny thing happens...we find abundance and likely discover that we are not in need of it any longer. Maybe it is because we are receiving it from other sources or maybe it is because we come to respect ourselves more.

When you feel lack, give what you want to get and live all the possibilities.

Give away your life; you'll find life given back, but not merely given back—
given back with bonus and blessing. Giving, not getting, is the way.
Generosity begets generosity.
Luke 6:38 MSG

APRIL 16

BE NOT-GIVING

Just like the rule: If you want something, give it. There is another "rule:" If you don't want something, don't give it.

If you don't want to be yelled at, don't yell at people.

If you don't want to be talked about, don't talk about people.

If you don't want to be treated rudely, don't treat others rudely.

If you don't want someone to hold a grudge against you, don't hold grudges against others.

You have heard the saying, hurt people hurt people. Often when we are treated poorly, we become hurt and frustrated and feel bad. Then we will show those "<feelings" ("less than" feelings) to the next person who gets in our way.

If you work to eliminate the behaviors you don't want in your life it doesn't mean your days will be rosy; it just means that when you encounter negative behaviors, you will be better equipped to handle them and probably won't pass them on as often. When you do pass them on (we are human) you will likely want to "rewind" and correct the situation. Eventually, you will probably notice that you don't encounter those negative situations so often anymore.

Dramatic behavior and negative energy rob you of positive possibilities. Use your words, time and energy positively and the positive possibilities are endless.

The world is circular… everything comes back around to you.
Unknown

APRIL 17
BE GOAL-ORIENTED

Remember: Thoughts → Feelings → Actions

Every choice matters. Even if we are living deliberately, we can get off track and end up making choices that are not the best for us. A simple way to monitor ourselves is to ask the question:

Are my actions in line with my goals?

> If you want to run a 5K, are you preparing or lying on the sofa?
>
> If you want to get another professional license, are you studying for it a little each day?
>
> If you want to attract new clients, are you taking steps daily to do that?

Revisit your professional goals and ask yourself: are my actions in line with my goals? If not, make a plan today to get the two working together. If you need help (and that's okay, we all get stuck and need help) contact your manager, co-worker or a coach today.

When we get our actions in line with our goals, we become energized and focused—with endless positive possibilities.

Many fine things can be done in a
day if you don't always make that day tomorrow.
Unknown

APRIL 18
BE LONGER-TERM

Every once in a while, stop and ask yourself: are my actions in line with my goals? If not, one of two things may be happening, either you are not "All-in" with your goal or you are looking at the short-term goal of instant gratification rather than the long-term goal of success and happiness.

If your goal is to lose fifteen pounds, do you: Take one bite of yummy cake and savor it? (Long-term Goal) or do you…

Eat the whole huge piece of chocolate cake? (Short-term Gratification)

We can easily give up our long-term goal for instant satisfaction. Every choice matters, and unless we remind ourselves of our long-term goal and choose our actions to line up with that, we will either become frustrated and sacrifice our goal completely or take much longer than necessary to get there.

If your goal is to double your business, do you: Actively and purposefully seek new business in your daily activities? (Long-term Goal) or do you…

Just try to make it through the day? (Short-term Gratification)

Try to avoid embarrassment in case they don't want to talk to you or you don't know an answer? (Short-term Gratification)

Be prepared and keep your goal in mind. Many painful mistakes are made and goals missed because we choose short-term gratification over our long-term goals. When you get off track (and you will, because we are human and imperfect), do what you need to do and get back on track. Don't waste time and energy beating yourself up. If you go All-in and choose your actions to line up with your long-term goals, you will make your possibilities happen. Don't short yourself.

Don't give up your goal just to feel good for a few minutes.
Unknown

APRIL 19
BE PRO-ACTIVE

1. List a goal you have
2. Now list *at least* three actions you will take that will move you closer to your goal.

List or think about why you have not done these actions before. Were you afraid? Was the timing not right? Did you choose other actions or responses that were not in line with your goal?

Sometimes we can prepare for an action or reaction by visualizing it in our minds.

For example: maybe my goal is to have a healthy, great relationship with a family member or associate, but this person often yells at me and I end up cowering or yelling back. After those interactions, I don't feel good and certainly don't feel closer to my goal.

A possible solution is to visualize what I want my positive response to be the next time that situation happens so I will be better prepared to handle it. Visualizing is basically practicing the difficult situation in your head, whether that difficult situation is your first public speaking occasion, learning to say no to someone, or developing new communication habits with someone.

Remember reactions don't "just happen." We can choose them just as we choose what to wear in the morning. Sometimes, we just have to learn to develop new ones for situations that don't leave us feeling good or closer to our goal.

Good goals and positive actions and reactions produce possibilities where impossibilities once were.

Visualize this thing that you want. See it, feel it, believe in it.
Make your mental blueprint and begin to build.
Robert Collier

APRIL 20
BE ASKING

Others should be able to tell what our goals are from our actions. Remember the question, "Are my actions in line with my goals?" Turn that around and ask others, "What do you think my professional/personal goals are?" You can watch some people and know their goal is to be excellent at their work. You can watch others and wonder if they even want to be there. If you asked others about your goals, would their answers reveal excellence? Would they say your goal was "to be a top producer" or "just to make it through the day?" "To increase your production?" or "To just be left alone?"

Would they say, "He is a sharp, attentive manager" or "I wouldn't want him to manage my mother's business affairs."

Ask yourself: Are my actions in line with my goals?

Ask others: What do you think my goals are?

The purpose is not to be concerned about what others think of you, but to be aware of words you say and actions you perform that work against you instead of for you.

Words and actions can reveal self-defeating/negative thoughts we weren't aware we were acting on. Without outside "assessment," we can easily miss little things we do and say that move us further from our goal rather than closer to it. Positive Possibilities come easier when our thoughts, words and actions are working *with* our goal, not against it.

I have always thought the actions of men the best interpreters of their thoughts.
John Locke

APRIL 21

BE WILLING TO BE DISAPPOINTED

A friend called and said, "I need business. So why do I not spend the first two hours of my day working on the deal I know I can get?" Then he answered himself, "Because I might not get it. And my confidence is already shot. So I would rather not put forth the effort in case I don't get it. I just don't want to be disappointed."

Sometimes we would rather be half-hearted with our goal and be "not disappointed" than go All-in and be intentional about the outcome.

Think of a time you didn't give all your efforts to a goal because you didn't want to be disappointed if you didn't get it—maybe involving a relationship, a job search, a prospect, a recruit. Do you wish you had done anything differently?

If you go All-in and don't get what you want, you can know you were not supposed to get it or not supposed to get it yet. But if you don't give a goal all you have, you will never know if you were the reason it didn't happen or if it just wasn't supposed to be.

Live this day so you can spend your energy on possibilities, not "what if's."

What if I had worked harder? What if I had done more research? What if...

Live and work All-in today and the positive possibilities will present themselves. Today will not happen again. Be deliberate about how you live it.

What do you want?

What can you do in the first hour of your workday to be deliberate about getting it?

Let your first hour set the theme of success and positive action that is
certain to echo through your entire day. Today will never happen again.
Og Mandino

APRIL 22
BE INACTIVE

Our recent focus has been on our actions in one form or another. One thing to point out is that sometimes our best action choice is inaction. To do nothing—yet. Being still about an issue is quite difficult for most of us, yet sometimes it is our best choice.

Sometimes we have to wait for conditions to be right. No matter how much you want to impress your company from Kansas, you should probably wait until after the hurricane to take them to the beach.

Sometimes we have to wait for another person to be ready for action or change or interaction. No matter how much you want to clear the air, you should probably wait until after the emotional hurricane to talk it through.

Sometimes we need to gather more information before making a decision of action. Actively gather information while waiting and don't let someone else pressure you into a crucial decision you are not educated enough to make.

Two important things to keep in mind when choosing inaction:

1. While you are being outwardly inactive, make sure your internal choices are positive and part of the solution.

2. Be prepared to act when the time is right. If you know it is time to act and do not, that is a symptom you could be avoiding the situation because you are fearful, rather than choosing inaction because it is the best choice.

Avoidance, procrastination, laziness and fear are not good reasons for inaction. We can easily slip from an intentional choice into one made from habit, and at that point inaction becomes a bad excuse instead of a good decision.

Make sure your choice of inaction is because you are being patient enough to wait, not because you are afraid to act.

Sometimes inaction is the best choice...just don't let it turn into a habit. We must be as intentional about "inactions" as our "actions."

If this is a time of waiting, don't just sit around. Get prepared to act, whatever that looks like, when the time is right.
Amy Lewis

APRIL 23
BE EXCELLING

You get up early and go to work every day. Even when you are tired or would rather be doing something else, you go to work. You also make sacrifices in order to do your work: you miss a family function or you don't get to attend your daughter's play. So if you are making the choice to be at work when sometimes you would rather be doing something else, why would you ever work against yourself when you are there? Why be at work and not be All-in?

Of course there will be days (or even seasons) that you are weary or sad and not your best, but overall, you will get more of what you want if you work All-in while you are at work. For example, if you work All-in and become a top-producer, you will likely have the ability to hire a team so you can get away for your daughter's class play. Whatever job you do, when you are a contributor, more freedoms come to you.

Over the next few days we will address various ways we work against ourselves in our work so that we can work for ourselves while we are there. Work with an All-in attitude toward your goals because otherwise you are really just working against yourself.

Work is a gift and we are happier people when we work and give ourselves to our work, whether it be cleaning a house, answering a phone or managing money. What we do doesn't matter as much to our happiness as how we do it. Work with an All-in attitude and experience the possibilities.

It's so hard when I have to, and so easy when I want to.
Annie Gottlier

APRIL 24
BE PRODUCTIVE

One way we work against ourselves is worry. Worry takes brainpower you could be using for something productive like making calls, staying educated on your profession, or learning something new. If there is an action you can take to eliminate or decrease the worry, take it. If there is not, surrender the issue you can do nothing about to address an issue you can.

If you think a client could be considering leaving you because of poor performance or lack of attention or because their new son-in-law is in your business, do the right things, then surrender the worry...then continue to do the right things. Your state of worry and angst will not help the situation; in fact, it could actually become a barrier between you and the client. And you could worry so much about that client that you end up neglecting other clients.

If you are worrying about passing a professional exam, study, prepare and let it go. If you know you have put in the necessary hours, there is no need to spend your pre-test brainpower on stress and worry. If you know you have not put in the hours necessary, there is still no need to spend brainpower on stress and worry. What's done is done. But you will probably learn you want to spend more hours studying the next time so you do not feel unprepared again.

Worry is fear about an outcome or that "something" will or will not happen. Fear paralyzes us; worry can do the same. Then we end up frozen and wasting time rather than working toward solutions.

We can be diligent about our responsibilities without worrying about them. We worry when we don't do the right things and sometimes we worry as a habit. Neither is helpful. Not worrying does not mean neglecting responsibilities; it means when you are concerned you didn't do something or didn't do it in the right way, you take the necessary steps to make it right and then you let it go.

Do the right thing. Let go of what you cannot control. And turn your attention to what you can.

Worrying is like a rocking chair, it gives you something to do, but it gets you nowhere.
Glenn Turner

APRIL 25
BE MORE PRODUCTIVE

Worry and angst pull productive energy right out of us. If you need to make their effects more tangible, think of it this way, worry means:

Three fewer clients you contact, (because you spend time in worry).

Two and a half fewer acts of kindness you do for your spouse (because you are thinking about you and your worry rather than about him or her).

One less encouraging word you say to your child (because you can't see her need, due to your worry).

And less money (because you are missing possibilities).

Worry leads to a sense of lack rather than abundance because you are giving and getting less than what is possible. Worry produces a < day (less-than day) and too many of those lead to a < life. (Less-than-what-is-possible life).

Pick something you are worrying about in the back of your mind and determine an action you can take to eliminate the worry.

Can you face it in some way? If not, let it go until it is time to face it. If it feels overwhelming, can you make a plan and take a first action? Do you need to apologize, return something, own a mistake, say thank you, or ask for help?

If you do not know what to do, call a trusted friend and ask for help/wisdom/advice. Sometimes just saying your worry out loud will help you release it.

When we worry, we are afraid. Fear is a bully who wants to keep us from our best, and worry is one of his best tactics. Don't let him bully you another minute. (If you are someone who thinks you have to worry or "it" will happen or that you have to worry because you are not a good spouse, parent or employee if you don't...you are getting bullied!)

Take action or let it go and Be More Productive.

The best way out of a problem is through it.
Unknown

APRIL 26

BE UN-SEPARATED

Another way we work against ourselves is guilt. Guilt is another bully who can push us around by playing on our shortcomings and mistakes, particularly the ones we know we could have made better choices in and didn't.

Here is guilt's tactic: Guilt separates you from the person involved and others. It wants you to disengage from a relationship or life. What happens if you have guilt regarding a client— whether it be for lack of contact or lack of performance—and you separate yourself physically and emotionally?

Your client is not going to know the depth of your sorrow; she is going to know only that she feels ignored and that you seem uninvolved.

It is the same with a friend or family member...if you miss your friend's event AGAIN when you know you could have put forth better effort to be there, you may try to avoid her in some way—if not physically, then emotionally. Your friendship will suffer until you truthfully address the issue. If you don't, your friendship can become shallow as you tiptoe around the hurts.

Guilt can occur just because we let someone bully us, but most often we feel guilt when we know we could have done better. Don't let guilt create yet another problem by creating separation between you and others. Own the issue, admit the truth to yourself and take an action of change to help that situation not occur again.

Remember we are not perfect. We are going to make mistakes. The quicker we acknowledge and own those mistakes and take action for change, the more powerful we feel and the better we will be able to serve our clients and those we love. Truth strengthens us.

Guilt makes us want to run to our emotional closet.
But we don't do anyone any good hiding out in our emotional closet.
Susan Goodman

APRIL 27

BE FORTHCOMING

Beth Moore says that silence breeds shame. If you cannot talk honestly about a subject, you probably have shame regarding it and if there is shame, guilt may not be far behind. So when you realize you don't want to admit something:

Own the issue: I did not contact as many prospects as I wanted last month.

Admit the truth to yourself: I am not on track with my goal and it is because I contacted less than half the number of potential clients I said I would.

Take an action of change: Schedule prospecting into your day and give it the same importance as an appointment with your top client. Tell your manager the number of people you will contact next month...say it out loud to yourself and others repeatedly. Set daily contact goals and meet them...no excuses. Give yourself little rewards when you meet weekly goals.

If you hide an issue or can't admit there is one...you've got a little problem that could mushroom into a bigger one. Your problem could be about prospecting, food or professional knowledge. For instance, you don't want to admit the actual number of prospects you contacted last month or the number of cookies you eat in a night. Or you just won't admit you don't know something because you didn't read the information. Silence breeds shame. Guilt is shame's companion. If you can't be honest about an issue there might be a behavior, habit or thought you need to change. There are several reasons you might not be able to talk about or admit something; shame, fear, pride, etc. The key is to recognize the symptom and effectively address the source, because whether the source is pride, fear or guilt, they all want to equally keep you from positive possibilities that accompany a joyful life and flourishing business. Don't let guilt create yet another problem in your life—besides the one you already feel guilty about—by creating separation between you and others. Own the issue, admit the truth to yourself, and take an action of change to ensure that situation will not occur again. And as always, ask for help if you need it. You have too much to do today to waste energy with negative emotions.

More people would learn from their mistakes if they weren't so busy denying them.
Harold J. Smith

APRIL 28

BE TASK ORIENTED

We procrastinate for so many reasons and fear or laziness is often the root. We are afraid it won't be perfect, or even good enough. We are afraid of some task within a project such as speaking at a seminar. Fear and just pure laziness are often the source of procrastination, but probably just as often you procrastinate because you are overwhelmed. You have so much to balance between the office and home that planning a seminar or implementing a communication process suddenly seems beyond your capability.

It is good to wait for the appropriate time, but if you find yourself making up excuses why you are not doing something, the right time may be here. We get overwhelmed with the magnitude of a project and find excuses (lies to our self) for not starting it yet.

When something feels overwhelming, break it down into smaller pieces. You don't have to learn all about estate planning overnight, but you could read one piece on the subject for ten minutes each day. Just that simple act will make you feel more positive toward your task and yourself. And when we put forth a genuine effort, somehow possibilities meet us halfway.

When we make just a short-time commitment, we will often get in flow and work longer and more efficiently than if we had dedicated extended time to a project. I don't know if it is energy or facing a fear or a little of both, but an engaged effort seems to multiply itself. Most things are changeable so don't let "perfectionism procrastination" keep you from getting started. Often, it is not as important for something to be perfect as for it to just *be*. Start your project today and let it evolve into what it is supposed to be. It could turn out just as you imagined or could become more than you ever thought possible. You won't know which until you take the first step. Begin today, because your project is not going to go away.

The best way to get something done is to begin.
Unknown

Start by doing what's necessary; then do what's possible;
and suddenly you are doing the impossible.
St. Francis of Assisi

APRIL 29

BE AN ALL-IN CONTRIBUTOR

To get the most out of this life means to contribute the most to it. To get every drop of happiness, prosperity and success this life has for us, we must continually ask ourselves how we are contributing to it.

1. Am I using all my talents?

2. What am I holding back?

3. What am I afraid of?

We all want to know our purpose in life, and it would be great if that came to us via letter or email. For example, "Ronald Reagan, your purpose is to work to end the Cold War." But those emails don't happen, and if they did we would probably go about our purpose all wrong because we would miss the lessons along the way. And if we miss those wisdom-producing lessons, we will be ill-equipped to handle "our purpose" when it presents itself.

If you will have an intention of positive contribution—to your clients, your office, your family, your community, and your relationships—the possibilities will come. What are you giving?

Ask yourself what you are contributing to your work and your life. When you give your full effort, purpose and possibilities reveal themselves.

What would happen if you forgot your self-imposed limitations and became an All-in contributor to this life?

In any situation, ask yourself: What strengths do I possess that can contribute towards accomplishing something in this situation? Then follow through.
Unknown

APRIL 30
BE CHARITABLE

If we know there can be purpose in problems, why do we struggle so? There are many reasons, but two are pride and judgment. Pride wants to keep us silent about our mistake. That silence can eventually produce shame. And shame, like fear, will make us shrink from possibilities.

Another reason is judgment. We don't want to share problems or mistakes, because we are fearful people will judge us and think we are unintelligent, bad or incompetent. Here is a quick "fix" to that. When we stop judging others, we will stop thinking others are judging us. It is a "get what you give" concept.

When we judge others harshly, we often judge ourselves harshly, too, without realizing it. If we have an attitude of "How can I help you solve this?" rather than, "How stupid can you be?" we will find we will be kinder to ourselves, also. And when we are kind to ourselves, we can see the possibilities within the problems.

Think about the mistakes you don't want to own up to. They are often either

1. Ones we are continually criticized for making.

OR

2. Ones we criticize others for making, if only in our thoughts.

Acknowledge, own, and fix mistakes. Carrying the mistake or "failure" around on our journey is exhausting and becomes part of the problem. Carrying the lesson with us is helpful, purposeful and part of a solution.

Remember, it is pride's job to destroy something (a relationship, an idea, a job) and shame's job to exaggerate (a mistake, problem, situation). Don't let them.

Admit your errors before someone else exaggerates them.
Andrew V. Mason

MAY 1

BE OF GOOD EFFORT

Positive possibilities present themselves more often when we are doing the right thing, being positive with our thoughts and attitudes and being honest about our intentions. Our actions, intentions and thoughts all matter—particularly our thoughts of ourselves.

We all have things we don't like about ourselves or things we are not proud of, but if we don't deal with those, we will miss out on possibilities and ways to contribute to this world. To be an All-in contributor you must deal with your opinion of yourself—and your concept of failure and success.

Sometimes we know we didn't "succeed" because we didn't put forth the effort that was in our control. And we need to own those times and move on.

But we don't feel successful about other situations because we didn't get to finish. That could be for reasons in our control or not. Either way, what matters is the effort. If you didn't get the opportunity to finish something meaningful to you but you know you gave your best effort, you can know you were successful. The world judges success by outcome when really success is simply to give your full effort to something regardless of the outcome.

If you give your full effort to a prospect and in the end he chooses another company, did you fail? Maybe from the world's eyes. But what if all the effort you put into that prospect was to prepare you for the better client that is coming next month? Every time you put forth full effort, regardless of outcome, you are building something good. If you are giving your full effort and are not achieving your goals, maybe you need to tweak a few things—your sales tactics, your investment process or your style. Those things are easily fixable and you have many people willing to help. When it comes to success, if you have attitude and effort, you are already there. Sometimes we don't feel that we are successful because we didn't finish something, but in the end we find out what mattered was the effort.

Satisfaction lies in the effort, not in the attainment. Full effort is full victory.
Mahatma Gandhi

MAY 2
BE ALERT

Are you more concerned with what you give or what you are going to get? We are human and certainly at times we make decisions based on what we are going to get; but overall, are you more concerned and have more care for what you contribute or what you receive?

When we are more concerned with what we get than what we give, we might be afraid of something. If we are afraid of losing our job or a client or a relationship, we don't contribute with an All-in effort. We worry about the future and what might happen rather than put our full effort to this moment and what actually is.

Pay attention to what you are contributing to your work and your relationships and this life. Are your contributions positive or negative? What energy do you bring to your office? Is it good or bad? What attitude do you carry in the door with you? Do you make positive contributions to the success of your associates and situations?

When we make positive contributions, positive possibilities present themselves. They don't always come wrapped in a beautiful box; sometimes they come in the form of a problem. But when we make positive contributions to our lives, we will start to look for the opportunities that come with the problem. Opportunities abound for you to grow, to strengthen a relationship or simply to learn something new.

When you make positive contributions to your work with your actions, words and attitudes, you will eventually get the promotion or the new client or the help you are asking for. What are you contributing?

There is a very real relationship, both quantitatively and qualitatively, between what you contribute and what you get out of this world.
Oscar Hammerstein II

MAY 3

BE CONTRIBUTING

How do we stay focused on contributing positively? One way is to take the focus off ourselves.

If we are afraid, we *probably* are not giving All-in effort. Being afraid usually indicates we are concerned with "me."

How will this affect me? What will they think about me? What if he/she leaves me? How will I…? And remember, when we make a decision based on fear, it is ultimately not going to be successful. (Or rather, let's say a fear-based decision is probably not going to be successful. Anything is possible.)

When we stay focused on what we can contribute to the company, the relationship, the client, or a solution, rather than what we can get for "me," we tend to spend less time going in circles (wasting time and energy) and more time efficiently building something good.

It is important to consider how something is going to affect you and others—and you need to make choices that are good for you—but be aware that sometimes the choice that is best for you is not the obvious one but the most contributing one.

A very real benefit of being a contributor is that when we give, we are not afraid to ask for what we need…the help, the favor, or the business. We may not get it, of course, but when we give with an All-in effort, we will boldly ask.

What are you contributing?

There is a very real relationship, both quantitatively and qualitatively, between what you contribute and what you get out of this world.
Oscar Hammerstein II

MAY 4
BE SERVING

Positive possibilities are everywhere, depending on our attitude and perspective. Possibilities exist in relationships, deals and even problems.

In your interactions today, ask a question:

How can I help this person? or How can I serve this person? or How can I contribute in a positive way to their situation?

Ask one of those questions even if you don't like the person. In fact, ask the question *particularly* if you don't like the person. Your internal response might trigger a new energy around your relationship that leads to more productive interactions or it might simply make you see them and yourself in a new light.

You don't have to act on the answer at that moment; sometimes asking the question now is preparing you for an opportunity in the future. Just be ready to act when your opportunity to contribute arises.

We seem to see the possibilities that obviously help ourselves, but we can sometimes miss those awesome possibilities that arise from sincerely serving another.

Seek to contribute today by seeking to help. Possibilities can be created by service.

The secret of success in life is for a man to be
ready for his opportunity when it comes.
Benjamin Disraeli

MAY 5
BE SMOOTH

Relationships offer so many possibilities for our needs being met—financially, emotionally, materially. But some relationships seem to only present problems, and often, those relationships involve the difficult people in our lives or, as I have heard them described, the "sandpaper" people of our lives. We all have them, those people that rub us the wrong way. (And even more importantly to remember—we are all sandpaper people to someone else, too!) Interactions with our sandpaper people create friction instead of smooth interactions. Results are still achieved, but often a negative energy flows around the situation that begins with the dread of having to deal with that person.

Things to help you with sandpaper relationships: Often there is a lack of respect involved with one party or both. Seek to understand why that is and work to resolve the issue. Honesty with yourself is a great place to start. Remember to look for the opportunities in the problems.

There will always be sandpaper relationships—people you rub the "wrong way" or they you. But with the proper perspective, those sandpaper relationships eventually help us to be better, "smoother" people, even if it happens just because we wear each other down! So while you will always encounter personality differences and difficulties, overall, an intention of positive contribution will create more productive interactions and favorable outcomes.

Think of people like sandpaper; the more they rub you the wrong way,
the more polished you get.
Unknown

MAY 6
BE SMOOTHER

It is always good to have questions/statements to keep yourself "in check" and moving toward your goal rather than in circles, wasting time and energy.

Below are three thoughts to help you check your words and attitudes toward the sandpaper people in your life.

1. What you don't like in the other person is probably a trait you also don't like in yourself.

2. Whatever words you are saying about that person, right now someone else is saying about you.

3. No matter how you feel about the person, someone else feels that same way about you.

These may not be completely accurate statements, but they can help you to be more conscious of your contribution to the negative situation, more careful about the words you choose to speak, less defensive in your attitude and more open to the possibilities that are ever present, even in difficult situations. If they were true statements, would you speak and think differently than you do now about the sandpaper people in your life?

There are many tactics for dealing with our sandpaper people, so if you need help with identifying solutions, get it. Remember, we are either part of the problem or part of the solution. Our attitude and intention have as much to do with which part we play as our words do. So as you seek out the coping strategies that work best for you, it helps to seek to have peace, not to "win."

A loving person lives in a loving world.
A hostile person lives in a hostile world: everyone you meet is your mirror.
Ken S. Keyes, Jr.

MAY 7
BE POSSIBLE

Anything is possible. Even smoothing a sandpaper relationship. But what if the difficult person is you? We can easily identify the sandpaper people in our lives and yet forget that we are sandpaper people to others.

Today, be aware of any sarcasm you use. Some is purely for humor, but often sarcasm is used to wrap up a truth we are not brave enough to say. Sarcasm is often cowardly and meant to make the other person feel small. The difference is in the intention—is it playful or penetrating?

Also be aware of when you verbally "beat up" on someone. Sure, it makes you feel powerful for a minute, but you will eventually feel bad for your behavior.

If you catch yourself being sarcastic or verbally beating someone up, stop, rewind and say, simply, "You know what, I didn't mean that" or "I'm sorry, what I meant to say was..."

Know how you feel and *effectively* express it. Masking through sarcasm or verbal bullying does not resolve anything; it just prolongs the problem and creates negative energy. And negative energy pushes out positive possibilities.

Anything is possible.

Kind words are a creative force, a power that concurs in the building up
of all that is good, and energy that showers blessings upon the world.
Lawrence Lovasik

MAY 8
BE THERE

Ninety percent of pursuing possibilities is in just showing up. That means showing up for the meeting or the date or the luncheon and then really being there. Being present in the moment where you are. If you thought of your "coolest" opportunities, you would probably find they came from just showing up somewhere with a "What cool thing is supposed to happen?" attitude.

Show up to work today and be there.

Show up to a meeting today and be there.

Show up to your home this evening and be there.

...with a "What great thing is going to happen?" attitude.

There will always be setbacks, there will always be difficulties, but you never know who is watching how you handle that situation. A potential client may be making a decision about doing business with you based on how you handle an undesirable situation. It is much easier to effectively deal with problems when we start with a "something cool can come from this" attitude.

Sure, you can still encounter great opportunities with your mind being somewhere else or if you have a bad attitude, but you will likely miss many more than you will find. Show up in mind and body and enjoy your possibilities.

I've found that luck is quite predictable. If you want more luck,
take more chances. Be more active. Show up more often.
Brian Tracy

MAY 9
BE AGILE

Just as we don't know who is watching how we handle a difficult situation, we also don't know the impression we are making on people. You are going to be shocked when someone comes to you years later telling you the impression you made on them and the positive difference you made in their life. Those are great to hear and make us feel good and purposeful, but we mustn't be blind to the fact that there could also be circumstances where we might have made a *negative* impact on others.

We are much quicker to be irritated or indignant and to mishandle an issue when we show up with a < (less than) attitude. When we come into a situation with a < attitude, we tend to create a < outcome: less than what we ultimately want, less than the best, less than what is possible.

At any point, we can stop and turn our attitude around, but we must want to, be willing to and actually do it. It seems impossible to do that because of opportunity-stealing pride, but once you turn your attitude around a few times, you realize how much more fun you have and how many more possibilities arise. When you realize you aren't showing up with your best attitude, you will want to stop, rewind and bring your best so you can give your best to those around you.

When someone comes to us years later to tell us the difference we made for them, we want it to be a good one.

If you keep showing up with a positive attitude, positive possibilities will too.

The greatest discovery of our generation is that human beings can alter their lives by altering their attitudes of mind. As you think, so shall you be.
William James

MAY 10

BE YOUR BEST

We want to bring our best into situations. In fact, it is our responsibility to contribute our best to our clients, our family, our associates. Not *the best*, but *our best*—for that day, that moment, that task. We are not perfect; we are people who feel and hope and fear. We don't always get enough sleep. We don't always eat when we should. Sometimes our commitments outnumber the minutes available in our calendar.

Problems are going to happen. Of course, you can work to eliminate over-booking that makes you chaotic and low-blood sugar that makes you crabby, and yet still there are going to be days you don't feel your best.

As you are getting ready for meetings, you are juggling schedules, saying goodbye to kids who want to know where their blue shirt is and handling problems that pop-up with clients (it is some universal law that the minute you try to leave the office, everyone wants you). You may feel scattered and overwhelmed and don't feel at your best. But when you show up with an expect-the-best attitude, somehow what you need will find you. You can come into a situation not feeling your best and still trust that you will receive what you need.

Don't confuse "your best," with "perfection." We are going to have off days, we are going to trip over words in meetings and we are going to be frustrated with someone around us and raise our voice. Correct what you can; let go of what you can't.

Phil Mickelson isn't going to shoot five under every round of golf he plays, but if he shows up with his best attitude every round, he still contributes to his overall success. Sometimes attitude rather than performance is the key.

Some days "your best" is not very good on a performance scale but can still be good-to-excellent on an attitude scale. Your best is not going to be at the same level every day and it is not going to be the same best as those around you. Do the best you can in this moment and possibilities will take care of themselves.

Always do your best. Your best is going to change from moment to moment;
it will be different when you are healthy as opposed to sick. Under any circumstance,
simply do your best, and you will avoid self-judgment, self-abuse and regret.
Don Miguel Ruiz

MAY 11

BE ON TIME

Show up with your best attitude *on time* or maybe even...*early*. For years, I was always a few minutes late. I would try to fit one more thing in before I left. Then someone told me being late was selfish and disrespectful. When we are habitually late, we are implying that our time is more valuable than another person's time.

Of course, we are going to be late sometimes because of circumstances beyond our control such as traffic, a sick child, technical difficulties, a client problem. But when we know we have done our part to be on time, we can trust that this extra issue happened for a reason and we can be released from the stress of being late.

For example: If you knew you were running late because of poor planning and then traffic made you even more behind schedule, you are still going to be a little stressed because you had not done your part to get there on time. (And we can't try to use traffic as the reason because it would just be an excuse and you would still be stressed.)

But if you left the office in plenty of time to get to your destination and ran into terrible construction traffic, you can be released from the stress and trust that you aren't supposed to be there yet because you had done your part to arrive—not just on time, but early.

Arriving on time (or ten minutes early) eliminates one more anxiety, frustration, or problem. It can help you be better able to handle issues that arise and often be more productive in interactions because your focus is on the other person rather than your excuses or late arrival.

If you are late again, don't beat yourself up; just do your best to do better next time. When you know you have done your best, you can be released from stress and guilt that unforeseen circumstances can bring and trust that those unexpected circumstances are a purposeful part of your day.

I give it as my deliberate and solemn conviction that the individual who is habitually tardy in meeting an appointment will never be respected or successful in life.
Rev. W. Fisk

MAY 12
BE PROBLEM-FREE

Fear paralyzes. Pride destroys—relationships, jobs, people, happiness, goals.

Having pride in our work with an intention to do it well is good. Being proud of your children and recognizing their gifts and achievements are good. Being prideful is not. There is a difference. When you want *yours* (your work, your child, your home, your car) to be better than others' in order to feel superior and make another person feel less than you, that is "bad" pride. The difference is wanting yours to be the best it can be *and* wanting that good for others, too.

I somewhere found "pride" defined as the love of one's own excellence, a desire to be more important or attractive than others, failing to acknowledge the good work of others. Excessive love of self.

We want to be excellent in all we do. We want to contribute the best we can to our work, the world and the people around us. But we don't want to admire our own excellence too long or place ourselves above others in importance. That is the "bad" pride. We can miss opportunities in the present when we admire too much or dwell too long on a personal achievement from the past. Appreciating and celebrating our accomplishments is good, but we can miss future contributions and achievements when we are too intent on admiring the old ones.

If you can't sincerely acknowledge the good of/ in another person, you might have a pride problem in that area or with that person. If you want someone else to do poorly or be unhappy, there could be a pride problem. If you won't say, "I was wrong," there could be a problem.

You are the only one who can know if you have a pride problem. We all have pride issues at some point and we always will. Pride doesn't go away just because we become aware of it. The key is to recognize when pride is a problem instead of a helper, because pride keeps us going in circles with our goals, relationships and possibilities. And we have too much to do to waste time and energy going in circles.

In general, pride is the source of all great mistakes.
Unknown

MAY 13

BE EXPRESSING

We often won't say what we need and want because of pride or because of fear it won't be given to us. Pursuing possibilities seems easier when we can kindly and honestly say what we need and want.

To do that we must:

1. Know what we really need or want.
2. Say *kindly and honestly* what we need and want to the appropriate person.
3. Be mentally prepared so that it is okay if what you want is not given to you. (This is important.)

We can't control the other person's response, but we also are more likely to receive what we need when we can express it.

For example: We realize we are feeling dissatisfied because we want to be appreciated by a friend, manager, or significant other. So rather than saying it, we will often withdraw, become silent, and "stew" about it. Then when they ask, "What's wrong?" We respond, "Nothing" and withdraw more. Nothing?!?! *That's not true!* You feel unappreciated and want to be appreciated.

What's that appreciation look like? A raise...recognition in a meeting...thank you's...your spouse picking up the dry cleaning?

If we feel dissatisfied with a person or situation, we must first understand why. It also helps to have three solutions ready that would satisfy your need in that situation. But also understand and be prepared that the person might not be able or willing to meet your need, and that is okay, too. There is also the possibility they don't think you need appreciation. In that case, you have the opportunity to open a healthy dialogue about expectations...yours and the other person's.

When you find you need something, at the right time (timing is important), express that need rather than "stew" about it. The pursuit of possibilities is not always in the getting; sometimes it is just in the asking.

When we tell the truth, there is a strong force pushing us toward success; when we tell a lie, even a little white lie, there is a stronger force pushing us toward failure.

Unknown

MAY 14

BE SOLUTION-ORIENTED

When we express a need or want and it is not given to us, a great opportunity arises for healthy discussion. That denial presents the ability to learn where our perspectives don't match up. Rather than walk off and make up inaccurate and unproductive stories in our heads, we want to stop and seek to understand.

You want financial help, but maybe your manager doesn't think you are meeting all your job requirements and doesn't want to give you a raise or marketing assistance.

You feel under-appreciated, but maybe your spouse thinks he/she does more than you do and is feeling under-appreciated, also.

You want your friend to babysit, but maybe your friend thinks she has kept your kids five times more than you have kept hers and doesn't want to.

If someone doesn't want to meet your request, don't get defensive. Pride wants you to take offense instead of seek resolution. Don't listen to pride. Instead, seek to understand the other person's perspective and discuss solutions that work for you both.

Maybe your manager didn't know about some of the extra responsibilities you have taken on. Maybe neither you nor your spouse realizes how much the other does and it is good time to really appreciate each other. Whatever the issue, there is often a solution if both parties will be honest about their intention, emotions and beliefs.

• Stay calm. Do not become defensive.
• Seek to understand. (Listen)
• When the time is right, discuss solutions.

It is okay to say, "Let's think about this for a day and talk tomorrow." After a good discussion, you may walk away with common perspectives and clearer understanding; or you may have a new goal to work toward.

Whatever the outcome, keep a good attitude toward your work and responsibilities. Feeding anger and misery because of your disappointment won't help anymore than "stewing" does. Be grateful if your desire is met but if it is not, be of good attitude in working toward a new goal. Good attitudes create good possibilities.

One's best success comes after their greatest disappointments.
Henry Ward Beecher

MAY 15
BE HAPPY

There is a saying, "Would you rather be right or happy?"

Sometimes we find we have stood our ground and "won" the fight but have lost happiness.

When you have argued with someone, try being the first to seek peace.

Even if the other party was wrong, you have some responsibility in the argument.

Ask yourself: "What is my ultimate goal/intention in this relationship?"

If your goal is to be right, then there is no need to seek peace. Your actions are in-line with your goal because you are right!

But if your goal is to have a fruitful, long-term, happy relationship with the other person, (and be happy yourself), then your actions will not be in-line with your goal until you stop blaming the other person and accept and own any part you played in the negative situation, apologize if necessary and seek reconciliation.

That doesn't mean you have to sacrifice your position; it simply means you are keeping respect and communication in the relationship and building a bridge between the two of you rather than a wall. You can respectfully agree to disagree.

Remember the other party does not have to accept your attempts at peace, and that is okay. Once you have done your part for peace sincerely and completely—pride can make your attempt half-hearted—you can be released from guilt or negative emotions and move on to happily pursue all your possibilities.

And keep in mind that a need to be right might not affect just you and the other person, it can also affect the energy, productivity and happiness of those around you.

Would you rather be right or happy?

Temper gets you into trouble. Pride keeps you there.
Unknown

MAY 16

BE HAPPIER

There is "good" pride and "bad" pride—or destructive and constructive pride. "Bad" pride is destructive to our happiness and possibilities and we want to recognize it.

"Destructive" pride feels like:

I want to learn about this, but I should already know it, so I won't ask.

I want to know about her success but I can't ask because I'm smarter than she is.

Mine is better. My car is better. My job is better. My family is better.

When he calls, I am not taking his call. He can just keep calling.

Lonely. Sad. Need to control. Perfectionism. I'm the victim.

"Destructive" pride looks like:

Calling a cab to go to work because you won't ask a co-worker to pick you up.

An escalating argument, rather than seeking to understand.

A person struggling because they don't want to admit they need something.

Someone sitting alone because they don't want to admit they need someone.

A relationship suffering. One or both won't admit their part in the problem.

Not admitting a mistake.

Not pulling the trigger on something because it is not "perfect" yet.

"Destructive" pride sounds like:

You can't do that to me. You'll pay!

Nothing's wrong. I'm fine.

I am right. You are wrong.

She can call me if she wants to talk.

What can he teach me? I've been here longer. I'm smarter.

I will never talk to her again.

The problem is, people eventually stop calling and stop communicating and stop feeling. And then we wonder why we are in the spot we are in. "Bad" pride destroys. If we will stop and do the opposite of what pride is telling us to do, we will find possibilities...and we will be happier. If we are always looking to be right instead of happy, we end up being right alone rather than happy with others.

Destructive pride leads to a < life. Less than what you thought. Less than what you wanted. Less than what is possible.

Would you rather be right or happy?
Unknown

MAY 17
BE OUTSTANDING

Good pride gets us out of bed in the morning with our work clothes clean and pressed and appropriate. It keeps us motivated to arrive early to work and stay a little late with an attitude of excellence. It can keep our car clean and our lawn mowed because we "take pride" in their appearance.

Good pride makes you do a great job on a task even if you are the only one who will ever know. It is about your personal self-respect and expectation.

It turns to "bad" pride when we have to pay more for our clothes than we can afford in order to look better than other people. Or when our car can't leave the driveway if there is a spot on it. Or when we miss our granddaughter's game because the lawn must be mowed every eight days for it to look perfect and this is the eighth day.

Constructive pride builds something good and helps others be good, too.

Destructive pride destroys and secretly wants others to feel or appear small in some way because it makes you feel bigger.

When you take good pride in your work, you are genuinely content with its excellence and you do not worry about another person's performance. On the other hand, destructive pride makes you look for fault in another's performance so you can feel better about yourself.

The difference can be very subtle because we can easily rationalize our thought patterns or words. But while you can try to fool yourself, destructive pride is not fooled and something will eventually be destroyed if you don't tend to it—from a relationship to a business.

While destructive pride is subtle, constructive pride is not. Good pride is intentional about building others up, building good teams, building a good book of business and contributing to our company. It is energizing and motivating.

Be deliberate about constructive pride today. I look at good pride as excellence. Have an attitude of excellence for yourself and an attitude of contribution toward others and you will find yourself building sustainable things in your life while creating possibilities for yourself and others.

Excellence is not a skill. It is an attitude.
Ralph Marston

MAY 18

BE PURSUING EXCELLENCE

What do you want to be excellent in but don't feel you are yet?

Clothing? Job Skills? Seminars? A hobby?

What can you do about it?

If it is clothing, get your outfit out the night before and make sure it is pressed and spot-free.

If it is job skills, take a class or look for help from an internal expert at your company.

If it is seminars, ask someone who is having success how they do it. Get a speaking coach to help polish you and your presentation.

If it is a hobby, look online, join a club involving that hobby or take lessons.

We can achieve a certain level of excellence in whatever we really want to do. There is usually a solution if we will take the time to look for it. If we don't put time and effort into it, we probably aren't as interested at being excellent in that area as we say we are. So admit that and move on. If we keep saying, "I want…" and don't do anything about it, we are wasting energy. Either commit or admit.

Commit yourself to finding solutions and work toward excellence or admit you really aren't interested in pursuing excellence in that area so you can move on to one you are willing to commit to.

Don't make excuses; make something incredible happen in your life right now.
Greg Hickman

MAY 19
BE CONSTRUCTIVE

What could you do today if you acted only on constructive pride?

Today, when you realize a thought or action is being made because of destructive pride, turn around and do the opposite.

Be *boldly constructive* today.

Ask for help on something or of someone you wouldn't before.

Give the compliment to someone you really don't want to give one to.

Tell someone what you need in a kind, confident, well-worded manner.

Ask others, "How do you think I can improve as a _____?"

Apologize...sincerely.

As you interact with others, silently ask yourself the question, "What can I learn from you?"

An attitude of "What can I learn from you?" will make you more engaged and energized and can even multiply your possibilities.

When you act on constructive pride rather than destructive pride, not only are you going to have more productive interactions and happier days but you are also going to eventually end up with more self-esteem. So others will view you as confident and maybe even more interesting.

Have a "teach me" attitude and be open to every possibility. You will find some you didn't know were possible.

Be boldly constructive all day today!

*Every person that comes into our life comes for a reason;
some come to learn and others come to teach.*
Unknown

Boldness has genius, power, and magic in it. Begin it now.
Johann Wolfgang von Goethe

MAY 20
BE COURAGEOUS

I once read that "fear crushes the treasures." If fear crushes treasures, it paralyzes possibilities. That is fear's job: to freeze you and keep you from your best. Fear comes in many subtle forms. One is jealousy.

When we are jealous, we are afraid we are not going to have "that" too. Whatever "that" is. "That" could be recognition, respect, beauty, clothes, home, relationship, success, or a corner office. Regardless of what "that" is, jealousy is not going to help you get it. In fact, it might even hurt you, because when we are jealous, we block "that" thing from coming into our life, but when we want the best for others, we end up getting the best for ourselves.

I don't know if this is actually true, but regardless, the standard is a good one to live by. Being jealous doesn't help you get any closer to what you want; in fact, it can make you take short cuts that can hurt you in the long run or it can just make you bitter. Bitter taints everything in our lives and automatically gives us a victim complex.

For example: An advisor walks by a great corner office and says to himself, "I am going to have an office like that office one day." While a jealous advisor walks by the same office and says to himself, "I am going to get that guy one day."

Which is the more productive intention?—"I am going to work hard and earn a great office one day, too" or "I am going to beat that guy and take over his position of success"?

A constructive rather than a destructive intention is going to be better in the long run for everyone. If you cannot be happy for someone, you probably have a jealousy issue and pride problem. None of us is immune to jealousy—because we are human. But jealousy is not going to get us what we want. It is the change in our perspective that will change our circumstance.

As a friend says, "Don't be jealous of someone unless you are willing to do what it takes to get there." ...which is usually a lot of hard work, sacrifice and facing of fears. The point is, don't be jealous at all. Just put in the hard work, self-examination and change it takes to make your own possibilities happen. Otherwise, you will let jealousy, bitterness and fear crush your treasures and your possibilities. ✒

When we are jealous, we block what we want from coming into our lives,
but when we want the best for others, we end up getting the best for ourselves.
Susan Goodman

MAY 21
BE DELIBERATE

Jealousy creates confusion and makes us think we want something we probably do not.

Have you ever wanted something, got it, then were disappointed because it didn't give you the *feeling* you thought it would? Or you got the feeling but the feeling didn't last? Oftentimes that is because what we really want is not the big house or the cool car or the trophy. What we really want is the feeling we believe comes with the material item. We get the thing but not the feeling, and we become disillusioned.

We think the big house will give us the security we want or the cool car will make our parents proud or the trophy will get us the respect we crave and when they don't, we are not happy and we don't know why. All those material items are great, but what we really want is the respect, security and happiness, but we don't always know how to get them.

Yes, a great-looking suit that looks sharp on you will boost your energy and confidence, but you didn't purchase energy and confidence with the suit. You already had those; they were just enhanced. A beautiful home is a wonderful gift and gives a sense of security and pleasure to come home to, but real security doesn't come from a house. So being jealous of a "thing" someone else has is not productive because the positive emotions you probably really want come from the hard work and self-inspection of deliberate living.

Jealousy creates confusion because we spend time and energy trying to attain someone else's life when what will really make us happy and fruitful is deliberately living our own. One way to eliminate the confusion that jealousy creates is to be grateful. Work deliberately toward what you want while being authentically grateful for what you have and what you are accomplishing.

Jealousy creates confusion. Gratitude creates possibilities. When you find yourself jealous, change your thinking to a "Good for you; I am going to work toward that, too" attitude and possibilities will come.

To cure jealousy is to see it for what it is, a dissatisfaction with self.
Joan Didion

MAY 22
BE PROCESSING

Another subtle but powerful form of fear is revenge. As human beings, our automatic response when someone hurts us is to somehow hurt them back. We want to teach a lesson and make sure they know how much we hurt by inflicting equal or more hurt on them. Our pride hurts (how could you do this to ME?); we are afraid of what people will say (did you hear about Susan?), of what we will "lose" (money, material items, a client, control).

When we have a vindictive intention, we end up even more unhappy and don't know why. We continue to blame the person who hurt us when, actually, we are the ones holding on to the pain. If we acknowledge our hurt and embarrassment (and any other negative feeling) and then work to heal from that, our wound will likely heal quicker and we get to move on with a more productive, happy life. But if we plot to "get the person back" in some way, our hurt will be prolonged; most of the time we will continue to blame the other person, when actually we have become the party responsible for our pain. There comes a point—and it is difficult to detect—where we become the one hurting ourself, and yet we still blame and continue in a victim mode.

Revenge takes many forms—words that will hurt as much as possible, deals or lawsuits that get as much money or stuff as possible, and even just in our thoughts of wanting the satisfaction of seeing the other person pained, embarrassed or simply unhappy.

Do not avoid or suppress feelings. We must express and process negative emotions—anger, fear, pride, resentment, bitterness, etc. The key is processing, and that may take an hour or a year. But the important thing is to seek to understand, process and heal—not to seek revenge. That small intention is important to our happiness.

As people of excellence, wanting the best in and for our lives, when we are hurt by a rude stranger or a family member or a manager, our response should be to stop, recognize we were hurt and make a deliberate decision about our response. Seek constructive solutions and truth rather than destructive revenge. We choose our response (both internal and external) to every situation…choose happiness and positive possibilities.

Those who plot the destruction of others often perish in the attempt.
Thomas Moore

MAY 23
BE FORGETFUL

While the urge to "get people back" is strong, it is not productive and it certainly is not going to create possibilities. Revenge crushes possibilities and creates more pain than is necessary. So when we catch ourselves wanting someone to hurt instead of be happy, we need to stop, be aware of the destructive intention and either admit that is what we are choosing or work to eliminate it.

Rewind. Stop and ask yourself, "If I could do it over, what would I do?" and then do it. Talk to the person involved and tell them how you feel. Make sure you are doing that with an intention of solution, not bashing and pointing out all their wrongs in the situation. That is still revenge.

Seek to understand. Most of us do not want to seek to understand. We want to operate on our assumptions so we don't have to accept responsibility. It is important to understand the other person and our part in the issue because if we don't, we could keep repeating the situation in the future and not know why.

Talk to your Truthtalker. We all need someone who will be on our side enough to tell us the truth. There are friends who just tell us what they think we want to hear; then there are friends who won't let us be less than what we can be. They will tell us the truth even if it is hard to hear. Find that person in your life. Truth can be painful and difficult, but ultimately it strengthens and energizes. When we get to truth, we can finally get to peace. And truth involves seeing and owning our part in the problem.

Own your part. Ask yourself, "How did I contribute to this situation?"

Forgive. Forgive the other person and forgive yourself for your part. Consider this quote from an unknown source: "When we forgive someone they don't get off scot-free; we do."

Once you forgive yourself and the other person, forget the problem and move on, because if you don't, you eventually become the one causing your pain, not the other person. You have too many amazing things to do to be wasting your time with revenge.

While seeking revenge, dig two graves—one for yourself.
Doug Horton

MAY 24
BE ENHANCING

To pursue all possibilities, it is helpful to know and understand what and how we feel. We can more easily manage our emotions rather than our emotions managing us when we are mindful. A simple goal that will help you is to leave people better than you found them...with a smile, a compliment, a kind intention or just looking them in the eye and thanking them. You don't have to do any outstanding act; just having a constructive intention rather than a destructive one makes all the difference.

Even if this is a way of life for you, you won't be able to do it all the time. Remember, we are human. We have days that we are not our best, and there are some people we actually have to psych ourselves up to leave better than we found them (like our sandpaper people). But if we will remember that a few people might have that same trouble with us (we are a sandpaper person to someone), we might be a little more forgiving of their not-so-nice behavior, because we will one day want that same forgiveness from someone else. The point is, don't beat yourself up. Either rewind, apologize and start over or just do better next time.

Whether dealing with a client, a family member, a CEO or a valet attendant, try out the goal of leaving people better than you found them, and possibilities might just start knocking at your door.

Beginning today, treat everyone you meet as if they were going to be dead by midnight. Extend to them all the care, kindness and understanding you can muster, and do it with no thought of any reward. Your life will never be the same again.
Og Mandino

MAY 25
BE RIGHT

People say fear is good because it keeps us from doing the wrong thing. The problem is that sometimes fear can keep us from doing the right thing. So what if you took fear out of the situation and simply asked, "Is this the right thing to do?"

Example: Maybe you are afraid to jump off a bridge. Take fear out and ask yourself, is jumping off a bridge the right thing to do? NO!

Maybe you are afraid to go out on a blind date with a friend of a friend. Take fear out of it and ask, is going on a blind date with a friend of a friend the right thing to do? Maybe.

Or maybe you are afraid of public speaking so you won't host a seminar. Take fear out of it and ask, is holding a seminar the right thing to do? Maybe.

The point is, don't choose not to do something because you are afraid. Choose not to do it because it is not the right thing to do. For instance: Don't make the decision to not drive 150 mph because you are afraid you will get caught...make the decision to not drive 150 mph because it is simply not the right thing to do.

When we don't do something because we are afraid we will "get caught," we can end up making some of those poor decisions anyway because someone (or ourselves) can convince us we won't get caught. On the other hand, when we make a decision to not do something because it is simply "not the right thing to do," it seems we end up with stronger character and decision-making skills. That might not be true, but it sure seems like it.

And if we take fear out of the decision-making, we don't take it into the situation with us. We make decisions based on what is right for us, rather than what we are afraid of happening or not happening.

We must always be smart and stay out of dangerous, illegal and bad situations. I can't imagine any of those that would be the right thing to do. Once you know a decision is a good one for you, go ALL-IN. Prepare, ask for help if necessary and leave fear out of it, because fear crushes the possibilities.

The right thing to do never requires any subterfuge; it is always simple and direct.
Calvin Coolidge

MAY 26
BE IN THE PRESENT

Possibilities are increased when we make decisions in the present moment. If we always made our decisions based on the past, nothing would change. How many times have you said, "I have tried that; it doesn't work." And maybe it didn't then, but it might now.

We live in an ever-changing dynamic world. Why do we think we can stay the same and still compete (or be happy)? Maybe you tried a particular prospecting tool three years ago and it wasn't successful. But maybe now is the time to try it again. Ask others how they have success with it and modify it for your personality, business and belief systems. Or don't. You don't have to do anything you do not want to do. But make sure you are making your decisions based on what is serving you and your clients, not based on avoidance because of fear or "no" because of pride.

The reason something didn't work before could have been your attitude or intention, your circumstances, execution, timing or that it just wasn't supposed to be. The point is to be aware and consider making your decisions based on what you want and current circumstances, not purely from the past.

Take a look at the traditions in your life, your business and your personal patterns. Ask yourself, "Do I like it or do I want to try something new?"

If you always say no to blind dates and you are still single and don't want to be, you might want to try something new. If you always say no to your manager's ideas and your business isn't growing, you might want to try something new. If you always say no to your friend and you aren't hearing from him or her lately, you might want to try something new.

"No" is not bad. No is very appropriate and necessary. Boundaries are good. We have to choose our lives and "no" is part of that. Just make sure you are being deliberate about your choices, not saying "yes" or "no" based on habit, fear or pride, but on what is the best choice for you and those around you.

We are creating our lives and businesses with our "yeses" and "no's," both internal and external. Be aware of them and the life you are creating with them.

It is not necessary to change. Survival is not mandatory.
Unknown

MAY 27
BE UNCHAINED

Not forgiving an offense is a bit like revenge in that, at some point, we become the ones causing our pain and anger. So to be less pained (or maybe completely pain-free), own your part in the problem, think about how you would have handled it all differently and forgive the person. For some things, it may take more time, but for most daily situations, we can simply choose to not be offended and choose to forgive.

Choosing to forgive doesn't mean you ignore the problem. If there is an ongoing situation you need to address then do so at the right time. Remember to seek to understand. Since we come from two sets of needs and two different perspectives, it is easy to get sideways. As hard as it is to believe, not everyone thinks as we do and we will help ourselves and our productivity if we seek to understand the other person's perspective. And the good news is we may also find ways we are creating our problem. Our pride may not like knowing how we are creating the problem, but it is much easier to change our behavior and eliminate the negative than it is to change another person's.

If you say you "can forgive but can't forget," you are fooling yourself...you have not forgiven the person who offended you and are likely choosing not to. The more truthful expression would be, "I can forgive, but I am choosing not to." You can choose to not forgive...we all have that choice. But when we choose not to forgive, at some point we must accept responsibility that we have become the cause of and major contributor to our own unhappiness.

I can forgive, but I cannot forget, is only another way of saying,
I will not forgive. Forgiveness ought to be like a cancelled note - torn in two,
and burned up, so that it never can be shown against one.
Henry Ward Beecher

MAY 28

BE A GOOD SPENDER

What we focus on has power in our lives. If we are worried (someone being seriously ill, our child in trouble, etc.), that situation has power in our lives. We spend energy and time on the concern, even if it is mainly in our thoughts. We can all relate to that.

All negative situations are similar in that way to varying degrees, and holding a grudge is no different. We let the situation and the other person have power in our lives by our unwillingness to forgive. Not only are we hurt, now we use our valuable time and energy to keep reliving the injury in some way. Then we spend energy avoiding the person, and we spend time thinking about how we will act if we do see them.

If we thought about a business building activity as much as we thought about someone who has offended us (or our sandpaper person) and take the negative energy we spend on that situation and use it for positive energy toward the success of an activity, we would rock! Think about it, if we spent as much time and energy envisioning the conversations with our future clients as we do envisioning our next (or past) interaction with "that person we are angry with," we would have more productive interactions and positive experiences.

If we are spending our time and energy on an old injury, we are not pursuing all our possibilities. When we forgive, we let it go and can spend our time and energy on making a positive impact in the present rather than on reliving a pain in the past.

If we don't forgive, that unforgiveness can turn into bitterness. And while you can pursue possibilities in any mood or emotional state, positive possibilities seem to just show up when we are focused on making a difference rather than making a point. When we are holding on to unforgiveness, we are often subconsciously trying to make a point, not a difference.

Become aware of anything in your mind that does not help you be a better professional, spouse, parent, employee, contributor—often that includes old offenses and new worries.

Release the issue and move on to thoughts and activities that benefit you and your clients in this day. What are you spending your thoughts on?

What we think, we become.
Buddha

MAY 29
BE UNCONFINED

In order to pursue all our possibilities, we need to be free. Unforgiveness keeps us bound up in a virtual prison. We can't see the bars, but we are incapable of stepping outside that little cell to explore what is possible. "I can't_____" is a good symptom of a freedom problem. When you say "I can't," replace the words with "I will not" or "I choose not to." For example, "I can't go to that restaurant; I might run into Jim." You can go, but you choose not to because you are afraid.

When we begin to let go of grudges and forgive, a whole new way of living and doing business opens up for us. When a client leaves us, we might hold a little grudge that can lead to a multitude of complications down the road. If we are holding a grudge, we will probably avoid that former client. And if we are not going places in order to avoid her, then we are possibly avoiding other clients or future clients, as well. Or we won't prospect someone we know is a friend of hers because we are still holding a grudge and anything associated with her is negative for you. Should she want to come back to you one day (after finding out just how good you are!) if you are still holding a grudge that is not going to happen.

The prison of unforgiveness keeps you operating in a little bitty box, dictating your actions based on negative, fearful thoughts rather than operating in a realm of positive possibilities. If you have insecurities or a tendency to avoid certain people, it could be because you haven't forgiven yourself for your part in a problem.

If you have trouble forgiving *another person,* imagine that when you refuse to forgive someone for an offense, you are giving someone else permission not to forgive you. When you want forgiveness, you must also give it.

If you have trouble forgiving *yourself,* imagine that when you refuse to forgive yourself for a mistake, you are modeling that behavior for someone you love. You do not want anyone you love being held back from possibilities and making a difference because they won't forgive themselves for a mistake.

Not forgiving ourselves or someone else keeps us pacing around a little virtual prison cell rather than freely exploring the possibilities and making a positive difference with the lessons we have learned. Life and business are simpler when we will choose to forgive others and ourselves.

To forgive is to set a prisoner free and discover the prisoner was YOU.
Unknown

MAY 30
BE UNDETERRED

A successful young woman shared this story:

"When I first wanted to become an advisor (from being an assistant), I was told by another advisor I shouldn't and that I wouldn't make it as I had three things going *against* me: I was young, female and attractive. A year into my business, I had achieved great success and won awards from my firm. I attributed this to a belief in myself and an extremely focused goal and work ethic. I was determined to prove that associate wrong.

"My associate noticed my success and came back to me, praising me for my efforts and told me I was at an advantage as I had three things going *for* me: I was young, female and attractive."

Once we make a decision to move forward, we must begin to make possibilities out of "problems." When we do that, we can make good things happen. This wisdom reminds us not to let other people's idea of obstacles stand in the way of our own success.

Life is a series of great opportunities brilliantly disguised as impossible situations.
Charles Swindoll

MAY 31
BE MOTIVATED

Yesterday, a businesswoman shared the three things she was told she had going against her. When she had experienced success in a short time period, the same person came back and explained her high accomplishments by listing the three things she had going for her. The pros were the same three characteristics this person had previously listed as her cons. The speaker didn't remember the original comments made to her.

We let negative words people say to us roll around in our heads and hold us back from moving forward when the sad thing is that often we are the only one who remembers them.

If you have unproductive words playing on the tape-recording in your head, either do something about them or ask yourself if you are choosing to hold on to them for some reason. Instead of letting other people's words de-motivate and de-energize you, use them to fuel your journey. You can turn their negative into your positive.

Give awareness today to any negative words or comments that replay in your head and keep you stuck instead of moving forward toward your goals. Those words probably reflect more on who the original speaker is than on who you really are.

When we judge or criticize another person, it says nothing about that person;
it merely says something about our own need to be critical.
Unknown

Change your thoughts and you change your world.
Norman Vincent Peale

JUNE 1

BE MINDFUL

We all have automatic responses to certain situations. I call these "default settings." Most of us believe that because our automatic responses are "automatic," we can't change them. The truth is, we can.

Default settings can be small things that make a big difference in our possibilities. Some are positive—gratitude, seeking to understand, returning calls—but there could be some you would like to change. For example, accepting compliments rather than deflecting them, saying "yes" rather than "no" or "I can't," or eating when you are bored or stressed.

If you can't recognize some of your current default settings, ask the people around you (your associates, children, significant other, friends) how you respond or act in certain situations, and most likely their answers will be a good start for understanding your personal default settings. Since awareness is the first step in changing the ones that are not serving you or your business, you will be well on your way to making changes you want to make.

Your "default settings" can be attributed to any number of things from personality to past experiences, and some are more difficult to change than others. But when we recognize a need and want to more than we are afraid to, we will let go of those that are not serving us and establish new ones that do. Choose your life rather than let it happen to you.

When patterns are broken, new worlds emerge.
Tuli Kupferberg

Happiness is a conscious choice, not an automatic response.
Mildred Barthel

JUNE 2

BE ABNORMAL

Sometimes we are afraid to make changes because they feel permanent or because we are afraid of what people will say. So try out a new default setting for just a day. Just test-drive it. You don't have to maintain the change if you don't like it and how it affects your attitude, business and relationships. Whatever your normal response is, try something new today. (Good and healthy, of course.)

If you normally will not apologize, try admitting your mistake or your part in the problem and offering a sincere apology.

If you normally say to yourself, "Oh no, another problem," try saying to yourself, "Where is the opportunity to learn or improve the relationship?"

If you normally cut people off in conversation, wait for them to finish and then take your turn.

If you naturally grab chocolate at 2:00 in the afternoon, try carrots.

Change a default setting just for today. If you like the results in your day and your relationships, work to keep it; if you don't like the results, don't keep that setting. Be fearless in making changes that make a positive difference in your possibilities.

The key to change...is to let go of fear.
Rosanne Cash

JUNE 3
BE RESPONDING

Possibilities are always possible—even in the midst of difficulties and arguments and struggles. How we respond in tense or negative situations can make the difference between more negativity and being able to find a solution...being disregarded and being respected...and between a relationship being broken or strengthened.

We have the ability to change the course of a conversation by our responses. So we should examine personal default settings, look at how we respond in discussions (disagreements) and think of it this way:

Decisions made in pain produce more pain.

Decisions made in pride produce more pride.

Decisions made in anger produce more anger.

Decisions made in respect produce more respect.

Decisions made in love produce more love.

It may not always be true, but it is a good way for us to manage our responses. Your response can either take a step toward resolving the situation and moving forward to grow the relationship and solve the problem, or you can be angry, difficult, and attacking and have to work on fixing the relationship in addition to the problem. In other words, you can become part of the problem or part of the solution. Your response makes a difference.

Possibilities are everywhere in all situations; choose the more productive response and you will be choosing more productive possibilities.

How people treat you is their karma; how you react is yours.
Wayne Dyer

JUNE 4

BE A LISTENER

Often we respond to pain with pain—you hurt my feelings, I am going to prove you are wrong or hurt you back. What if we responded to pain with patience and when someone disagreed with us, we listened?

Granted, there are going to be situations where we raise our voice because the only way we feel heard is by responding in a like tone. But when those become the norm rather than the exception, people can turn a deaf ear to us and tune us out rather than hear us out.

What if when our kids bickered, rather than yelling and telling them to stop, we stopped and sought to understand?

What if we asked questions and actively listened to the answers—being aware of what is not being said while listening to what is? Then we sought creative solutions? The issue probably isn't going to get solved overnight, but your children will likely feel more respected while learning how to express how they feel. What if when an associate starts "attacking" again, rather than immediately starting in with your side, you listened and then responded?

Active listening helps us to not only gather accurate information and get to the truth of a matter easier, it helps us remain calm because we are not seeking to be right; we are seeking a solution. Listen instead of lashing out and discover new possibilities in relationships and seemingly impossible situations.

Life is a series of great opportunities
brilliantly disguised as impossible situations.
Charles Swindoll

JUNE 5
BE SIMPLE

The pressure and stress of business along with the busyness of life can lead us to forget to appreciate the little things, the moments and the people around us. There is a simple solution to that. Thank you.

Genuine gratitude brings us back to the present moment, a feeling of fullness with appreciation and a multitude of possibilities. How do you feel when your spouse thanks you for picking up the dry cleaning? What about when your significant other gets you a card or simply thanks you for always being happy to see him or her? How do you feel when your manager thanks you for the work you did to help someone out or just for your positive attitude? What about when your kids really thank you for breakfast?

We all thank people for big things, but the little things we live through everyday contribute to our overall attitude and direction of relationships, responsibilities and work. The little things affect our lives and possibilities in a big way.

Recognize the little things all day today. Take nothing for granted. Feel gratitude for your car and that you got to work without any problems. Be grateful you have work to go to. Thank those around you for their attitudes and help. And don't just say, "Thank you." Say, "Thank you for..." As you do, you may notice a new recognition of your own attitude and service to others in the little things.

Make sincere "thank you's" a default setting in your life. The simple awareness of wholehearted gratitude will create possibilities—even in places where you thought none existed.

If you want to turn your life around, try thankfulness.
It will change your life mightily.
Gerald Good

JUNE 6

BE ALIGNED

When situations get "sideways" or tense, what is your automatic response? There are many productive ones; utilize any that work for you. If you don't have one that helps, stop and ask yourself, "What is my intention?"

For example: what is my long-term goal? To double my assets, have a loving marriage, raise confident, contributing children?

Then ask, what is my short-term intention? To win the argument or find a solution, to fight or have a great day, to get my way or do the right thing? To make the other person feel small or make them feel valued?

Once you identify your intention, get your thoughts, words, and actions lined up with it. (This part takes a little longer but is worth it in the long run.)Anything else will keep you going in circles rather than toward your goal.

There are always possibilities, but when we are going in circles, the same ones keep popping up. When we step out and move toward our goal, we find new possibilities we haven't seen before down that road. Find new, positive possibilities.

The possibilities are numerous once we decide to act and not react.
George Bernard Shaw

JUNE 7

BE SLEEPING

Sometimes happiness just happens, but probably many more times, it is a choice. If happiness isn't happening for us, we need to examine our happiness habits. Some are unique to the individual, but most of us share some basics that affect our days and how we feel in them.

One big factor in our happiness is sleep. How much sleep we need is unique to each of us, but we all need it. If we don't get enough good sleep, we are less energetic, less productive and quicker to be dramatic or frustrated because of concentration problems. We see the glass as half empty, and we can have difficulties seeing the possibilities sitting right in front of us.

If you are not getting enough sleep, what can you do? If it is because you like watching the late show, record it. If it is because you awake with angst, seek a solution. People have found many solutions that help; some seem unconventional, but they have worked for someone, so maybe they will for you. If you awake with anxiety or thoughts running through your head, keep a piece of paper and pen by the bed. You don't even have to turn on the light; just scribble what is in your head. There is something about writing it down that lets you let it go—as if our brains say, "Okay, I don't have to work to remember that anymore. It's written down so I will remember to worry about it tomorrow." I know people who have found their sleep solution in tapes. Whether it is a tape of people talking them to sleep or the sound of running water, if it works, play it! Things as simple as exercise and meeting your responsibilities can be good sleep factors. Or you may need to see a doctor; medical issues such as hormones could be causing your sleepless nights.

Sleep is so good and such an important component to overall health and happiness that if you are not sleeping, seek a solution. Read a book, see a specialist…or peruse a prospectus. If we don't sleep at night, we could end up sleep-walking through our days.

To achieve the impossible dream, try going to sleep.
Joan Klempner

JUNE 8

BE CHOOSING HAPPINESS

To pursue all our possibilities, it helps to be deliberate about our life and that includes our happiness. What makes us happy?

Maybe the biggest factor in our happiness is simply taking responsibility for our happiness rather than looking to others to make us happy; owning our lives and our choices rather than blaming others...in other words, personal responsibility.

Contrary to what we *want* to believe, others are not responsible for our happiness. Not our boss, not our spouse, not our children or friends. They contribute to our happiness, but they are not responsible for it. There is a big difference. One makes them part of the fullness of your life, the other makes them feel guilty for the emptiness of it. If we want someone to feel guilty, then we probably have an emptiness that needs filling, and no matter how much we want someone to fill it, they can't. Sadly, we can end up making them feel guilty when they simply aren't thinking and acting the way we want them to.

We need people in our lives and it makes us happy to be with those we love. We just need to make sure we are happy simply being with them, not happy only when we can control them.

As we start developing more happiness habits in our lives, the first place to start is with the realization that we are ultimately responsible for our own happiness. Not others, not circumstances—us. Who or what have you been blaming or trying to control?

We pursue possibilities but we choose happiness.

Take your life in your own hands, and what happens?
A terrible thing: no one to blame.
Erica Jong

JUNE 9
BE ACCOUNTABLE

Blaming steals our joy and our possibilities. Taking responsibility for our lives and happiness is hard because when we do that, we have to stop blaming others for our problems and fears and unhappiness. It is much easier to say, "You did blah blah blah," rather than, "I did..." Rarely does a personal situation arise that we do not have some part in its happening and its outcome.

If we don't take responsibility for our part in a situation, we will likely repeat it. We will find ourselves months or years down the road in a similar situation and wonder how we got there. When we begin taking responsibility for our contributions to a negative situation, something magical may happen: we could become aware of and begin to change those behaviors that get us there.

When you find yourself in situations you like, ask yourself how you got there and repeat those thoughts/actions/attitudes/intentions. You will probably find those involve some form of positive. Contrast that with the ones you don't like and often blame someone else for. They probably involved some form of negative on your part in thought, action, attitude, word or intention. Even if someone else started it, you could finish it differently.

Remember our intention is where it all starts, so blaming in our thoughts and intention is just as debilitating to our happiness as blaming with our words and actions. New possibilities start with owning instead of blaming.

It is not only what we do, but also what we do not do,
for which we are accountable.
Moliere

JUNE 10
BE SEEKING

Possibilities seem to multiply when we own our contributions to unpleasant situations. A celebrity was recently interviewed about a public break-up and what she learned. The break-up was very painful for her, so she said she made a list of the negative things he did. For example: *He* changed. *He* would withdraw. *He* didn't pick up his socks. *He* didn't consider my needs. *He* was selfish. And then she crossed out "He" and wrote "I." She realized the same things she blamed him for in their relationship, she had also done.

Often you will find the things you don't like in others are things you see or have seen in yourself in one form or another. The behavior may not look the same on the outside, but the underlying motivator may be exactly the same on the inside.

Truth is a happiness habit. So when she discovered the truth, it instantly began to free her from the negative effects of blame. If her goal was to blame and seek some form of revenge, she could have kept going in the same negative circles with her thoughts and behaviors. But since her goal was happiness, she sought the truth of the situation, stopped circling the same old stuff and starting moving toward her goal of being happy.

When she stopped blaming her ex-boyfriend, she was freed from the "negative" of the situation and could move past the pain to focus on the positives of the relationship and actually be grateful for having it for the time she did. Whether it is boyfriends, spouses, friends, clients, or the guy who works at the dry-cleaners, when there is a broken relationship, it helps us begin to forgive when we own our part in the problem. Taking responsibility starts the process of forgiveness. And forgiveness lets us see our new possibilities rather than trying to relive old ones. You have too much to do today to spend time in a cycle of blame.

Forgiveness is the only way to break the cycle of blame and pain in a relationship... It does not settle all questions of blame and justice and fairness... But it does allow relationships to start over...
Philip Yancy

JUNE 11

BE ADVENTUROUS

Not all happiness habits are as difficult to develop as taking responsibility for your life. Some are actually fun, like adventure. Adventure is relative. To some it is climbing Mt. Everest; to others it is climbing the bleachers at a high school basketball game. Adventure isn't as much about danger as it is about simply taking a chance.

Dictionary.com defines "adventure" as *an exciting or unusual experience; to take the chance of. Dare.*

Trying new things helps us explore new possibilities. If we are closed off to trying something new, whether it is a new food or a new way to work, we are likely more closed off to pursuing all our possibilities. The degree of adventure doesn't matter as much to our possibilities as the experience and the attitude behind it.

Make it a habit to try new things:

Try a new recipe.

Take a new route to work.

Add something different to your wardrobe.

Sign up for a racc.

Register for a car driving experience.

Take a yoga class.

We don't have to be Indiana Jones to experience the exhilaration and positive effects of a little adventure. It is often just the willingness to try new things that opens the doors to new possibilities.

The only question in life is whether or not you are going to answer a hearty "YES!" to your adventure.
Joseph Campbell

JUNE 12

BE REAL

Many of us work in professions that encourage comparison in various ways. There is a healthy kind of comparison and there is an unhealthy, unhappy kind.

Comparing to improve yourself because you like what you see in someone else or in their life is good. But comparing to find ways for others to improve your situation may not be so good. When you compare and find that you lack something and want it given to you rather than earning it, that is definitely not a healthy kind. And here is the real signal of the not-so-good kind of comparing – when you find yourself not wanting that other person or group of people to have "it" either or not wanting the best for another person.

The first type of comparing accepts responsibility for the choices that landed you where you currently are as well as takes responsibility for your future. The second type does not accept responsibility but blames someone or something else. This type of comparison grows envy and entitlement and is certainly not a happiness habit.

One good way to know the difference is simply how you feel: are you happy and energized or unhappy and angry? Are you happy for the other person or are you unhappy for you? If you find yourself unhappy for you and your situation, then you are likely comparing in an unhealthy way and could end up jealous and looking for a way to feel entitled to what he or she has rather than earn it on your own.

We can create problems in relationships simply because someone has more than we do (more windows in their office, more money, more happy than you feel) and we want to be given what they have rather than work to acquire it ourselves.

The problem is, if we don't work for it ourselves, we probably still won't be happy and we won't know why. Comparing with an attitude of happiness for the other person and working on personal improvement for ourselves creates possibilities and we will find talents and solutions we never dreamed of. But comparing with an attitude of jealousy and entitlement will block possibilities and happiness. Remember that question regarding pride: would you rather be right or happy? Would you rather be jealous or happy?

We must be careful how we compare; it can make all the difference in our efforts and our happiness.

To cure jealousy is to see it for what it is—a dissatisfaction with self.
Joan Didion

JUNE 13
BE UNLIMITED

If you are going to compare up, you have to compare down. He might have the cooler house, but you have a better car. And we must remember that particularly in the context of material comparisons, it is often the feeling, not the "thing," that we are looking for. The feeling of happiness, success, security, and enjoyment that we attach to the cooler house is what we're after, not the house itself.

When we are jealous, we could block that thing we want from coming into our lives, but when we want the best for others, we often end up getting the best for ourselves. Jealousy can block what we want, as well as our possibilities. We are either energized or angry by seeing others happy with things we want. If we are energized and happy for them, we are probably living abundantly and working toward healthy goals. If we are angry, then we are likely living in jealousy with an attitude of lack.

Looking for ways for *you* to improve yourself and your situation is great. Looking for ways for *others* to improve your situation is likely not going to go so well. You will spend days, weeks and maybe even months of your life trying to justify being entitled to what another has in some way, rather than being grateful for what you have now and working toward it yourself. If we put the same energy into building on our own possibilities as we did trying to "take" from another (the corner office, the house, the lifestyle, the business, their laughter), we would find ourselves with self-respect as well as the stuff we want. We can all "have." There is no limit on joy, love or corner offices in the world.

Many of us would put in the hours of labor if we were "guaranteed" those hours would get us what we want. But it's the more important work of putting aside pride, entitlement, jealousy, greed and fear that we are not willing to do. Work with an intention of building in your own life rather than one of taking from another. Not only will you be more productive and energized, but your joy, energy and possibilities will thrive in that attitude of grateful abundance.

If you compare yourself with others, you may become vain and bitter;
for always there will be greater and lesser persons than yourself.
Max Ehrman

JUNE 14

BE THE HAPPIEST

The quicker we can get to the truth of an issue, the happier we will be. Somehow when we get to the truth, we get to a level of peace. That sounds easy, right? The problem is, we often don't want to get to the truth because we might find we don't like it. The truth may reveal our selfishness or desire to control or something else we don't like about ourselves. Lies and half-truths to ourselves keep us going in circles. Truth moves us toward our goals and new possibilities.

When do you feel happiest, most productive and energized. When you are going in circles or moving deliberately toward your destination? Let's say you vacation in Paris but spend the majority of your time stuck in a traffic circle and don't experience the parts of Paris you planned. Are you going to be satisfied with your trip or feel cheated and frustrated that you spent your time, energy and money going in circles?

When you look back on your life, do you want to be joyful and satisfied or feel cheated and frustrated? You are the only one who can get you off your personal traffic circle and moving toward the experiences and possibilities you desire in life. Excuses and lies to yourself will keep you in the traffic circle. Truth will move you toward your goal.

Truth examples:

When I am jealous, I am really just not happy with my choices, or myself, and want to blame you and "get" you.

I am unhappy with my own choices and I won't admit that. It is much easier to blame someone else or a situation.

I want money and I would rather take an opportunity to get it from you than to earn it myself.

The next time you hear a criticism or read something that you want to deny, instead of defending yourself examine it. Say out loud or internally, "Maybe you are right. Maybe I did..." When you examine the situation, you might discover, "I really didn't feel that way." Or "Oh wow, I am responsible for _____, and I didn't realize it!"

There is no guilt or condemnation in a truth, just a freedom that allows us to get off our traffic circle and move toward our goals, purpose and possibilities with a new truth we are not embarrassed to share. When we seek the truth, we will find new possibilities. What is the truth?

The truth is more important than the facts.
Frank Lloyd Wright

JUNE 15
BE RESPECTED

When we lie to ourselves, we lose our self-respect and often the respect of others. We can lie to ourselves, thinking that is what we have to do to keep respect, but we can actually end up losing it.

The next time someone makes a statement about you that you don't like, don't defend it. Examine it. See if there is any truth to what they are saying. There may be some or there may be none, but find out because the truth reveals what you are afraid of. If you are not moving joyfully toward your goal, it might not be a good goal or there is a lie involved somewhere. Seeking the truth is a great way to get off your personal traffic circle and move deliberately toward your goals.

When we are struggling, we might be lying to ourselves. Get to the truth of the matter.

I don't like you and I want you to suffer. I don't like myself and I want you to suffer. I don't want you to like that person because I don't like him. I don't want you to be happy because I am not. I want to be liked the most. I want every penny I can get. I am staying (in my job, relationship, routine) not because I am happy, but because I am afraid I won't succeed at another.

I don't want to be responsible, I want somebody else to fix this. I don't want to be vulnerable. I am afraid if you really knew me you wouldn't like me. I know this isn't right but if I don't find out for sure, I can claim ignorance.

Once we get to the truth of the matter, we may find that is not what we really want or the person we want to be and can then adjust our thoughts and actions accordingly. The truth is the first step to moving deliberately toward our goals, and it has a great side effect: we stop wasting time and energy going in circles. We will have more productive and enjoyable interactions with others, more respect for ourselves, and new possibilities we couldn't recognize before.

If you are struggling in an area of your life, stop and ask yourself: what is the truth?

*Above all, don't lie to yourself. The man who lies to himself and listens
to his own lie comes to a point that he cannot distinguish the truth within him,
or around him, and so loses all respect for himself and for others.
And, having no respect, he ceases to love.*
Fyodor Dostoyevsky

JUNE 16

BE CONGRUENT

Sometimes our perspective is diluted by our pride, fear, guilt or experiences. Select an area you are struggling in and ask people around you what they think the truth is. You will get another perspective you may not have been able to see before.

Those areas where you are struggling and don't have peace, probably have a lie involved: you are likely saying one thing and thinking or doing another. When our thoughts, words, intentions and actions are congruent, we are moving toward our goal and most likely have peace about it. When one of those is not in line with the others, we could be going in circles.

For example: you are *saying*, "I am working for that big account," but *thinking*, "I may not get it and don't know what to do with it if I do." Then you don't really work hard to get the account because you are afraid of it. So you say that you are working hard on that account, but you really aren't. You say, "I can do it." But *think*, "I'm not good enough and I can't do it."

You say one thing but fight with yourself because you believe something else.

If you say, "I like her" but think, "I want to be liked more than her." Or "I don't want her to be happy," then you are struggling.

You are saying one thing but have a completely *different intention*. So you are saying one thing and doing something else.

Pick an area you are struggling in and ask people around you what they think is the truth. They may not be right, but they will give you an idea of what your outward signals look like. Remember, the truth can be difficult and painful to get to, but is ultimately strengthening and energizing. Seek the truth and the possibilities will find you.

Until we get the inward (thoughts and intentions) lined up with the outward (actions and words), we will likely be struggling with others, ourselves and our goals. Pursue the truth and you will automatically pursue possibilities.

All truths are easy to understand once they are discovered;
the point is to discover them.
Galileo Galilei

JUNE 17

BE FREE

We have spent several days looking at difficult truths we might rather not examine.

In areas of struggle, what is the truth you haven't admitted? *I want to be liked the most. I am going to get him fired. I want her to fail. I don't think I am enough...pretty enough, smart enough, etc.*

Write your truth on a piece of paper and look at it. It may feel uncomfortable or silly, but writing down our truths forces us to examine them and take responsibility for them.

Is it what you want? If it is, keep it. If it isn't, decide on the truth you want (and remember if it's an area you are struggling in, you are already wanting to change something). When you know the truth you want, write it on a piece of paper and put it on the wall (or computer or door). You can change the direction, joy or prosperity of your life by deliberately changing one "truth" and intention.

For example, it is hard to put on paper, "I want to be liked more than (person you are jealous of)." You will probably find that is not what you really want or who you want to be, and you will change that truth to something else. On the flip side, it may also be hard to write down, "I want (a person I am jealous of) to be liked as much if not more than me." But when you genuinely want that and change your thoughts, words, actions and intention to that truth, then your attitude toward the person will change and you will find peace with your new truth. You won't need that sign on the wall anymore because you will sincerely live it—in all areas of life.

Change *I want her to fail* to *I want to help her succeed.*

Change *I am not good enough* to *I am more than enough for what I propose to do, and I rock.*

If you need help changing your truths, call a friend or therapist. You have too much to accomplish to waste time and energy around lies and excuses.

The truth helps us get to new possibilities rather than wasting energy in old excuses.

The truth will set you free, but first it will make you miserable.
Attributed to James A. Garfield

JUNE 18
BE FREER

A reader shared that her peace was interrupted. Her mind was focused on a person and situation rather than on her work and the present moment. She was struggling a little in that relationship and was wasting time and energy because of it:

"A vague feeling of insecurity was growing in me and beginning to affect other parts of my business and life. I liked this person and couldn't figure out what the problem was."

"As I sought to understand, I became more frustrated until finally I got to the truth. I realized I had become jealous of this person. It was that simple. The moment I realized the truth, I had peace. I wanted to change this truth and did. As uncomfortable as it was, I went right to the person and said, I have a confession to make: I was jealous of you. I was relieved because I was released from jealousy and the other person was relieved because she sensed something was wrong and couldn't figure out what it was."

The reader thought the truth was, *I like you*, but it had changed to, *I am jealous of you*, and once she was courageous enough to be honest with herself, she was free to be honest with others.

We are constantly checking our truths. If you don't have peace, you probably don't have the truth. You don't have to tell it, but you do have to know it. Your happiness, productivity and possibilities depend on it.

Honesty has a beautiful and refreshing simplicity about it. No ulterior motives.
No hidden meanings. An absence of hypocrisy, duplicity, political games
and verbal superficiality. As honesty and real integrity characterize our lives,
there will be no need to manipulate others.
Chuck Swindoll

JUNE 19

BE UNSELFISH

Because of the nature of your job and the care you put into it, you might catch yourself needing to be in control...everywhere...and of everything. When that happens, it is not your job responsibilities or the emotional attachment that exhausts you; *it is the subtle need to control the situations and people around you that wears you out.*

Some have developed an energizing art that allows them to take responsibility for their part and for themselves then let go and let what is supposed to be, happen. To let go doesn't mean you shirk responsibilities or that you don't plan and do your part. It means you allow others to experience and develop their part, too, rather than orchestrate it for them.

As important as it is to control what we can, it is equally important to learn to surrender what we cannot.

I can control how I spend my time, how I run my business, and what I put into my mouth. I can encourage and support how *others* spend their time or run their business and what they put into their mouths—but I can't control it.

The difference between encouraging support and wanting to control another person can be as simple as looking at our intention. *Do I want her to wear her hair this way because it really looks great or because I am embarrassed of her when she wears it the other way?*

Do I want her to make this decision because it is best for her or because it means she will spend more time with me instead of the person I am jealous of?

One way to spot control is a selfish intention: is it about me or them? *Is my pride involved? Am I afraid of what people will think, that someone else will be liked more than me or that I won't be perfect?*

Note that encouraging support can still say, *no, don't eat that...it is not good for you* or *I don't think you should go.* The difference is the intention behind the words. And as much as we would like to, we cannot rationalize control into encouraging support. It's a fine line, but we all know the difference.

Self-control is an excellent characteristic and is energizing. Everything-and-everyone-else-control is de-energizing, if not downright exhausting. To pursue all our possibilities means to sometimes allow situations and those around us to *just be* rather than for them to *be* as we want them to. Be aware of when you are trying to control another person today, then stop and change your intention. Control can fill up so much space in a relationship or situation that there is no room for respect, excitement...or possibilities.

To exercise some sort of control over others is the secret motive of every selfish person.
Wallace Wattles

JUNE 20
BE STRUGGLE-FREE

The need to control is not only de-energizing, it also stifles positive possibilities.

Another symptom of control is struggle. When you are struggling with *another person*, it could be a symptom that you are trying to control them and the situation.

When you are struggling with *yourself*, it could be a symptom you are trying to control a situation that isn't supposed to be the way you want it to be.

Whether you are struggling with another or with yourself, stop and ask yourself what you are trying to control.

If we are not happy or peaceful, it could be a sign we are trying to control something in a way it shouldn't be. We may be operating in a way that seeks to get rather than give. (If you are saying the words, "You should be giving _____ to me!" You are likely not taking personal responsibility for yourself, and that will always create a control struggle.)

We may want to be angry, but to surrender or be forgiving could be the better choice. The desire to control may be keeping us angry and unhappy.

Be aware of what you are trying to control and just experiment with letting it go. You can always, "take it back"…but you will likely find that you don't want to. You might find you like the new possibilities more than the old control.

The harder you fight to hold on to specific assumptions,
the more likely there's gold in letting go of them.
John Seely Brown

JUNE 21

BE SURRENDERING

In a game of tug-of-war, two sides pull on the same rope from opposite ends. The object is to muscle the other person over to your side; usually the one with more strength wins. But even though the teams know the side with more muscle will likely win, neither one will let go. One team operates with muscle and the other on pure pride. And while the exhausting struggle could go on for a long time, neither team will let up or let go.

Our control issues are similar to a game of tug-of-war, with one difference; often there is no winner until both sides let go. If we want someone to let something go, we may have to let go first.

If you are trying to control how your twenty-nine-year-old daughter wears her hair, there is the possibility she might be wearing it a way you don't like just to annoy you.

When the struggle begins, you may find the best thing you can do is to let go...surrender. Love and accept her regardless of how she wears her hair, and you may end up giving her enough space to change it.

When we try to control someone, we can end up working against ourselves. No matter how much muscle we have or bullying we do, the other person might not let go because that is the only "control" he or she may feel they have. Or it could just be they don't want to give in because of pride.

Here is the cool thing about surrendering and letting go...when we let go we might find that we actually start to like her and her hair. The thing we wanted to control so badly is suddenly not so bad after all. It may take more muscle to win the tug-of-war struggle, but it takes more strength to let go in a battle of self-centered will.

In tug-of-war there is only one winner. In letting go, there are two.

When you find yourself in a game of tug-of-war, let go and let the positive possibilities flow.

There's an important difference between giving up and letting go.
Jessica Hatchigan

JUNE 22
BE OPEN

Have you noticed that when your hands are clenched in frustration, anger or control, the rest of you is clenched, too?

Not just your body is tense, but also parts you can't physically feel, like your spirit.

When our hands are clenched, a couple of things happen:

1. We keep something in, holding on tightly, trying to control it.

2. We keep everything else out.

When we try to control something, we do not just hold on; we clench tightly, keeping it from growing and expanding because we are trying to keep things out, like other people, ideas and change.

Holding onto something tightly (control) keeps it in the dark rather than bringing it out to the light. We don't let it breathe and flourish, so, as a result, it stays small and contracted. Instead of becoming what it was meant to be, it eventually withers in the darkness of our clenched hands (or controlling spirits).

Unclench your hands and your heart and mind will open too. When we hold something tightly, we can end up strangling it, but when we let go, we can breathe new life into it—whether "it" is a person, a relationship, a situation or even just a moment. When we let go and let something "be," we can end up with something bigger and more wonderful than what we dreamed when we held it in the dark, small confines of our control.

Let go and you may find that not only does what you were trying to control become more wonderful, but that your life becomes more creative and vibrant. When our hands and spirits are clenched in control, we are not only holding onto a person or situation, we are simultaneously keeping out new and wonderful possibilities in areas of our own lives.

An intention of trying to stifle another's journey winds up stifling our own.

Let go and allow the possibilities to come—for everyone.

The harder you fight to hold on to specific assumptions,
the more likely there's gold in letting go of them.
John Seely Brown

JUNE 23
BE AWAKENED

When we have a struggle, internally or with someone else, it could be we are being selfish, when we should be seeking to be fair. Everyone's idea of what is fair will be different, but here is a great way to test out fairness. When we point a finger at someone else, we need to turn it around and point at ourselves, too. If we examine the situation closely, we will likely find we did that behavior first. And if so, that is where the struggle may be.

For example: "He lied to me!" Did you lie to him six months ago about how much that handbag cost?

"My friend lied to me!" Did you lie to her with an excuse first?

Often the behavior we are upset with is our own; it just looks different on someone else. Controlling struggle says, "What about me?"

When we try to get our financial security, our position security, our dream security, or our happiness from the wrong source, we are likely going to struggle. For example, we get angry with someone (life partner, business partner, friend, relative) for a "breakup." They burst your dream and hurt your pride. But what about you? What if you burst their dream by not being whom they wanted, too?

Don't waste your time and energy struggling and striving to control others when you could multiply that energy by spending it on building for yourself what you are trying to get from someone else. If you feel you lost potential financial gain, spend your time and energy finding new ways to create that gain yourself, and you will probably find more than you thought possible. If you feel you lost your dream, spend your thoughts creating a new one. Change your bad thoughts of him or her to good or neutral thoughts and feel your struggle subside.

Remember boundaries are good: we need to "breakup" with someone we aren't supposed to be with (business partner, significant other, friend, florist). But blaming them rather than taking responsibility for ourselves increases our struggle and decreases our positive possibilities.

Just because we decide to walk away from each other
doesn't mean we have to turn and fire.
Unknown

JUNE 24
BE AN OWNER

Sometimes when we struggle with wanting to control something or someone, it is really ourselves we are struggling with because we aren't happy with our choices. Instead of acknowledging our responsibility and letting go, we blame the other person or situation and continue holding on, because often we would rather not own our part and continue to struggle, than to accept responsibility and have peace.

Your business partner may not have your same values and philosophy, so you are frustrated and angry with him/her...and frustrated with yourself because you chose that person. Now you realize you should have asked more questions and had more conversations to provide clarity.

Maybe your relationship with your spouse or boyfriend/girlfriend is broken and you are angry. You are likely unhappy with yourself also, because you know you could have made better choices in your actions and reactions.

Whether it is a business or personal relationship or situation, we have responsibilities for its deterioration or its not turning out how we wanted, as well as the other person. The sooner we acknowledge that, the sooner we can let go and move on to give that energy to building what we want for our future instead of blaming and feeling angry about our past.

Owning our part doesn't mean we physically stay in a relationship we shouldn't stay in. It means that when we don't physically choose to stay in it anymore, *we don't emotionally stay in it either.*

Look at situations you are struggling in; maybe you weren't who you should have/could have been, too. Accept responsibility for your part and feel your struggle subside. As you do, you will feel your happiness and joy return.

If we are struggling with another, it could be we are really struggling with ourselves for our own choices we wish had been different. When we stop blaming and start owning, it makes all the difference... not just in our struggle but in our lives.

When we blame, we increase our struggle. When we fully accept our responsibility, we increase our possibilities.

Forgive yourself for your faults and your mistakes and move on.
Les Brown

JUNE 25

BE AT PEACE

Another control struggle we might have is when we try to take responsibility for someone else and his or her happiness. We can encourage and support, but a person's happiness or unhappiness is ultimately his or her choice. It goes without saying that we want to be helpful, *but sometimes the right thing to give someone is simply the responsibility for their own happiness choices.*

Those of us with a high level of responsibility want to take responsibility (and control) for other people's happiness. We want to make others happy, which can lead to struggle, because when we make decisions only to soothe others we can wind up with an internal conflict and not realize its source.

And here is the bigger reason: what that person thinks will make him or her happy in the short-term often doesn't generate happiness in the long run. So we have to ask ourselves, "Am I making this decision just to soothe and avoid drama? Is this good for the long-term or am I enabling? Is this decision the right thing or am I feeding the monster of co-dependency?"

You can help and encourage, but you can't do it for them. Their life and happiness are their choices. When they want you to make decisions based on their gratification rather than on what is best, you have to step back and re-examine the situation.

As hard as it is, there may be a point we have to be still and let them work the issues through. If not, that individual may always expect someone else to be responsible for providing entertainment, money, peace of mind or a place to blame when he or she isn't happy. Not only will that expectation not lead to happiness, but worse, he or she may never fulfill their purpose.

This is a conundrum with an answer only you can know. If there is anger, guilt, or any fearful emotion involved, take a step back and examine the "right thing." The right thing to do will ultimately make you happy, too. If you are struggling with this, seek wisdom with making good decisions. We can give help, support and encouragement without taking upon ourselves the personal responsibility of another.

When we try to take responsibility for someone else's happiness, we may end up taking their possibilities, too..

It is not easy to find happiness in ourselves, and it is not possible to find it elsewhere.
Agnes Repplier

JUNE 26

BE BOLD

Don't give up. Whatever is happening in your life right now that makes you want to quit, don't.

Stop and ask yourself, "What am I afraid of?"

That it will be too much work?

That I am not going to like what I find out?

That I will be embarrassed?

That I will "fail?"

That I will succeed?

That it won't be "good enough"?

Then decide what to do about it. For example: Call a trusted friend or someone you think has knowledge on the subject. Pray or meditate. Talk to your manager. Write down times in the past when you felt like this and pushed through to find your answers or success. Contact your team and tell them you need particular encouragement through a problem. Choose a good attitude. Read stories about people who have persevered to have the success you are working toward.

Sometimes it is an action game…sometimes it is a waiting game. But regardless of what stage you are in, if you know something is not done yet, keep pushing through. Don't give up.

It may be time to move on to something else and that is okay to do. New seasons in life come with a new purpose and we certainly don't want to stay stuck when we can be moving on.

But when we just want to quit because something is hard or we feel tired, misunderstood or afraid, that is no time to quit. It is often the pushing through that rewards us.

Possibilities and perseverance travel together.

Who are you going to help if you give up?

Most people never run far enough on their first
wind to find out they've got a second.
William James

JUNE 27

BE CHOOSING BETTER

When we know we have prepared and feel confident with our product (whatever that is—an idea, an investment, a value, ourselves), we can often handle and process rejection easier. When we aren't so pleased with our product or ourselves, we can get stuck with the rejection and want to quit.

If you find you aren't pleased with your product, your preparation or your skills, do something about it, from gaining more knowledge to addressing perfectionism and insecurities to changing your attitude and adjusting your goal. Take a class, hire an expert, talk to your manager or someone else who wants to see you succeed.

Sometimes our fear can take us down longer roads to our goal. We can get so stuck on how we think something should be that we miss what is supposed to happen and ultimately what is the best for us. When we are rejected (and we will be in life), we mustn't let bitterness, resentment or insecurities settle in. They will keep us going in circles rather than moving forward—and unhappy rather than joyful.

"Unhappy" can signal that our focus is about us and what we receive rather than what we contribute. When we are self-centered and concentrate on what we are getting, we will want more—more recognition, more money, more than someone else—and we will likely be unhappy. But when we focus on what we give, we are more concerned with how we contribute to the world, our company, our clients and our relationships. And as a benefit, we will likely end up happy.

If we make that shift, we will often find that not only do more possibilities show up, but our purpose does, too.

We can either get bitter or better. It's our choice.

I think all great innovations are built on rejections.
Louis Ferdinand Celine

JUNE 28

BE TRAVELING LIGHT

Think of a time you moved on to a new season in life because it was what you were supposed to do—like moving on to another company or to a new strategy or a different relationship. Moving on to a new season in life is progression, moving forward.

Next, think of a time you were in a difficult or confusing situation and you surrendered it instead of giving up. Actively and truly surrendering a difficult situation brings peace and a multitude of new possibilities.

Finally, think of a time you were in a difficult situation and you quit.

When we quit something because it's hard or because we are angry or because we "can't," it is as if we leave pieces we were supposed to take with us and we always want to go back and get them.

Quitting (because of pride, anger, weariness or revenge) may leave us stuck and unable to quit emotionally what we have already quit physically.

But when we move on from something in peace because it is complete, we are free to move forward physically and emotionally.

When leaving something—whether it is piano lessons, a job or a relationship—leave in completeness because it's time, rather than quitting in anger because you feel tired and frustrated.

I heard it said once that how we leave a place is how we enter the next. Don't leave something in negativity; you will likely carry that negative with you.

Positive emotions and attitudes are weightless. Negative ones are heavy.

Possibilities are easier to pursue when we aren't carrying a lot of extra weight. Travel light.

Between you and every goal that you wish to achieve, there is a series of obstacles, and the bigger the goal, the bigger the obstacles. Your decision to be, have and do something out of the ordinary entails facing difficulties and challenges that are out of the ordinary as well. Sometimes your greatest asset is simply your ability to stay with it longer than anyone else.

Brian Tracy

JUNE 29

BE MAKING ROOM

Sometimes new wonders and possibilities wait on us to make room for them in our lives—and in our closets. Do you have room in your closet or do you need to clean it out and pass items on?

Just like people, things need to be loved and "used" or useful. If you haven't used, loved or admired something in your clothes closet in over two seasons, then bless someone else with it. Someone somewhere is waiting for that piece of clothing and it can't get to that person until you are willing to pass it on. Some of my most worn pieces have come from my friend's closet. I love to be around when she does her annual "cleaning out and passing on."

How many of us have clothes that have hung in the closet for over a year with the price tag attached? A friend or family member might be in need of that item.

What about that sweater that was so loved that it is showing it now—stretched out, worn out and in need of rest. Let it go. You will find other sweaters.

What about the skinny clothes that we all hope to get back into? We could one day, but if they aren't classic styles, we might not be able wear them even if we can fit into them. Pass those on to someone who can wear them and be stylish now.

Pick a time to clean the clutter out of your closet, but don't try to do it alone. It takes less time and less emotional energy when someone is there to encourage us to pass an item on that doesn't need to be in our closet any longer (or never should have been). Ask a friend to come join you to clean out your closet and tell her you will return the favor.

Feeling and being lighter has to do with not being wasteful. Being wasteful may not just be about tossing things out; it could also be about wasting something's beauty or usefulness. If you aren't admiring or using an item, consider letting it go so that someone else can.

When we clean out space in our closet or our lives, we make room for new wonders and possibilities to replace the wonderful past ones.

Anyone who has ever cleaned out a closet and taken stuff to Goodwill knows how liberating it is. You feel lighter; your mind feels clearer.
Cecile Andrews

JUNE 30
BE UNCLUTTERED

Not only do we need to occasionally clean out our closets, but we also need to clean out our minds. Just like an old sweatshirt gets tossed off into a corner and smashed behind a shoe rack, old hurts and unhelpful memories get stuck in our brains. And just like the sweatshirt, you may not be aware they are there, but they are still taking up space.

Look at it this way: we have only so much space in our brains and we don't want to waste that space on junk.

A lady shared a story that she had said something she wished she hadn't to someone two years ago and still felt burdened by it whenever she saw the person. If you have a situation like that, work to talk to the person or let it go, because you could be the only one remembering it.

If someone once said something that offended you that you still recall, let it go. If we are not willing to forgive an offense, then how can we expect someone else to forgive us? If we are still holding on to it, isn't it because we want to for some reason? We want to have "evidence" against the person so we don't have to acknowledge good things about him or her. We want to be upset with them or think badly of them. We want them to still be the bad guy or the dingy girl.

Sit down with pen and paper and plenty of time and start writing any negative clutter that is taking up space in your brain. Wounds, words, offenses, times you have offended and anything else that causes you embarrassment or pain. Then work to let them go. If there are some you are having trouble with, get help. There are therapists waiting to help you clear out the clutter in your brain and spirit so you can experience the new possibilities waiting in your life.

Eliminate physical clutter. More importantly, eliminate spiritual clutter.
D.H. Mondfleur

JULY 1

BE ABUNDANT

There is not a limited amount of joy, love or corner offices in the world. It is when we try to take what someone else has (position, respect, love, happiness, material items, money) rather than earn and receive our own that limits are established.

We are the ones who establish the feelings of lack in our lives, or the abundance of our lives, with intention and attitude.

For example, if we don't want a friend or relative to like another person, we are the ones who are limiting love and joy in our lives. Instead of being happy for others and allowing abundance of love to flow, we are limiting it by believing *there is only so much love and only so many happy moments in life. I want those moments and don't want that other person to experience them.*

Sadly, not only do we limit ourselves with that thinking, we limit others' happiness, too, because we are seeking to control the sources of their love and happiness: *you can get some here but not over there, because I want to give you what you need. I don't want you to get happiness from that other person.*

It is the same with money. *There is only so much business, so I have to make sure you don't get any.* When I am more concerned with taking yours than getting my own, I limit my possibilities. If I work to find my own, I may find undiscovered potential.

Now, granted, I don't think we walk around consciously saying, "I want her clients" or "I don't want anyone to like the new person in the office or the new neighbor on the block." But it is the subconscious thoughts wandering around in our brains that contribute to the truths and intentions that shape our actions, lives and happiness.

Joy, love and rewards for our work are limitless. We set limits when we hunger after another person's position, influence, affection, happiness, material possessions or wealth rather than earn and reap our own rewards.

Don't let the subtle thoughts of jealousy and fear create lack in your life.

In what areas do you feel lack? What are you afraid of?

If we live and work with an attitude of abundance for us all, we are contributing to all our good, but when we work to take what another has, we are limiting everyone.

Abundance is, in large part, an attitude.
Sue Patton Thoele

JULY 2

BE EMPOWERED

Another happiness habit is taking responsibility. It isn't always easy, but it is necessary if we are going to be free to pursue all our possibilities. In his book, Shift: *Change your Mindset and Change your World,* Steve Sax says that "the average person can accomplish extraordinary things...if you accept the responsibility that comes with freedom...."

"When my kids were young, one thing I would impress upon them is that if you don't accept responsibility, then you don't have freedom. When my kids were old enough to have a car, I helped them with a down payment, but they had a structured plan that they had to follow. They had to help pay for their auto insurance. They had to take care of the maintenance on the car and they had to have a monthly payment. That's how I found out what it's like to be an adult in this world. I didn't want to rob them of their freedom. They might have thought that freedom was, "Hey I don't have a car payment." No. That's not what freedom is. Freedom is, "I have a car payment. How does that work? It works because I'm not depending on somebody else to do something." When you can do things for yourself, that's real freedom."

"Don't be a parasite in this world. You become a free person by doing things for yourself and that means paying your own bills. That's part of being free. I wanted my kids to learn this lesson and today I'm so fortunate that my kids are wonderful young adults who just thrive on their independence. I'm so grateful for this because I know they're free now."

This doesn't mean we don't delegate or ask for help. We can't do it all. It means we need to own our "stuff" rather than expecting someone else to. Not just the material needs, like a car, but the responsibilities and choices of our lives that determine whether we are a contributor or a "parasite..." free or imprisoned. Is there any area in which you feel imprisoned rather than free? Do you look to someone else to fill a need or maybe look for someone to blame or fix it for you? How or what can you do to take responsibility in that area? Change a behavior or simply an attitude?

We want to be free to pursue all our possibilities, and freedom starts with responsibility.

Don't give up your freedom. When you lay your problems at the doorstep of somebody else, you've just given up your freedom.
Steve Sax

JULY 3

BE DISCOVERER

Looking at truths is not intended to condemn us or to make us feel guilty but to help us spot the areas that create problems in our lives and in our personal peace.

Have you ever encountered a situation where a friend said they wanted something and you realized that even if they were given that, they wouldn't be happy?

Often what we think we want isn't what we really want. That "thing" may satisfy us for a while, but we will still need to find the true source of our dissatisfaction or we will continue with Band-Aid solutions that don't work...and continue with a life in which we aren't happy, satisfied or at peace.

Getting to the truth isn't fun, but it is necessary if what we really want is peace and joy along with our possibilities. Which brings us back to the original intention: getting to the truth around a problem situation most always involves acknowledging something about ourselves we don't want to.

So after we find it, what do we do with it? Celebrate!

Discovering truth isn't to make us feel bad about ourselves, it is to help us know what to do to feel good again. We might need to forgive ourselves or another, change our perspective, educate ourselves on a subject, acknowledge pride, correct a problem in our business or relationships, or own a mistake.

There are few things so exhilarating as discovering the true source of a problem or fear, even if the true source is you.

Don't feel bad about a truth you don't like about yourself. Celebrate that you spotted it so you can stop wasting time and energy circling your goals and possibilities. Ask for help or choose to change it yourself and keep growing well.

To the question of your life you are the answer,
and to the problems of your life you are the solution.
Joe Cordare

JULY 4

BE IN-LINE

Are your actions in line with your goals?

Occasionally it is good to step back and ask yourself

1. What are my goals?

2. Are my actions in line with those?

If you want to grow your business by x percent, are you increasing your business-building activities by xx percent? If you want consistent communication with your clients, do you have the plan in place to help you? Are you following it? If you want to lose ten pounds, are you walking thirty minutes a day and eating well?

If we don't do what we know we are supposed to, we waste time and energy and we cheat ourselves. If it is not important to you, tell yourself the truth about it and either change your truth to make that goal important or move on to another one.

Keep those "someday" goals on another list, but don't lie to yourself that you are committed to it when you are not. Doing this can create frustration for you and others. If you tell your manager you are going to host a seminar each month and want her time and financial support, but months go by and you have not done even one, frustration—and worse—disrespect could grow.

If you have a goal you know you are not working toward, do one thing today that moves you toward that goal. One thing is not so hard but can make the difference between a possibility missed and a possibility pursued.

How am I going to live today in order to create
the tomorrow I'm committed to?
Anthony Robbins

JULY 5
BE A WRITER

As you begin to pay attention to your own stories and what they say about you,
you will enter into the exciting process of becoming, as you should be,
the author of your own life, the creator of your own possibilities.
Mandy Aftel

We want to pay attention to our stories and what they are telling us for many reasons. The most important could be to see if how we think of ourselves matches who we are and who we want to be.

Do the same stories keep happening in your life? If so, why do they keep happening? If they are good ones, keep adding that good in your life. If they are unpleasant, why do you continue in that pattern?

As we examine our stories, we can choose to change what we don't like. Some parts of situations are beyond our control, but much is not. One thing that is not beyond our control is our choice of response.

We can choose care or bitterness. We can choose to honestly discuss an issue or pout. We can choose to share as much love as possible or be controlling and jealous. We can be honest with ourselves and others or lie.

When we lie to ourselves we probably aren't accepting our part in our story because we don't want to. It is much more comfortable to have someone to blame besides ourselves.

Some of our stories aren't pretty. In fact, they are flat-out ugly. But here is the reality: we can have pretty stories and still not be "pretty."—and we can have really ugly stories and have grown to be a beauty. It depends on Whom we believe and who we have chosen to become.

Think about your stories. Which ones keep coming up that you would rather not keep telling? What can you do to change that story?

Begin to be deliberate about your choices rather than letting life happen to you and create not just your life, but your possibilities, too.

Everyone is necessarily the hero of his own life story.
John Barth

JULY 6

BE AN EDITOR

If we have stories we don't like, why do we keep writing them (by living them)?

There are many reasons, but a common issue is that we aren't willing to take a risk to make a change. The risk usually involves being vulnerable and losing something. We become fearful of change because we are often unable to see the possibility of something better replacing what we will give up. We often don't want to give up what we know for something we don't—even if we are not satisfied where we are.

So you: Will not admit you were wrong about something and will keep pretending you are satisfied with a situation when you are not.

Will keep having the same defensive argument rather than admit the truth.

Will settle for less than your best because you don't want to take a risk.

You feel you could lose your position, pride or control if you risk changing a story you don't like, when you might actually end up gaining something so much better:

"I am afraid I will lose respect if I tell you the truth." You might, or you might gain peace of mind and a friend who can help.

We may be risking discomfort or embarrassment, but we are hoping for the "profit" of replacing the story we don't like with one we do: replacing a fear story with authenticity, joy, laughter.

Most of us would like the freedom to write our own stories, rather than pride, fear and guilt writing them for us. Fear stories are exhausting. To write our own stories means that sometimes we have to take risks: try that new marketing plan, step out and do a speaking engagement, talk to our children about uncomfortable topics.

We all have stories we don't like, and at some point we may become willing to take the risk to change those.

If you need help changing a story, ask for help. We have too much to do to be writing stories in our life that aren't productive, contributing and energizing. When we change stories that aren't productive, we can create possibilities that are.

Unless you are prepared to give up something valuable, you will never be able to truly change at all, because you'll be forever in the control of things you can't give up.
Andy Law

JULY 7

BE YOUR OWN AUTHOR

One way to rewrite a story we don't want to live any longer is to be still long enough to know how we really feel. When we go on autopilot and act out of habit for too long, we can miss emotions or signals that tell us we need a change.

Once we know how we feel, we can begin to express and act from that awareness, but the problem is many of us would rather act on an old "default" setting than on the truth.

For example:

> It is much easier on our pride to argue than it is to say, "My feelings are hurt" or "You were right."
>
> It is much easier to bark at someone than to say, "I am afraid."
>
> It is much easier for us to avoid an issue than to talk about what is emotionally or physically separating us from others.
>
> It is much easier to eat the pie than to say, "I am bored and lonely."
>
> It is much easier to make assumptions than to seek the truth.

The issue with "much easier," is that it won't change a story we want to change. If we stay with the same "easy" we will be living the same stories.

If we want to change a story, we must determine who we want to be and how we really feel, and then act on those determinates rather than on unproductive substitutes. Be courageous enough to change a story that isn't serving you and others, and you may experience possibilities you didn't know were possible.

After living with their dysfunctional behavior for so many years
(a sunk cost if ever there was one), people become invested
in defending their dysfunctions rather than changing them.
Marshall Goldsmith

JULY 8

BE ENCOURAGING

One of the most important aspects in changing your stories is to allow others to change their stories, too. When we let others grow and change, we grow and change. When we keep others in their same old past roles and behaviors, we keep ourselves in the same old roles and past behaviors—the same old stories.

There are times that we don't want others to change for the better; we want to keep them in their previous ways, pains or situations. As you read those words, you probably are thinking that just can't be true...when would we not want someone to succeed, improve their life or be happier?

When we speak poorly of someone who is making positive changes in his life, we may not really want him to change his story. We may want him to be unhappy because we are still unhappy with him in some way. When we bring up old behaviors someone no longer exhibits or activities they no longer participate in with the intention to make them feel small or to wound them in some way, it shows that we don't want them to change their stories for the better.

If you want to keep others "down" rather than build them up, you may be jealous or need to forgive them for something. Examine why you wouldn't want another person to change their story from a "bad" one to a "good" one; then do what you need to do in order to start helping change their story to a better one. When you help them change theirs for the better, you may find your story is already becoming better, too.

Be aware of your thoughts and the stories they create in your life. To change our stories, we have to change our thoughts, words, actions and intentions and allow others to do so, too. We don't want to hold anyone back, even in our thoughts; because when we hold another back, somehow we end up chaining ourselves to them.

Don't be stuck in old patterns and old possibilities; move forward and take everyone with you.

We are always growing and, hopefully, learning and choosing to change for the better. Allow others to be better and experience new possibilities that only building up another can bring.

One man cannot hold another man down in the ditch
without remaining down in the ditch with him.
Booker T. Washington

JULY 9

BE CHANGING YOUR STORY

We all have stories in our lives we want to stop writing and telling. We want different, better ones. So if that's the case, why don't we just do it? One of the reasons we don't change those stories is the "what if's."

The thought of change can trigger that internal dialogue of "Oh, no. What if _____ happens"?

Have you ever noticed that our "what if's" are almost always negative?

We don't ever say to ourselves:

"What if I am the 1000th customer and I win a brand new car!!"

"What if I walk into a meeting and my client says, you have done such a great job, I am bringing you ten new clients!"

"What if they really like me?"

"What if I look better at 50 than I did at 30?!"

It is good to be prepared and deliberate in making decisions. The problem comes when we begin the endless tape recording in our head of negative "what if's" and they keep us from moving forward to change a story we want to change.

Don't waste time and energy on negative what if's. Change your negative what if's to positive ones and your story may just start to change, too.

Of all the people I have ever known, those who have pursued
their dreams and failed have lived a much more fulfilling life than
those who have put their dreams on a shelf for fear of failure.
Author Unknown

JULY 10

BE FEARLESS

Habitual "what if's" are driven by fear. They can be a constant stream running through our thoughts and will steal possibilities until we become consciously aware of those "what if's" and choose to change them. "What if" fears start controlling our lives early. They may not always block our goals, but they certainly waste energy and steal joy.

What if I don't get into this college? Then you get in and it becomes, Oh my goodness, *what if I fail?*

What if I don't get married? You get married, then it becomes, Oh no! *What if I get divorced?*

What if I don't get this job? Then you get the job and it becomes, *What if I get fired?*

Do you see the habit? You can go on and on...you just replace the words following "what if" with whatever is happening in your life and add the worst-case scenario.

How many times have those things happened? If they did, how did you contribute to the issue? Do you think your fear contributed to the "failure"? Maybe. Did your fear and angst help you do your job better or be happier in life? Probably not.

So what if we learned a new habit? What if we learned to enjoy the moment rather than fear the future? Because often, what we are afraid of doesn't happen, it just robs us of the opportunities to enjoy our life, relationships and business. And possibly the biggest issue with "what if" fears is they can keep us from fulfilling our purpose. We don't want to miss our purpose and possibilities because of a bad habit of the "what if's."

Do the right thing, make changes when necessary and trust in the rest. Not only will you see more possibilities, you will have more fun, too.

Fear is a habit; so are self-pity, defeat, anxiety, despair, hopelessness and resignation. You can eliminate all of these negative habits with two simple resolves: I can!! And I will!
Unknown

JULY 11
BE SUPPORTIVE

When we take steps to make good changes in our lives, we often find people around us who don't want us to make changes for the better. Your changes may be met with resistance by others because sometimes people don't want what is best for you, but what is comfortable for them.

They don't want us to make healthier food choices because they won't get to meet us at the ice cream shop anymore.

They don't want us to go back to school because we might get a better job than they have.

They don't want us to grow because we might out-grow them.

They don't want us to ask questions and learn about the new products available because we may outperform them.

They don't want us to be happy because they aren't happy.

They don't want us to change because they don't want to change.

The issue is this: people (ourselves included) often look at how something affects them rather than how it affects the person making the change.

So how do we make sure we are not one of "those people" who are more concerned with "How am I affected?" than "How can I help you be a happier, more productive person?"

First, we can ask: What is really best for my friend or associate? How can I be part of their solution instead of the problem? How can I encourage him or her?

It is okay to acknowledge how a friend's change is going to affect us...and even be sad about what we think we will lose. But then turn it around and begin to celebrate the positive possibilities in your friend's or family member's life. Because when one thing ends, something better comes—if we will only let it.

When one door of happiness closes, another opens; but often we look so long at the closed door that we do not see the one which has been opened for us.
Helen Keller

JULY 12

BE INNOVATIVE

The easiest way to begin a change you want to make in your life is to make a change in your environment. Removing yourself from the "problem" areas is a good start, as well as adding and removing items or activities that will help you succeed.

Maybe you are trying to eat healthier and you have identified the office as a problem area. You don't have to change your place of work, but you can change whom you go to lunch with or what you keep at the office for snacks.

You may be trying to change how you manage your time, so bring an egg timer to your office to time phone calls that can get away from you. Use the timer to get you started on tasks with the tactic of "I am going to work for ten minutes on this." Perhaps you want to strengthen your marriage or family relationship, so maybe you need to read some books or articles…or add family time or playtime with your kids…or a commitment to kiss your spouse or significant other when they walk in the door.

As you move forward, if your solutions don't seem to be working, then change something else. If you don't see improvement immediately, don't be discouraged, because if you are working toward your goal with an honest intention of change, you are making a difference even if it isn't evident yet.

The change in your environment doesn't have to be drastic. Small things can be the beginning of big change.

No one is in control of your happiness but you; therefore, you have the power to change anything about yourself or your life that you want to change.
Barbara De Angelis

JULY 13

BE PAIRED UP

Possibilities often come in pairs—you and at least one other person. We are supposed to need others. So why do we keep trying to do "it" alone, whether "it" is carrying an awkward piece of furniture or making a change to your business.

You have people all around you willing and wanting to help you *exceed* your goals, yet you may sometimes ignore that they exist. We don't get extra gold stars for doing it alone. So why do you not ask for help?

Is it because there are some goals you really don't want to achieve? If that is the case, then admit it and move on, because you are wasting your time and energy and others', too. But the minute you are ready to commit to that goal, bring it back in and work toward it with full desire—and help.

Is it because of pride? Remember, pride destroys anything it can—your back from lifting that piece of furniture or your business from choosing not to utilize all the resources available. Doing it alone is not more noble, just more exhausting.

What goal do you have or what change are you trying to making that isn't going so well? Whom can you ask for guidance or ideas? Contact them today. Sometimes possibilities come in "pairs" and solutions from honest conversations.

When something is missing in your life,
it usually turns out to be someone.
Robert Brault

JULY 14

BE VULNERABLE

Yesterday we looked at the importance of "pairing-up" to make changes or complete goals in our lives, yet there are times that we may prefer to do it ourselves.

Sometimes there is a fantastic satisfaction that comes from accomplishing something ourselves, but other times there is no satisfaction in completion, only a satisfaction in the *exclusion of others* (I don't need *your* help. No! I can do it). Know the difference. Because the first leaves you filled and joyfully satisfied, whereas the latter may leave you with a "satisfaction" but it will be empty, and it will be one of those times that you aren't happy and won't know why.

When you are making real and lasting changes in your life, you will need help, at least one other person for support or guidance or accountability. You probably have family members, friends or a manager who will encourage and guide you. If you don't, there are trainers, coaches, consultants, designers or other "experts" whose sole professional purpose is to help you make the changes in your life you want to make. *They want to help you as much you want to help your clients.*

When it comes to pursuing your possibilities, never underestimate the importance of the right question, an honest answer or just a high-five and an atta-girl. Asking for help isn't a weakness but a vulnerability, and while we don't like being vulnerable, it is a moment where possibilities are born.

Remember, we all stumble, every one of us.
That's why it's a comfort to go hand in hand.
Emily Kimbrough

JULY 15

BE YOUR OWN ACTION FIGURE

As you are changing the stories you want to rewrite in your life, a simple way to monitor yourself is to continue to ask the questions,

"Are my actions in line with my goals?"

"If someone looked at my actions, what would they think my goal is?"

If someone looked at your marketing activities, would they say your goal is to increase your business by five percent or fifty percent?

If someone looked at your actions and interactions with your spouse or child, would they say your goal is an awesome, loving relationship, or to just make it through the day or to drive them out of the house?

Are your actions in line with your goals?

When we get our actions and goals lined up, our possibilities aren't far behind.

An idea not coupled with action will never get any
bigger than the brain cell it occupied.
Arnold Glasgow

JULY 16

BE UNCLOGGED

Possibilities flow when we are allowing good to flow through us into our lives. If we are not letting kindness flow through our lives to someone else, we have a "clogged sink" that we need to unclog.

We allow good to flow through us, to others and back again…or we block it. What happens when the sink clogs and we turn off the faucet? Everything stops. We are like a faucet as we control what we turn on and off in our lives. We don't have full control of what happens to us, but we do have control of our reactions and how and what we contribute to situations.

This may seem like a confusing example, but stay with it. If you become offended by a co-worker, family member or friend and you *hold onto that offense*, eventually more offenses pile up and resentment or anger gets piled up with it. You find you don't let love flow freely to that person anymore. You probably don't want to do the little kind things you once did; you don't want to help them with a problem or even see them be happy.

When something happens that hurts our feelings or our pride and we don't resolve it, but instead choose to hold onto it, we get a little bit of junk lodged in the sink. And when we choose to be jealous, offended, vindictive, prideful or unforgiving, more junk piles on.

Initially, a little love, kindness and fun can still get through, but if left unresolved, eventually, everything good and kind stops. The junk has accumulated and keeps the good stuff from flowing through. Then, sadly, everything gets piled up inside of us at one spot, waiting on something to unclog it. That "something" could be you blowing up on someone. Or on the flip side, that "something" could be a simple choice of forgiveness or finding the first piece of junk that got stuck and dealing with it. Or it could simply be a conversation with someone you need to forgive—maybe even yourself.

If we are not letting good flow through our lives to someone else, we have a clogged sink we need to unclog. When we turn off our faucet, we turn off our possibilities. Don't let the little pieces of junk turn into a big mess that blocks what you really want in your life.

*It has long been an axiom of mine that the little
things are infinitely the most important.*
Sir Arthur Conan Doyle

JULY 17
BE UNENCUMBERED

Emotionally clogged sinks don't just clog your emotions; they clog your possibilities, too.

Emotionally clogged sinks block good stuff. When we are emotionally clogged, the love doesn't flow through, kindness doesn't flow through, and no fun gets through either. It all gets stuck. Then we wonder what happened to the fun, laughing, loving, productive person we once were. He is still there, but he and his possibilities are stuck in the sink.

Our possibilities flow when the positive is flowing through our lives. We turn the faucet on and off with how we choose to deal with things and react in situations. When the sink gets clogged, we turn the faucet off and nothing good gets through us.

No matter how hard we try, eventually things are going to get messy, and at some point we are going to have to clean up our mess.

If you have lost your laughter with someone or you consciously do not want to do kind things for him or her, or you find you are avoiding the person, you might just need a little emotional Drano.

We all need help, or a new perspective, to clear out an offense or pain and allow the positive to flow freely again. Sometimes we can't unclog a relationship because the other person isn't ready, but we can be unclogged so that we are prepared when the opportunity for resolution presents itself.

We don't want to miss a minute living and working in love, laughter and kindness, pursuing all our possibilities.

It's not what happens to you, but how you react to it that matters.
Epictetus

JULY 18

BE EMOTIONAL DRANO

When we are emotionally clogged, we need emotional Drano.

Everyone has different ways they empty out what is stuck. *How* you do it doesn't matter as much as *that* you do. Just make sure it is appropriate and works for the other person involved, too.

Some ways to unclog:

> Call a trusted friend who will give you wisdom, not just tell you what you want to hear.
>
> Make sure the words are for venting and processing, not to put someone down. Otherwise, you will add more junk to the clog rather than clean it out.
>
> Talk to the person you are having issues with. If it is not the right timing for conversation, write a letter; you don't have to send it.
>
> See a counselor, therapist, coach or clergyman.

Some ways to stay unclogged:

> Journal.
>
> Pray.

As soon as you realize something is stuck, talk about it immediately with the person involved.

You have too much to do to be wasting positive possibilities that are blocked by junk that isn't good for you anyway—like pride, jealousy, selfishness and old wounds. Stay clog-free and your possibilities will flow.

If you don't manage your emotions, then your emotions will manage you.
Doc Childre and Deborah Rozman

JULY 19

BE SPACE CONSCIOUS

There are times we don't like someone because of something that person has done to us, but there are other times we don't like someone because we want something they have. We don't like them, not really because of who they are but because of the space they fill: maybe it's the position they have worked for, the person they are married to, who they are friends with or the house they live in.

We don't like them because we decide they aren't doing their job the way we would do it or because they spend time with people we want to spend time with, or because of the power we perceive they have.

If you have these feelings and do nothing about them, you contribute to your own clogged sink, and maybe even theirs.

We think it is okay to be angry, judgmental or jealous of someone as long as we don't say anything to them. But when we are thinking it or saying it to others and not to the person involved, it is still harmful. (If you are the one "not liked" and you are willing to talk, but the other party isn't, that is another day's message.)

We have all done it, and even after we know better, we can be drawn back in to that behavior without realizing it. Forgive yourself and, when the moment presents itself, apologize. Or if you still have those feelings, seek to understand the person. Maybe instead of beating up on that person, you could help him or her do the job better or help that person make better choices.

If we just want to beat people up, we need to take a step back and examine why we won't discuss our problem with the person. It could be we want to have a problem with them simply because of the space they fill. And when that is the case, we are really the one with the problem and don't know it.

A sink clogged = possibilities not pursued.

Be not angry that you cannot make others as you wish them,
since you cannot even make yourself as you wish to be.
T.A. Kempkis

JULY 20
BE INTENTIONAL

If there is someone you don't want to do kind things for, that is likely a symptom that you have a clogged emotional sink.

But what if we want to give goodness to someone who doesn't want to receive it from us? Well, unless we are stalkers, they have an emotionally clogged sink, and if we aren't careful, we could catch it.

Remember, they might not like you because of something you did or because of a space you fill or because they are afraid or jealous of you.

So what do you do about it? Sometimes that person is not interested in communicating with you, only about you.

If he or she will not honestly communicate with you, it is quite easy to slip into that same pattern. Then processing or venting turns personal and to gossip.

If we are venting with an intention to make things better and still have everyone like each other, that can be a way to unclog. But if we are venting with an intention to make the other person feel bad or have others dislike him, that is an ill-intention and we might as well say, "I don't like that person and don't want you to either."

That little bit of truth—at least admitted to ourselves—might begin to unclog our sink. Sometimes we can't help but laugh at ourselves and our selfishness when we get that honest, and genuine laughter can work wonders on a clogged sink.

Beware, emotionally clogged sinks can be catching; before long we might find ourselves doing the same negative behaviors we don't respect and that frustrate us when others do them.

We have to be careful not to let our positive possibilities go down the drain because we got caught in someone else's emotionally clogged sink.

A lie does not consist in the indirect position of words, but in the desire and intention, by false speaking, to deceive and injure your neighbor.
Jonathan Swift

JULY 21

BE AT EASE

As much as we would prefer not to, we will have problems with others. We are human, a condition that gives us a lot of opportunities to learn and grow from mistakes, particularly in relationships.

Who do you need to clear an emotional clogged sink with?

If you can talk to that person, do it today. If you can't, write a letter (that you send or not) then choose forgiveness and start fresh with a great attitude and positive emotions flowing again. If all you can do to unclog is change your attitude, make that choice today. You don't have to keep the attitude if you don't want to, but you may find it feels so good to be clear of clogs that you will work to stay that way.

What if the person you need to clear out the clogged sink with is yourself?

A reader wrote that she was having more success with a desire she has had for a long time. She said that, "Finally, I think I am clearing out my clogged sink."

You are clearing out emotional clogged sinks with others; now do the same with yourself. Forgive yourself for a mistake, be kinder to yourself in areas where you struggle, be honest with yourself, accept responsibility, face something rather than avoid it.

Remember, when it comes to our emotional sinks, anything negative that is stuck just leaves less room for the good stuff to get through. Do you need to clear out anything today?

Clear your sink and get ready for the new possibilities to flow.

I discovered I always have choices and sometimes
it's only a choice of attitude.
Unknown

Our lives improve only when we take chances, and the first and most
difficult risk we can take is to be honest with ourselves.
Walter Anderson

JULY 22

BE LIGHTER

We all make mistakes. We can hope that as we continue to learn lessons we will make fewer now than we did yesterday. But we are supposed to make mistakes. That is not an excuse; that is a fact. We are imperfect, so mistakes will come. We do not have all the knowledge in the world or all the skill in the world or every virtue, so we have to learn and develop as we go.

As we grow and change, we will know more next month than we do today. The important thing is to make sure the changes we make with that knowledge are ones that make us better, happier contributors to ourselves as well as to those around us. If our changes make only us and our situation better, but not our clients' or company's, they are probably not good changes.

What is your relationship with your mistakes? Do you take ownership, look at how you could have done better and move on? Or do you hold onto them, beating yourself up?

What about with others' mistakes? Do you move on or do you hold onto them, blaming and beating that person up?

Keeping mistakes in your handbag to pull out and wave over the person who made that mistake isn't a good idea. We have enough of our own mistakes without carrying around other people's, too. That will only weigh us down and hold us back. Forgive the person and lighten your load.

When we forgive someone else for his or her mistakes, we start to forgive ourselves for our own. We decide the "weight of the world" we will carry with many factors. One of the heaviest is unforgiveness. Once we truly forgive an offense, we will want to continue forgiving, because we realize how much unforgiveness has been weighing us down and slowing us up.

Don't carry around more than is necessary. Forgive, give grace and move on quickly with a lighter load to pursue your purpose and possibilities.

As we grow in wisdom, we pardon more freely.
Unknown

JULY 23
BE HELPFUL

If we take a minute and look back, we often find that the things we aren't proud of in our lives are things we were judgmental about at one time or another.

Could it be that what we have been judgmental about, we will eventually experience so we cannot be judgmental anymore? Remember that old expression: "We become what we hate"? Maybe the statement is really: "We become what we judge."

If you examined your pains, problems and difficulties, would you find many are related to situations you were once judgmental about?

For example:

My child will never act like that.

Why doesn't that guy work harder?

I will never...

That will never happen to me.

I can't believe she…

He's stupid.

The things we are judgmental about might be the lessons we need to learn.

Take a minute to bring to mind what you are judgmental about and begin to work to let that judgment go. If we seek to understand now, maybe we won't have to experience the pain of the situation later.

Seek to help, not to judge or criticize. You could end up being the one you help in the long run.

We are all full of weakness and errors; let us mutually pardon each other our follies.
Voltaire

Don't pick on people, jump on their failures, criticize their faults—
unless, of course, you want the same treatment. Don't condemn those who are down;
that hardness can boomerang. Be easy on people; you'll find life a lot easier…
Luke 6:37-38 MSG

JULY 24

BE FLEXIBLE

The great thing about our opinions or behaviors is that we can change them at any time.

Any given moment, we can change our mind or behavior. We can correct mistakes and learn new ways to operate...this very moment. But many of us won't.

We don't want to change because the change may affect our:

Pride

Position

Pocketbook

Social life

Even when we know something else is the right thing to do, we will often want to avoid a truth so we don't have to change. But when we think back on our lives, the moments we tried to cover up something or avoid the truth are likely the times that created the most pain and problems.

So with that in mind, wouldn't it make sense to embrace change and better ways of living rather than staying the same because of stubbornness or fear of change? Changing for the better is usually the better option, even if it does change our social lives or pocketbook.

We would probably rather be happy with a new set of friends than still unsatisfied with the same old drama. But we are afraid to let go of what we know. Maybe we feel we need to make a change to our business that will cost in the short-term. But who is to say that in the long run we won't end up with a bigger bank account because of our better decisions?

Make good choices instead of fearful ones and you will find possibilities where there were none.

Faced with the choice between changing one's mind and proving that
there is no need to do so, almost everyone gets busy on the proof.
John Kenneth Galbraith

JULY 25
BE RELEASING

There are times we do everything right and still do something wrong. With all the rules in the world, there are bound to be times when we have the best intentions and still get it wrong.

When you know you did the best you could, you have to let the problem go. Learn from it so you don't have the same one again, but let it go or else you may stay stuck—and stuck can lead to anger or shrinking back.

When you know you could have done better, accept that and do better next time.

We can let our pains and mistakes keep us from moving forward, but when we do, we are not serving anyone. And since possibilities and purpose are often found in serving others, we could likely miss ours.

Forgive yourself. Forgive someone else. Then repeat that cycle as many times as necessary over your lifetime. (For some of us, it could be daily.)

What do you need to let go?

Something you did...something someone else did...something that no one "did," it just happened?

Let's make this our "let it go" day and let possibilities fill the space that pain once did.

When you make a mistake, don't look back at it long. Take the reason of the thing into your mind and then look forward. Mistakes are lessons of wisdom. The past cannot be changed. The future is yet in your power.
Hugh White

JULY 26
BE RESPONSIVE

There is a space between a "problem" and our response. That space makes all the difference for our feelings, interaction and, potentially, outcome.

What we do with those moments before we respond will determine if the situation escalates or de-escalates—if it flows to a solution or if it stalls, if we have peace or angst.

For example, when you get an email that feels attacking or impatient, do you respond that way or do you take a step back and reassess? Oftentimes how we read an email is how we feel, not always how the person writing it feels. Expecting the best of the words helps us to get our emotions and fears out of the way and see a new perspective in the email.

When someone offends you or hurts your feelings, do you automatically respond back with an intention to hurt their feelings, too? If you do, do you have a productive and satisfying interaction with that person? I would guess no.

Revenge of any kind isn't going to help the situation and expecting the worst likely isn't either.

Take as long as you need to be clear-headed between the problem and your response. We are going to mess this one up quite often because we are human and not robots with perfectly calculated reactions. When we respond in a way we wish we hadn't, we can rewind and ask to start over or for forgiveness. But we will make things easier on ourselves if we will work with that space to choose gratitude or seek to understand or some other response that can help us make the best choice of reaction we can at that moment.

Between stimulus and response, there is a space.
In that space is our power to choose our response.
In our response lies our growth and our freedom.
Viktor Frankl

JULY 27

BE THOUGHT-CONSCIOUS

As we become more aware of how our thoughts affect our actions, health, relationships and most every part of our lives, we want to become more aware of what our thoughts are.

We can miss the significance of not just our unconscious thoughts, but also our conscious thoughts. Journaling helps us find unhealthy and untrue ones and process them. But many of us think, who has time for journaling? So if you are one of those time-crunched people, instead of journaling, you can simply look for signals in your daily activities, for example, pay attention to the words that come out of your mouth.

"I am afraid..." – Most of us say those words and don't focus on what comes after them. Listen to yourself say what you are afraid of. If it is something you don't want to fear anymore, face it and replace the thoughts. Or if you won't face it, acknowledge that you want to keep that fear. (There are many options but this is only a brief daily reading so find one that works for you. Get help if you need it.)

For example: a woman wanted to change careers, but was afraid of becoming homeless. She recently divorced and didn't feel the security of another person to fall back on and didn't want to be dependent on her children financially or emotionally. So one day she faced her fear by going to a homeless shelter. After facing her fear, she took the risk of changing her career. She became quite successful in business and life—accomplished, educated and interesting. And it started with finding out and facing what she was afraid of.

Another woman realized her automatic internal response to experiences was "no." No, I don't need help. No I don't want to try something new. She decided to have a no-fear week and chose her first internal reaction to be "yes" or "okay." Then she would contemplate her verbal response and whether it would be yes or no. When she changed her internal response she could make a decision on the individual circumstance rather than on habit, fears, pride, guilt or any other negative emotions lurking around in her brain.

There are many options in dealing with fears. When you find fears you were unaware of, work to find a truthful, lasting solution and you will find great new possibilities along with it.

Nothing in life is to be feared. It is only to be understood.
Marie Curie

JULY 28

BE MORE ACCURATE

Another signal of what is directing us is "I want _____, but____."

I want... but... When we say, "I want to take a class but I don't have time right now." Stop and ask if that is true. Is the issue that you don't have the time or that you really don't want to? A woman shared that she got her MBA while she worked and was a single mom of three kids. When asked how she did it, she responded, "Pure determination." Stop and ask yourself if you really want to take the class. If you do, make it happen. If you don't, move it out of your brain until the right season.

"I *want* to increase my business *but* the market is bad." Other people improve their business in difficult markets, so call and ask how they do it. If you aren't doing activities to increase your business, stop and ask yourself why not. What are you afraid of? Don't use excuses.

"I *want* to be better organized *but* I don't know how." There are many people you can hire to create workable systems or at least start you in the right direction and show you what is possible. If you are doing nothing to work toward being more organized, then maybe your words might be, "I want to be more organized, but it really doesn't matter that much to me right now."

Sometimes what we say we want really isn't what we want. We can fool ourselves with the excuses we make. Listen to what comes after your "but's" today and see if it is true or just convenient and then work to be more accurate with your words. Be truthful with your words; your life and possibilities tend to follow in their direction.

Don't make excuses. Make something incredible
happen in your life right now.
Greg Hickman

JULY 29
BE ABLE

Another signal of what is hanging out in our brains is the words, "I can't do that." Why can't you?

As long as something is not wrong or illegal or hurtful, why can't you? Why can't you wear a red coat? Why can't you train for a triathlon? Why can't you break out of your normal routine? Why can't you begin a new career? Why can't you take that class you have wanted to take? Why is that "too big" a goal for you? Why can't you go out on a blind date? Why are you not good enough?

Sometimes it's fear or pride and sometimes it is just a perception that we have of ourselves and what we are supposed to present to the world.

Take a risk sometimes and step out and try something new—from a hairstyle to a marketing idea.

Pay attention to when you say the words, "I can't" or "I can't do that." And then look at your beliefs and thoughts that led to those words. Do you need to work on your self-esteem? Do you need to reassess your risk tolerance? Or do you just need to change your words from "I can't" to "I don't want to"?

"I can't" can spill out to many areas of our lives and subtly direct our actions to underachieving rather than contributing, experiencing and accomplishing all that is possible for us.

*If you think you can do a thing or think you
can't do a thing, you're right.*
Henry Ford

JULY 30
BE CLEAR

W hat directs our days makes up our lives.

One way to be more deliberate about our lives and choices is to have a vision. If we don't have a clear vision of what we desire our lives to be, then our unconscious thoughts and feelings can have more control in our lives than we might want them to.

For example, if you don't have a clear, defined vision for your work and its purpose, you can end up making decisions based on money and pride rather than integrity and purpose.

Or if you don't have a clear understanding of your vision for your marriage, you may end up drifting away from your spouse and just using that person for financial security.

Or what about your kids? We can easily let frustration, busyness and selfishness build a wall rather than a bridge between us, and before we know it, we are no longer engaged in their lives.

Our vision can and will change. The point is to not let it change based on whims, negative emotions and unconscious thoughts. Be as deliberate as you can and recognize when you are choosing to allow pride, fear, guilt or frustration to make your decisions rather than what you know to be right for you.

Be conscious of your decisions and you will be more conscious of your possibilities.

Dissatisfaction and discouragement are not caused
by the absence of things but the absence of vision.
Anonymous

JULY 31
BE A VISIONARY

Having a vision of your life and business helps to direct your path.

What do you want your relationship with your spouse to look like? Your family, your clients? What do you want your business to look like?

Now consider what actions would lead to that vision...

Maybe a "date day" with your child?

Date night each week with your spouse?

Set time for conversations with far away friends/family?

A communication process with clients?

Weekly meetings with your manager?

There are a multitude of actions that will promote your vision. After you know ones you want to take, share them with the appropriate people in your life. Do you and your spouse have the same vision? You and your clients? What about your manager or partner?

It is important to share your vision because if one person has one vision while the other desires something else, there will be confusion and dissatisfaction.

Unless there is communication and solutions, you will be going in circles with frustration rather than working toward a common goal with peace and passion.

Vision without action is merely a dream. Action without vision just passes the time. Vision with action can change the world.
Joel Barker

AUGUST 1

BE A LEARNER

How do we learn? Sometimes we can read about a subject and get it. Other times we watch someone else or listen to another who has knowledge in the area. Occasionally we just know things. But most often we have to experience something to learn it, no matter how much we may not want to.

We have to live a loss to know we will survive it.

We have to experience a success to learn how to accomplish.

We have to go through problems to have a new knowledge that we will need later.

What we learn and how well may depend on our internal and external choices. Choosing to hang onto pride, anger, bitterness, avoidance, jealousy or anything negative will most likely not lead to a joyful, productive outcome. On the other hand, choosing to live through it with a positive attitude and productive actions and thoughts will help us learn what we need to learn, most likely, on the quickest, most direct path.

None of us wants to go through difficulties, but we must; difficulties are part of living. But our difficulties often don't have to be as hard as we make them. The internal choices we make as we live difficulties can be the difference between seeing our possibilities and missing them, between moving through a painful difficulty and being stuck in it.

Sometimes we just have to live it to know it.

To live remains an art which everyone must learn,
and which no one can teach.
Havelock Ellis

AUGUST 2

BE LIVING NOW

We can experience something and still not learn how to live well through it. We can stay stuck going in circles rather than moving toward what we want. A good way to help us get unstuck or just more aware of what we want is to experiment with new ways of living.

For example: What do you want your life to look like in ten years? Imagine it, write down your vision and start living that way now.

If you still want to be angry with someone in ten years, then go ahead and be angry with him or her now, but if you want to be happy, start clearing out your issues with that person today. If you decide you want to be bitter or jealous or tired or lonely in ten years, keep choosing it now.

If you want to be debt-free in ten years, start clearing it out now.

If you want to be laughing more, start laughing more now.

If you want to be loving to the people around you, start now.

If you want to be financially responsible, start now.

If you want to be holding hands with your husband, start now.

If you want to be respected in your field, live the behaviors and values that bring respect, now.

If you want to be accomplished in something in ten years, practice now.

If you want to be happy and joyful and energized in ten years, start choosing it now.

You aren't going to snap your fingers and these things simply exist as they do in your vision; habits can be hard to break. But you can begin to live what you want and develop new habits, because hard to break is completely different from impossible to change.

You are the one who chooses how you are going to live, and your choices now are making decisions about your life down the road. You may not be able to live fully in action how you want because of current circumstances, but you can in attitude. Begin today to live in action—as best you can—and attitude the way you want to in ten years, and future possibilities may begin to present themselves now.

When we put off for tomorrow what we can do today, we are putting off possibilities that are ready to be pursued.

To change one's life: Start immediately. Do it flamboyantly.
William James

AUGUST 3
BE CHANGING

There are always going to be emotional pains and situational difficulties, but we tend to make them more difficult than they have to be.

Have you ever noticed situations stop being so difficult when you change a negative emotion or attitude to a positive one?

Yes, it takes time to process emotions and we certainly don't want to deny or avoid them, but we also don't want to hold onto negative ones any longer than is necessary. When we keep moving through the typical emotional process, we come out better on the other side—quicker and happier.

But when we get stuck and our anger turns to bitterness, resentment, fear or revenge, then we are not only stuck in negative emotions and past situations, we are also stuck in our lives. Our relationships may struggle, and we might find ourselves wondering why our goals aren't coming to fruition.

We have to experience our emotions and live through the pain of a difficult situation, but when we find ourselves stuck rather than healing, we might need help. Forgiveness, kindness, gratitude and wanting happiness for others are good ways to begin to change your pain. If you still need help, get it. Being stuck emotionally can be more confining to our possibilities than being stuck physically. It is like being stuck in a room with a jammed door. We have to push hard to get unstuck and on to where we are supposed to be.

Remember our emotions are choices. For us to move through the difficulties of life rather than staying stuck in them, positive emotions and intentions are a great place to start.

Everything is okay in the end. If it's not okay, it's not the end.
Unknown

AUGUST 4
BE STEADFAST

There are just some things we have to live to know. Once we learn the lesson, we get to move on with a new knowledge and understanding that we will likely need down the road.

How many times have lessons you learned in the past helped you deal with issues in the present?

Perhaps something you learned in a mistake you made with a client last year helped you avoid a problem for several clients this year.

Something you learned in that difficult situation you were embarrassed by helped someone else through a difficult situation.

Something you learned about fear helps you live better and more peacefully.

But as it is human nature to quit just before we reach a goal, we can often quit just before we learn a lesson. Just because something is hard doesn't mean it isn't purposeful. In fact, because it is hard is exactly the reason we may need to examine it because some of our biggest possibilities exist in the toughest situations.

When something is hard, we may make it harder than it has to be with our fear, pride or pain. We can't control someone else, but we can work hard to control how we contribute to a problem.

When something is tough, look at how you can make it easier with action or attitude. If you don't have a solution or are too close to the situation to be clear-headed, seek advice from someone you trust and respect. We are not perfect; it is okay to need help. In fact, we are supposed to need help, support and encouragement.

Don't quit on a lesson until you learn it. Likely, it is one you are going to need down the road to pursue a possibility and make a difference.

Don't be discouraged.
It's often the last key in the bunch that opens the lock.
Author Unknown

AUGUST 5

BE SHARING

Sometimes we just have to live something to know it, but other times we can listen to learn.

Turning your pain into purpose is a big part of healing for you, and it helps others.

Consider one thing that you didn't want to live through but, by the time you got to the other side of that situation, you had learned something important. Write three pieces of knowledge you can share when you encounter someone who is living through the same.

They may just have to live it to know it, or they may learn something from you that helps them have a smoother ride to the other side.

Regardless of how others use the information, writing down the lessons helps us.

And if we find any bitterness, revenge, deceit, anger or anything else negative in our words or attitude, that is a good sign we still have more to learn.

Commit yourself to constant self-improvement.
Unknown

AUGUST 6

BE ON THE OTHER SIDE

Some of us innately know how to be successful at business, but we struggle in our personal lives. Or we are great in relationships but not so good at being successful professionally. We can take the class or buy the book, but sometimes we need to experience success to truly believe it is for us. Sometimes we need to live it to know it.

To do that, we have to overcome laziness or fear and move forward. We have to take a risk and believe. We have to do the little things that move us toward our needs and desires. Unfortunately, most of those little things begin with the scary internal decision to risk our pride and hearts to go "All-In" with what we want.

So if we know we want it, why don't we go All-In? Well, it is much easier to use the busyness of work or a painful past relationship as an excuse than to think no one wants us (that is not true; you are wanted but that is the crazy stuff that goes through our heads). Or it is easier to just talk about doing something you have always wanted to do rather than actually do it and risk "failure."

So what is the difference-maker for success? There are a few, depending on the situation, but a common one is going All-In. If you think back on times you wanted something but didn't achieve it, you may find you weren't All-In. You might have held back from giving yourself to the goal completely in case it didn't work.

We have to step out and be willing to risk the comfort of what we know for the possibilities we can't see yet.

Of course, we must be prudent and have boundaries; going All-In doesn't mean going crazy. It means we are moving toward what we want within the parameters of what is right and within our value system without emotionally holding back or using excuses.

Here's the part to watch out for: we can experience something and still not learn what we need. When we find ourselves still stuck going in circles without peace, we can be sure we are still living through it. When we are through it, we will know it and we will be better on the other side.

The person who risks nothing, does nothing, has nothing, is nothing,
and becomes nothing. He may avoid suffering and sorrow,
but he simply cannot learn and feel and change and grow and love and live.
Leo Buscaglia

AUGUST 7
BE PRIDE-LESS

By my own unscientific analysis, when it comes to possibility blockers, fear is number one and pride is a close second. Pride is so subtle we can miss it, and when we do, we miss possibilities, too.

If you have difficulty praising someone…

If you have a hard time telling someone how you feel…

If you won't ask for help…

If you sulk instead of working things through…

If you won't admit a mistake or issue...

If you won't go back to a business, church or family function (because you got mad)…

You could have a pride problem. And remember, it is pride's job to destroy anything it can: relationships, jobs and happiness.

If you have trouble spotting pride, look at problems that arise in relationships or your work or just in day-to-day interactions today. Examine your attitude prior to the problem.

"Pride comes before a fall" is true. You may laugh out loud at spotting the pride moments in your life or you may not want to admit them. If not, then, likely, pride is still alive and working to keep you from your possibilities.

When we realize that we are acting out of pride, if we will turn around and do the opposite of what pride is telling us to do, we will be lighter, happier, more productive people. That isn't always true, but often is, and regardless of whether we can immediately experience the happiness, we will be working toward new possibilities.

In general, pride is at the bottom of all great mistakes.
John Ruskin

AUGUST 8
BE PERSISTENT

Sometimes it appears what is blocking our possibilities is a person. Granted, people can desire to make us unhappy or unsuccessful because they are unhappy, jealous or fearful—and it can work for a while. But at some point, we have to take a step back, recognize the truth and then push through.

The person who wants you to be unsuccessful or unhappy just wants to be miserable herself. If you are doing your best, you have to quit worrying about him or her and push through to your possibilities. If you don't, you may miss not only your possibilities, but your purpose, too.

We often allow others to block our possibilities, but eventually we have to step back and learn what we are supposed to learn to keep moving forward. It may seem like others are blocking our possibilities, but when it comes right down to it, we are.

It may feel like something is standing in our way—the guy down the hall, a family member, a past relationship—but eventually we have to take responsibility and realize that ultimately we are the ones who are choosing not to pursue our possibilities.

The minute we accept responsibility instead of blaming, we see a whole new future ahead of us. And maybe even new possibilities with the person (or thing) we were blaming for our situation. Once we stop blaming that person and being critical, we may actually start liking him or her. After we push through the blame, we can go after our goal with energy and enthusiasm.

A woman shared the story that she had a terrible break-up with her fiancé who she had moved to a new city to be with. For several years, she was bitter and resentful and couldn't move forward with a new relationship. Then something happened to make her realize that she was actually equally to blame. Yes, she had moved to a new city for him, but she had made the choice. He couldn't have made her move across the country anymore than he could have made her marry him. She made the choice but blamed him.

When you find yourself circling with a goal, take a step back, identify the truth of your choices in the situation, stop blaming and move forward. We don't want to get to the end of our lives and wish we had...

Be persistent about your purpose and your possibilities will be, too.

It's easy to point when you can't heal it.
Don Walk

AUGUST 9
BE NEW

Guilt and blame hang out together, and they enjoy blocking possibilities.

Guilt separates us physically and emotionally, and blame puts responsibility somewhere else besides where it belongs.

If any guilt has crept back into your life, deal with its source, give forgiveness where you need to and release others from any guilt. Then ask forgiveness where you need to and receive grace. If any blame has returned to your life, turn the pointing finger around and look at yourself.

We have some responsibility in the situation. The sooner we find it, the sooner we get to fix it or heal it or change it. And then we get to joyfully move on to new possibilities.

The best years of your life are the ones in which you decide your
problems are your own. You do not blame them on your mother, the ecology,
or the president. You realize that you control your own destiny.
Albert Ellis

Dr. Miller says we are pessimistic because
life seems like a very bad, very screwed-up film.
If you ask, "What the hell is wrong with the projector?"
and go up to the control room, you find it's empty.
You are the projectionist, and you should have been up there all the time.
Colin Wilson

AUGUST 10
BE PRESENT

Today is a gift. That's why it's called the present.

We have all read those words numerous times in various inspirational stories and emails, but do we fully grasp the meaning?

If we aren't as mentally here as we are physically, we are missing the real "present," and that is the peace and possibilities that come from living in the "present moment."

When we live in the past with memories, there is often pain and regret, maybe bitterness: I wish...if only...

When we go to the future with our thoughts, there is often fear: what if...?

When we live in the present moment, we are more likely to make choices that serve us and our clients now instead of allowing fear and worry to make these choices for us.

So live this moment right now.

Leave the pains, frustrations and wrongs of yesterday in the past.

Leave the worries, fears and expectations of tomorrow in the future.

And live this moment right now.

Decide if you like the person sitting across from you based on this moment and not on what he did five years ago (or even yesterday) that you still hold a grudge about. You could find a new beginning in this moment.

Enjoy this moment and don't drag your future worries and expectations about what might happen next week into the now. You could have a fresh start right now.

One step at a time. One breath at a time. One moment at a time.

We want to learn from the past, prepare for the future, but fully live this moment.

Live this moment right now. Be fully present in this day without bringing yesterday or tomorrow into it and feel your joy, creativity, energy and possibilities expand.

How simple it is to see that we can only be happy now,
and there will never be a time when it is not now.
Gerald Jampolsky

AUGUST 11
BE FULLY ENGAGED

Engaging in the present moment helps us be fully present in it.

We have been told that multi-tasking makes us more efficient. But does it really? Many of you multi-task and often you don't have another option, but for those times you do, take it. Rather than multi-task, do one thing and become fully engaged in the task, conversation or activity at hand.

We have become so attached to multi-tasking that it can become a habit we do even when it isn't necessary. Yes, there are times you have to put on mascara with a toothbrush in your mouth while calling for your kids to get in the car. But for those other times—when you can stop emptying the dishwasher and focus on your child or spouse when they are trying to talk to you—do it.

When you are on the phone with your client and don't need to be reading something unrelated, don't. Be fully engaged where you are with whom you are.

Engaging in the present moment offers many benefits:

Actively listening to clients helps you hear what they are not saying as loudly as what they are saying and you can help them work through their needs easier.

Being present moves you through tense moments because you are dealing with the issue at hand rather than automatically bringing past hurts or future fears that do not belong in it.

You are often more deliberate about your choices and words.

Awareness in the moment is a first step to many solutions.

Multi-tasking can create more work for you than simply engaging in now.

You won't have to go back and re-build a relationship because the person felt de-valued when something else was more important than hearing them out.

If you are using multi-tasking to avoid something, you will eventually have to go back and deal with it anyway, so you might as well do it now.

Engaging in the moment helps you engage your possibilities.

Thinking is the hardest work there is, which is probably the reason why so few engage in it.
Henry Ford

AUGUST 12
BE IN THE MOMENT

One of the most powerful things we can do for ourselves and our possibilities is to learn to live in the now. When we make decisions in line with our goals in the present moment, it seems we don't have so many problems in later ones.

What does it mean to take care of this moment?

Do you have any clients you need to call or write? Maybe they had an event in their life you need to acknowledge with a card, or maybe you just need to check in.

Are you happy with your marketing initiatives and do you feel comfortable with your processes and strategies?

If not, take steps toward these today.

Do you want to lose weight? Make the decision about eating the apple pie that will be in line with that goal.

Do you want healthy, loving relationships? Make the loving decision now.

How many times have we looked back and said, "I should have..."?

Now think of the times you can look back and say with satisfaction, "I did..."

What made the difference between a regretful "I should have..." and a satisfied and joyful "I did...."?

Live your goal right now with today's possibilities and tomorrow's will take care of themselves.

If you want to take care of tomorrow, take better care of today.
We always live now. All we have to do is entrust ourselves to the life we now live.
Dainin Katagiri

AUGUST 13

BE WISE

Yesterday we talked about taking care of the present moment and what that looked like.

So on the flip side, what might it look like to *not* live in the present moment? It could look like:

> Not calling a client because you are afraid of his reaction. (You are guessing at his reaction based on past reactions you or someone else has had to similar situations.)

> Still being angry over something that happened in the past. (So many reasons for this one, but all are about the past and none are helpful to our joy or to today.)

> Still being stuck in past pains and mistakes. (Keeps us from moving forward with what we know now and our purpose.)

It is not that we will always live in the present. Unless we are living alone on a mountaintop, it is quite difficult to not let the past or the future get in. What makes the difference is what we do after the realization that we are living in the past or future.

When you realize, do you stay angry? Do you keep blaming and playing the victim? Do you let guilt separate you again? Do you let your past pains and mistakes keep you from moving forward to your purpose and possibilities?

Or do you make a different decision this time? When you realize you are habitually living in the past, make a deliberate choice to live in the present.

One good way to live in the present is to allow others to live in the present. Don't keep others in their past with your thoughts, words, intentions or actions.

When we allow others to learn and grow and be excellent, we are likely more able to allow ourselves to learn and grow and be excellent...in this moment.

What can you take care of today so that tomorrow takes care of itself?

Living in the moment means letting go of the past and not waiting for the future. It means living your life consciously, aware that each moment you breathe is a gift.
Oprah Winfrey

AUGUST 14
BE QUESTIONING

We can avoid conflict and be more efficient with our time by asking questions instead of making assumptions.

Ask the experts what the rules are.

Ask your friend what she wants to do.

Ask your child how he feels.

Of course, sometimes you can ask questions, but those you ask give you inaccurate information (unintentionally, of course) and you still wind up with problems. But you did your best in the situation, and that is all you can do.

No matter how hard we try, problems will arise, and even when we have done our best to find true answers, we can still have a tendency to shrink back when problems come. But who does shrinking help? As a great woman says: if you are making a difference, you are likely going to have some controversy.

Keep moving forward, keep asking questions, keep making a difference.

The way to keep yourself from making
assumptions is to ask questions.
Don Miguel Ruiz

AUGUST 15
BE ENGAGING

Few of us really enjoy walking into a large event where we don't know anyone. And when you consider that very few in attendance enjoy it either, you often end up walking into a room full of "fear." Not the "I am afraid to be here" kind of fear, but just the little bit of angst and insecurity that can lead to a feeling of awkwardness.

A simple shift in intention can make a difference by changing your perspective and bringing you back to the moment.

When we are walking into that room with angst, it is because our focus is on "me." What will they think of me? Who will I talk to? Is this outfit appropriate?

When we shift our focus from "Who's going to make me feel good?" to "Who can I make feel good?" and "Who in this room needs attention?" everything changes.

We not only come back to the present moment, we now have an intention that is not about us. And remember the great benefit of giving: what we give, we somehow get back. If we genuinely seek to give a comfortable feeling with an attitude of interest to others, we will somehow end up being comfortable and interested—and enjoy our evening, too.

Everyone just wants to be "loved." Even people who are aloof (could be they are just afraid) or arrogant (could really be they are confident but have insecurities) just want to be loved. We don't have to engage people we don't want to, but we could be missing out on the most interesting part of the day.

If we do our best to leave people better than we found them, possibilities will find us.

You can make more friends in two months by becoming more interested in other people than you can in two years by trying to get people interested in you.
Dale Carnegie

AUGUST 16
BE EXCITED

Life gets busy and worrisome and messy. In the midst of all that, it can be easy to lose excitement about something or someone that you want and need to be excited about. Are you excited about your work each day? When we are not excited, we are not energized, passionate or really present in what we are doing. And since we have only this life in which to make mistakes and make a difference, we need to actively assess our excitement in how we are living it.

As you build excitement in your life, keep in mind that it is not just your life you will be energizing; you will energize others, too. Our emotions are contagious and we are responsible for what others catch from us. If we take genuine passion and energy into a meeting or a project, others will be fueled by it, too.

We want to be deliberate about our excitement and conscious of ways it can be depleted so we can be prepared. Some Excitement Squelchers Are:

People who don't want you to be happy, productive or successful. You may not be able to avoid them, but be aware of them and prepared for their attitude and responses. Don't be deterred from your goal or purpose.

"No" people. People who have a first response of "No, that can't be done," rather than "Let's talk about that," can drop a wet rag on excitement. You are not someone who lets "no" stop you from at least exploring possibilities.

Attacking others in our thoughts, words or actions. Unkindness will deplete positive, energetic excitement. It may raise adrenaline or your heartbeat, but likely not your genuine excitement. Don't confuse a power trip with being excited. If we get excited about attacking people, we may want to take a step back and re-examine intentions and goals. Genuine excitement seeks to build up others, too.

Yes, it is easy to let life's pains, attacks and situations beyond our control get us down—we are human—but it is also in our control to put activities and support in place to get us through those times and be excited again. Don't let the burdens of your day steal your joy and do not let others or yourself rob you of your enthusiasm.

Get excited about your work and your possibilities will meet you there.

If we expect to create any drive, any real force within ourselves, we have to get excited.
Earl Nightingale

AUGUST 17
BE WELL-INFLUENCED

Are you excited about your environment?

Do you love to come home to your house or could it use some warming up?

What about your office? Is it inviting to you and clients? Could it use a plant or a painting?

Research findings have shown us that color and other aspects of our surroundings impact physical healing, mental attitude, and productivity. Experientially, we know the same; we are influenced by color and beauty and sound.

The elements of design include harmony, unity and repetition. So why not use our physical environment to inspire those same things in our work and lives?

We can successfully serve our clients in the frumpiest of offices, but if we want to be excited about our spaces, we can take steps—even small ones—to create environments that excite us, calm us or inspire us. It doesn't have to be expensive—add a plant, a picture, or good lighting.

If you are less than excited about your physical environment, what can you do today to increase the comfort and beauty of your spaces? Call someone to help or just take the time to assess your surroundings and do it yourself.

Just one thing.

If you love your spaces, help those of us who are in need of your expertise. Remember, what we give eventually comes back to us, so you can expect help to come down the road for those areas that aren't so natural to you.

We are constantly creating our lives. Work toward creating spaces that you like to be in.

Beautiful spaces create beautiful minds.
Heidi Ketvertis

AUGUST 18
BE RESTORED

To be excited about our lives is to be grateful. It is hard to be excited about anything if we aren't grateful for it in some way.

So as we seek to bring a sparkle to our spirit and a quiet excitement to our days, gratitude is a vital element.

When you find you aren't energized or excited about something today, stop and be grateful for it. Gratitude is restorative and rejuvenating.

Be grateful your spouse is there to have a disagreement with.

Be grateful you have an office to go to. That you work for a great company. That you have a job...with insurance and income.

Be grateful even for problems because, as much as we would like to avoid them, they give us opportunities to learn and grow. Some of our most difficult moments are our most educational and preparatory if we will step back and look for the lesson we need to learn rather than always focusing on the lessons we want others to learn.

Be grateful for arms, legs, cars, stoplights, people—even problems. We can either be miserable and complain through them, or grateful and looking for the opportunities to grow in our jobs, relationships and lives.

Be grateful and you may find what was impossible just yesterday is your new possibility today.

There are two ways to look at life.
One is as though nothing is a miracle; the other is as though everything is.
Albert Einstein

AUGUST 19

BE LIGHT

The burdens of our days were not designed to steal our joy and excitement, but we let them.

We all experience difficult situations. If ten of us gathered in a room together, each one of us would have a story of difficulty and pain happening in our lives right now that we are feeling our way through. (And I don't know about you, but there are several moments I would like to rewind and do over as I feel my way through problems I haven't experienced before.)

The burden feels heavier when we think we are the only one responsible for the problem, but remember, when dealing with adults, everyone involved has a responsibility in the problem. Own your part and let others accept responsibility for theirs and carry their own load. Healing seems to come faster for everyone that way. Others can't heal and grow if we keep taking their responsibility for them. We can carry it for a bit, and we can always walk along with them, but at some point, we have to let them be accountable for their part in a problem.

On the other side of that, if you have been making someone else carry one of your burdens, take it from them and lay it down (and you will learn and grow). Don't let someone else live in guilt, pain, embarrassment or the past when you have the ability to take that pain from them. Take it and lay that burden down. Then everyone is freed up to pursue his or her own possibilities with renewed energy and excitement.

We can easily manage if we will only take, each day, the burden appointed to it.
But the load will be too heavy for us if we carry yesterday's burden over again
today, and then add the burden of the morrow before we are required to bear it.
John Newton

AUGUST 20

BE BELIEVING YOU CAN

There is little we can accomplish when we don't believe. But there is much we can when we do.

Granted, some things just aren't meant to be. But for those things we really desire to experience and contribute in our lives, believing is a vital element.

Yes, we tire of waiting, but maybe we are supposed to learn something while we wait. Or maybe it isn't our time yet. Perhaps we must change an attitude or behavior to prepare for our goal. Or maybe we just need to believe again.

Sometimes we won't really believe a desire will happen for us so we won't be hurt if it doesn't. It is as if we believe we aren't worthy or aren't good enough anyway; so if we don't really try, we won't really have failed.

Look at a goal that you are struggling with. Do you believe it can happen for you? Do you believe you can learn to play tennis? Do you believe you can have a good relationship with someone you currently don't? Do you believe you can serve a client with substantial needs as well, if not better than, anyone else?

Do you believe you can...

    find a way to build a needed program in your community?

    change the way things are?

    make a difference?

    grow your business?

    help clients?

    get organized?

    create processes for your business?

Believing is a vital part of accomplishing.

For those goals and possibilities you have lost faith in, determine if they are good for you and if they are still something you want. If they are, make the decision to believe in them again. Happiness is often a choice; sometimes, believing is, too.

Little seems to happen when we don't believe, but possibilities are endless when we do.

Four things for success: work and pray, think and believe.
Norman Vincent Peale

AUGUST 21
BE CAPABLE

One piece of advice given to people who are slightly depressed is to sit up instead of slouch, lift your head up, look people in the eye and smile. Our attitude and outlook can be affected by our body and actions. Think of believing the same way. When you lack confidence in an area in which you know you are supposed to be working toward a goal, act as though you can do it. Walk with your head up, feel confident in the areas where you know you possess skills and let that confidence spill over to public speaking, talking to new clients or going into situations where you don't know anyone.

Don't try to be something you aren't, but do believe you can. Prepare for the event by building a foundation in that area, gaining the knowledge you need and practicing what is necessary. Then believe you can.

Little seems to happen when we don't believe, but possibilities are endless when we do.

Whether you think you can or think you can't—you are right.
Henry Ford

AUGUST 22
BE BRAWNY

As we stretch ourselves and learn and grow, there will be times we want to shrink back or just quit and stay as we were. Even if "where we were" doesn't feel like where we are supposed to be anymore, it feels safe.

But what if it is not as safe as you thought it was? What if the discomfort you experience with growth is necessary for you to learn and expand yourself in order to handle what the future holds for you and what the world needs from you?

We are going to make mistakes and experience pain whether we stay this size or grow. We have this idea that our pains and mistakes will grow in proportion to our personal growth. Maybe they will, but somehow we will grow through them and, thus, with them. Everything can be used to make us better and help us learn.

Expect the best as you believe yourself through new growth stages, and your possibilities will grow with you.

It is not the mountain we conquer but ourselves.
Edmund Hillary

AUGUST 23
BE HERCULEAN

We want to prepare, but busyness, lack of focus, procrastination and feelings of unworthiness get in the way. So as we examine different areas where some of us could be more prepared than we are, identify your own specific areas and take action toward gathering what you need to be prepared for the opportunities that will come.

In your business:

1. What do you have angst over?

2. What do you hear yourself mention to others that you need?

3. When have you felt "inadequate" in the past? Do you avoid that particular area or are you working toward improving your confidence and being prepared?

Look for common areas and patterns in your answers above. Do you need to take action, change your thinking or both? What do you want to prepare for, create, or change? For example, I want an explainable investment process, a timely seminar I am ready to give, a client-communication process that I stick with through good and bad times, or a communication plan to utilize when a change of some kind needs to be communicated to clients quickly.

Create an action plan that includes blocking off time in your schedule to work toward your project.

If you need help, get it. There are so many people who want to help you prepare for all the possibilities waiting on you to be ready for them. Some possibilities don't present themselves until we prepare for them.

People only see what they are prepared to see.
Ralph Waldo Emerson

AUGUST 24
BE A BEGINNER

Sometimes we don't prepare because we feel overwhelmed by information. "Where do I start? I am never going to learn it all."

You are right, you are not going to learn it ALL—and you aren't supposed to. None of us will know everything, so we can release ourselves from that pressure. But we still can (and must) learn and grow.

Granted, the constantly changing technology, products and laws can make us feel inadequate. When someone mentions a new regulation or a new capability in your technology system, you can cringe, thinking that you should know that. When we cringe we tend to feel embarrassed rather than curious. So instead of taking that opportunity to learn and prepare, we walk away without asking, "Where do I find that?" or "Tell me more about that. I wasn't aware of that change."

When you hear something you don't feel informed on, take a "teach me" attitude and ask appropriate questions to learn.

If there is a topic you feel overwhelmed and under-prepared with, commit ten minutes each day to read an article or information on the topic. Ten minutes is completely doable. You won't be an expert quickly on the subject with this technique, but you will feel more adequate and may actually end up giving more time to it, thereby feeling more prepared than you thought.

For instance, if you need to learn more about estate planning, take ten minutes a day. If you want to be familiar with your technology, take ten minutes to explore; just click on a topic and see where it takes you. (Then if you find something you like, write it down!) The important thing with this approach to preparing is to begin now before a specific need arises.

Sometimes, preparing is just beginning.

It wasn't raining when Noah built the ark.
Howard Ruff

AUGUST 25
BE STARTING WELL

When we are unprepared, we waste time and energy, but just as important to note, we may also waste a lot of love.

We can certainly be rushed and still make those around us feel loved, but if we aren't doing that, we may want to examine why. If your mornings are consistently rushed and your frustration is being expressed more than your affections, then you might want to consider how you can be more prepared physically or mentally.

If there are things you can control, like getting lunch items gathered the evening before and the next day's clothing out of the laundry and into one spot, then do. For those things you can't control, be mentally prepared to be rushed and still loving. That looks different for different circumstances. As difficult as it may be to choose a patient reaction, it is possible—if not in the moment, later.

We are human; we are going to be crabby, unorganized and subject to other negative states and emotions as we grow and learn in this life, but when we catch ourselves behaving differently than we want to (maybe frustrated instead of affectionate), we need to stop, rewind and say, "I am rushed and frustrated, but I love you and want you to feel that, too." or "I am sorry I snapped at you this morning. How can we make our mornings easier?"

When we are in a rush, we may not take the extra time or focus to give attention and kindness to the sales associate behind the counter or our child that is scooting out the door. That is okay, but if you find this behavior occurs all the time rather than occasionally, stop and ask yourself if that is how you want to live your days.

A reader said yesterday that she has a new goal to get everything done for the next morning by bedtime—from clothing assembled to gifts that need wrapping so that her days start in the way she wants them to continue: energetic and peaceful rather than frustrating and chaotic. (And if she oversleeps, she can still get where she is going on time.)

Your days are busy enough without starting them off with less energy, joy and peace than is possible. What is possible for you?

Lose an hour in the morning, and you will be all day hunting for it.
Richard Whately

AUGUST 26

BE IN THE GAME

We want to expect the best...and prepare for not getting it.

No matter how charmed life is or how gifted you are, you will encounter times of "failure." We are imperfect beings, so there will be times we will say the wrong thing and do the wrong thing. We will lose some clients and some deals to the competition even when we are as prepared for success as possible. And there will be times we will flat-out mess up. We have to prepare for those moments of "failure."

How are we going to respond? Will we admit any mistakes we made or will pride keep us in denial? Will we turn around and apologize or will we point fingers and blame? Left to our natural responses, we will likely be defensive or avoid self-reflection. When that happens, we don't always know how to pick ourselves up and get back in the game.

If we don't learn how to recover from our mistakes or even, simply, the inevitable disappointments of life, then instead of jumping back up with new enthusiasm, we might stay down and act out as the angry victim instead of the educated journeyman equipped with a new wisdom.

Give yourself grace; then learn the lesson and file the new knowledge away, because you are going to likely need it again in the future.

When we "prepare" for our responses to difficult situations and our own missteps, we are more likely to be deliberate about our reactions, allowing us to move through the situation rather than staying stuck in the disappointment or embarrassment—or a moment that is already over.

Preparing for our response to problems helps us to move forward rather than staying stuck. Possibilities are in the lessons learned not in the moments that have passed.

The problem is not that there are problems. The problem is expecting otherwise and thinking that having problems is a problem.
Theodore Rubin

AUGUST 27

BE MORE PEACEFUL

Pick one thing you have been dreading or worried about and prepare for it. What is one thing you can do to prepare?

Is it a test?

> Study one chapter each day (or whatever schedule fits in the time frame).

Is it seeing someone you don't want to see?

> Then mentally prepare in a multitude of ways—visualize how you want to react, know what you want your intention to be and line up everything else to that, meditate or pray, etc.—or see a counselor.

Is it a situation?

> Can you do anything to prepare for it in action? Do research or write a speech. Do you need help of any kind that a professional could provide? With the struggling economy, most of us could use more income, so if you have a need and can pay someone to help you, it would be a win-win.

Is it putting on a bathing suit for a vacation in two weeks?

> Buy a fabulous cover-up and don't take it off if you don't want to.

When we have angst about something, it could help us to ease that angst to prepare for it by doing anything from processing with a friend…to educating ourselves on the topic…to preparing our attitude.

When we are prepared, we are often not as afraid. Pick something you are afraid of and do one thing to prepare for it. Then work to let the fear go and embrace the possibilities.

Luck favors the mind that is prepared.
Louis Pasteur

AUGUST 28
BE WISER

I read once that problems are gifts. I was in the middle of a problem with a friend when I realized problems can be gifts if we will let them be. They come like a "warning" for us to make a change so we can avoid a bigger problem.

For example: A problem with a client (no matter how much we don't want to have any problems with clients, we will; we are human) can lead us to put a system in place to help us avoid that same issue with multiple clients.

Or a problem with our car may help the mechanic to find a bigger problem that would have cost more money had it gone undetected.

Or a problem with a friend may help us change a behavior that will help us be a better friend.

We can choose to be bitter or better in response to a problem. And as easy as bitter may be in the moment, it is not too much fun over a lifetime (or even a week). So don't let bitter have even a full day of your time and energy.

We are all human. We are going to have angry responses. But don't hold onto anger and don't feed it. Let it go, because if you think about it, anger and bitterness do not get us any closer to what we really want over the long run.

Focus on the solution and "better" will come more easily.

When there is a problem... ask yourself, "Where is the lesson?" And work to implement it. Possibilities are in problems and they come alive in the lessons.

Every problem has a gift for you in its hands.
Richard Bach

The difficulties of life are intended to make us better, not bitter.
Author Unknown

AUGUST 29

BE DECIDING

I ran across an excerpt from Victor Frankl's book, *Man's Search for Meaning*. Mr. Frankl was in concentration camps for several years during World War II. Below is an excerpt from the book talking about choosing not to be a victim of his circumstance. If you would like to read the whole excerpt, you can find it on the PBS website. As we are looking at our responses to problems and struggles, Mr. Frankl's is an example of what's possible. Most of us can't even imagine how horrific it was and I in no way want to diminish the pain of those who experienced the suffering; I am only trying to help us learn to deal with our own.

"The experiences of camp life show that man does have a choice of action. There were enough examples, often of a heroic nature, which proved that apathy could be overcome, irritability suppressed. Man can preserve a vestige of spiritual freedom, of independence of mind, even in such terrible conditions of psychic and physical stress. We who lived in concentration camps can remember the men who walked through the huts comforting others, giving away their last piece of bread. They may have been few in number, but they offer sufficient proof that everything can be taken from a man but one thing: the last of the human freedoms—to choose one's attitude in any given set of circumstances, to choose one's own way."

"And there were always choices to make. Every day, every hour, offered the opportunity to make a decision, a decision which determined whether you would or would not submit to those powers which threatened to rob you of your very self, your inner freedom; which determined whether or not you would become the plaything of circumstance, renouncing freedom and dignity to become molded into the form of the typical inmate. ...Even though conditions such as lack of sleep, insufficient food and various mental stresses may suggest that the inmates were bound to react in certain ways, in the final analysis it becomes clear that the sort of person the prisoner became was the result of an inner decision, and not the result of camp influences alone."

Fundamentally, therefore, any man can, even under such circumstances,
decide what shall become of him—mentally and spiritually.
He may retain his human dignity even in a concentration camp...
Dr. Victor Frankl

AUGUST 30
BE GROWING

Problems arise for many reasons but often because we miss something due to language difficulties or assumptions or we just don't think about a situation from a perspective other than "good."

We can end up with miscommunication, misinformation, and misunderstandings because of what we "miss."

Problems also arise because we just mess up. We let a conversation turn to gossip and we end up with words we wish we could take back. We let disagreements get out of hand and end up—again—with words we wish we could take back. And sometimes with words we wish we could say, like, "I'm sorry. Can we start over?"

We are going to mess up and we are going to miss stuff. Don't miss something again by letting an opportunity of forgiveness, resolution or discussion for solutions pass you by.

Whether we miss something or we just mess up, our problems can lead to stronger relationships and better processes, if all parties want to put the work toward it that is needed. If all parties aren't willing, it simply becomes something to outgrow.

A new point of view is worth 80 IQ points.
Alan Kay

Man does not simply exist, but always decides what his existence will be, what he will become in the next moment.
Dr. Victor Frankl

AUGUST 31
BE FACTUAL

We have enough real problems today without making new ones up about tomorrow. Certainly, we must prepare and think through decisions the best we can, but we have a tendency to play a game of "what if" with ourselves that is likely not productive.

Looking at various scenarios for the purpose of decision making is prudent.

Letting the negative "what ifs" play in our heads isn't so productive. They bring us down, stress us out and make us less able to engage in the present moment.

Fear encourages us to make up negative scenarios for the future around a problem; we can then end up acting on the fear rather than the facts.

Ask yourself, "What is the real issue?"

"What are the parts I am making up about it?"

Don't let fear and pride rob you of your possibilities that are in each moment.

Real difficulties can be overcome;
it is only the imaginary ones that are unconquerable.
Theodore N. Vail

SEPTEMBER 1
BE RELEASED

What if there is a direct correlation between our need to control and how-out-of-control we feel? ...That the more out-of-control we feel, the more we feel the need to control others and their lives?

If you think about that, does it make you want to change anything? Do you want to control people and situations more, or do you want to feel more in control yourself?

Don't get me wrong, controlling what we can is important: our attitude, our words, our actions, our self-esteem, our pride, our fear, our responsibilities, our attitude, our schedule, ourselves.

But trying to control what we can't is exhausting. Trying to control your significant other, how your associate wears his hair, or how someone stacks the dishes in the dishwasher can be exhausting because we have put ourselves in charge of everything and everyone around us. That is a big responsibility.

Our way is surely the best way, but they still have their own journey through life to figure that out. (That was a little humor—which, if I have to point it out, may not be so humorous.)

We don't have to choose to like what someone else is doing or enable them in how they are behaving, but we can choose to support and love them, regardless. (Of course if someone is involved in illegal or unhealthy behavior, seek help.)

Make your choices of action and attitude and allow others to do the same.

Think about it: the need to control may be a signal that we believe we have a higher likelihood of controlling others than we have of controlling ourselves and our attitude and actions. That could be the root of a problem that has a solution... and that solution likely begins with "me."

This life is yours. Take the power to choose what you want to do and do it well. Take the power to love what you want in life and love it honestly. Take the power to walk in the forest and be a part of nature. Take the power to control your own life. No one else can do it for you. Take the power to make your life happy.
Susan Polis Schutz

SEPTEMBER 2
BE IMPERFECT

Control does not equal perfection.

Sometimes we have the perception that if we can control the people and situations around us, we will be perfect.

Well, that likely isn't going to work out so well, is it? Because, first off, we aren't perfect and can't be, so striving for perfection rather than excellence is going to wear us out.

And secondly, if we are trying to control others instead of ourselves to achieve our "perfection" (which is unachievable), we are going to wear them out.

Trying to control things that aren't ours to control will just leave everyone weary. Control what you can and what you are responsible for and lay the rest down.

No one is perfect... that's why pencils have erasers.
Unknown

SEPTEMBER 3
BE FLOWING

When it comes to communication, many of us are like salmon...when a disagreement occurs, we immediately turn and swim upstream rather than going with the flow for a bit. When we immediately go against the flow, we end up weary and likely further away from our partner and a resolution than when we started.

As you are paying attention to controlling your responses rather than letting negative emotions do it for you, try going with the flow instead of against it.

When someone makes a comment you don't understand or do not agree with, rather than immediately object or argue, try going with the current of the conversation for a little while. Go with the conversation to seek to understand before you begin to make an objection. Hear them out and seek to find out why the other person feels a certain way.

Not only might you find out something new you didn't know, but you will also likely uncover the root of the problem along with a solution more quickly than you would have. You will use less energy, improve your relationships (the people you are speaking with will feel heard and valued) and be more productive with your time and resources.

Possibilities and resolutions seem to come more quickly when we listen and seek to understand. Sometimes it is better to go against the current, but when it comes to conflict, it is often better to go with the flow for a little while.

Seek first to understand, then to be understood.
Stephen Covey

SEPTEMBER 4
BE REPETITIVE

When we seek to understand, we are seeking resolution, respect and solutions.

A really simple and easy way to seek to understand is to repeat back what we feel the situation is or what we hear being said. Often the issue lies in perspective. Until we know the other person's outlook, we can be arguing the wrong argument.

Have you ever been upset with someone over a comment they made? Did you seek to understand the comment or did you make assumptions? People aren't perfect, so before we become angry with someone, shouldn't we seek the perspective behind the comment first? If we find that we don't want to seek another perspective, it could be because we don't want to learn any evidence that might make us change our own. But keep in mind that if we want others to give us a chance to explain and expand, we have to be willing to do the same.

Summarizing or repeating back what we have heard helps us to:

Actively listen

Be present in this discussion rather than reliving past ones

Base the discussion on what is real rather than on what we imagine it to be

And it helps the other person:

Understand what you are hearing from them

Clarify what they mean or how they feel

You may come to a mutual understanding or you may still disagree. But remember, disagreeing doesn't have to result in an argument. We can disagree with someone and still like them. If someone has to think just the way we do for us to like or respect him or her, we might have a problem that is not only affecting our happiness, but also our possibilities.

A good listener tries to understand what the other person is saying.
In the end, he may disagree sharply, but because he disagrees,
he wants to know exactly what it is he is disagreeing with.
Kenneth Wells

SEPTEMBER 5
BE QUICK

When we seek to understand, it gives us a chance to control our emotions, rather than letting them control us. And the time we take to understand gives us a chance to readjust our judgment.

We are often quick to judge. What if we were quick to help? Or quick to seek solutions? Quick to listen… quick to be kind?

We all have our times we are slow to process through an unpleasant situation or problem. Slow is okay as long as we are still moving. Stay focused on moving through instead of staying stuck in the negative.

When it comes to day-to-day activities and interactions, it could be what we are "quick" with makes a bigger difference in our possibilities than we imagined. Be quick to be positive today and you could experience solutions and positive possibilities faster.

What are you quick with?

When we judge or criticize another person, it says nothing about that person;
it merely says something about our own need to be critical.
Unknown

SEPTEMBER 6
BE CHOOSY

I read somewhere (paraphrased) that fear makes us shrink back when we should be stepping forward—not stepping forward in false bravado or biting comments, but stepping forward in honest words and action.

If we are stepping forward in anger, jealousy or resentment to make someone feel small, we are still acting in fear. We have all done it. We step forward to tear down rather than build up, to lash out rather than reach out. But when we react in anger, what are we stepping into? What path are we walking on? What door are we going through? What kind of life and relationship are we choosing?

We don't want to shrink back, but we probably don't want to step forward in anger either. So sometimes the best choice may be to stand still and gather ourselves so we can step forward on the path we really want rather than having to backtrack and start over. We are human, so we will step down the wrong path more often than we would like. Being still long enough to choose our direction can save us a lot of time and potentially create for us more possibilities.

Watch where you are stepping today…into problems or possibilities.

When anger arises, think of the consequences.
Confucius

SEPTEMBER 7
BE SUCCESSFUL

Shrinking is easy to do. We are wounded by a comment and instead of saying, "That hurt my feelings," we shrink back. Or we are afraid of a situation and, rather than step forward to seek truth, we may want to avoid it.

For example, you may be having a discussion with a family member who says something that hurt you. Do you shrink and withdraw (and at some point lash out in anger) or do you have a calm, honest conversation when you are able and the time is appropriate? When you think a client could be upset, do you shrink back (and continue to wonder if they are unhappy with something) or do you step forward and make the call to connect and give information?

Remember, the truth may be hurtful and difficult initially, but eventually it can strengthen and energize. Truth, even if difficult, sets us on a path toward a goal. But lies and avoidance keep us going in circles—with the same problem, the same goal—instead of moving forward and growing with new goals.

If you aren't completing goals and creating new, exciting ones, identify where you are shrinking back and going in circles rather than stepping forward and moving toward your objectives. What are we creating in our lives when we shrink?

You can avoid reality, but you cannot avoid the
consequences of avoiding reality.
Ayn Rand

SEPTEMBER 8
BE PROCEEDING

Remember, the truth may be hurtful and difficult initially, but eventually it is likely to strengthen and energize. Truth, even if difficult to hear, sets us on a path toward a goal, but lies and avoidance keep us going in circles—with the same problems—instead of moving forward and growing with new goals. Why do we do that? Why do we go in circles with old goals instead of accomplishing them and moving on to new ones?

The truth is that sometimes we don't want new goals, because we know new problems come with them. We can shrink back from new goals because we don't want new problems. We are acquainted with the problems that come with this level of business or exposure, but we don't know the problems that come from a larger book of business or a bigger reach with increased exposure. Instead of stepping out with our skills and talents, we hide them behind our fears.

If you are not moving toward your goals, what are you afraid of? List the potential "problems" and identify solutions. Talk to your manager, truthtalker, coach or friend today and ask for their support with these potential problems and others that may arise.

Obviously, we want to do the right thing and work well to avoid complications, but some will eventually arise because we are human in an imperfect world (and, don't forget, problems are one way we learn and grow). As you move forward with the knowledge, skills and purpose you have been given, it is likely you will also be given the ability to overcome the issues that come with your new goals, just as you got through the problems that came with the old ones.

We have enough real "problems" in our daily lives without letting pretend ones keep us stuck where we are instead of moving forward to where we could be.

Happiness is not the absence of problems; it's the ability to deal with them.
Steve Maraboli

SEPTEMBER 9
BE LONG-TERM

In our normal everyday activities, we can shrink back in fear when the better choice might actually be to step out and move forward.

We want to be aware of how we are moving forward. Just as we can shrink back in fear, we can step forward in fear, also—and that is rarely a productive path to start down.

Acting on revenge, jealousy, or anger is stepping forward in fear. That action will not get us closer to our goal—well, maybe a short-term goal of getting our way, which makes us feel as though those tactics work for us, but not our long-term, happiness goals.

If we are getting what we want because we are acting on negative behaviors, we are likely actually alienating and destroying relationships rather than building them. However, this destruction is masked because we are getting what we want right now, so we think all is well. Acting on revenge, jealousy or anger may get us what we want in the short term, but it will eventually catch up with us.

For example, we may be succeeding in having the person we are jealous of be excluded or alienated, but in the long-run, our need for control can destroy the very relationships we are trying to "protect." Or when we step out in revenge, we may get short-term satisfaction (when the other person "gets what they deserve"), but if we continue that behavior, we will likely end up unhappy and probably not know why.

When you step forward, know which path you are choosing.

A well-beaten path does not always make the right road.
Proverb quote

SEPTEMBER 10
BE EXPANDING

Shrinking makes things contract—smaller. Do you want to be small? A small heart, a small mind? You don't have to be loud and large, just be open to possibilities, not closed to opportunities. Shrinking says "I am closed for business."

With our kids or spouse, we get wounded and retreat (contract) when love and kindness and patience are likely the better choices.

With an associate or family member, we get offended and choose not to forgive (contract) when forgiveness and grace are the better, more productive choices.

It takes courage to forgive others because, to do so, we often have to acknowledge our part and forgive ourselves, too. If you will not forgive someone, take a look at yourself. What do you need to own in the situation and forgive yourself for?

It is much easier to contract and play the victim than expand and own our part in the problem. "If I forgive, will I still get what I want?" "If I forgive will I still be able to control others and the situation?"

Another example of shrinking and contracting is when we avoid and shut down. It is easier to avoid discussing an issue than to expose that our position has no validity—that we can't back up our argument—so we just shut down and become angry.

If you can't back up your position beyond phrases like, "I deserve it." "You owe me." or "I want it," then you might want to reconsider your position and request.

When you have a valid position, you likely won't mind having a discussion. When you don't have a valid position, you will likely find yourself contracting and angry in order to avoid a discussion.

As we learn to spot moments and seasons of life that cause us to shrink back in fear or anger when we could move forward in kindness, grace and courage, we can learn to choose our actions and reactions and decide who we will be.

Because moments string together to a lifetime, do we want to live our lives in ways that are joyful and open to others and possibilities or bitter and contracted into self? More possibilities and happiness seem to find us when we are open rather than closed.

$\mathcal{L}$❦

Life shrinks or expands in proportion to one's courage.
Anais Nin

SEPTEMBER 11
BE TRUTHFUL

It takes courage to be honest.

When someone is rude to us, we can either shrink away in silence, bite back and allow the situation to escalate or step forward with a calm, honest response.

There are appropriate times for all these responses, but the most productive and the most difficult habit to develop is the calm, honest response.

One of the reasons it is hard to do is because it is sometimes hard to know what "honest" is. When negative emotions and fear get involved in a situation, it can be quite difficult to weed through the emotions and get to the facts. Getting to the very heart of how we feel and what "honest" is becomes a chore because we first have to clear out the thoughts that come with anger, frustration, pride and revenge before we can get to honest. It is almost as if the negative emotions want to cover up "our truth" in order to keep us negative and angry because they know that when we finally get to truth, a situation can begin to be resolved.

One of the best ways we can "get to honest" is to develop a habit of looking at our part in the problem rather than blaming. Blaming is so much easier, but in the long run, it isn't really fun and is rarely productive.

We can escalate a situation or defuse it with our response. What do we want to choose?

When we tell the truth, there is a strong force pushing us toward success.
When we tell a lie, even a little white lie, there is a
stronger force pushing us toward failure.
Unknown

SEPTEMBER 12
BE TRANQUIL

Something that helps us to step forward instead of automatically shrink back is honest words with others and honest thoughts with ourselves.

Many of us don't take the time to find out how we really feel and believe about a topic or situation. So instead of being prepared with an answer we shrink back because we don't have an honest response, or maybe, worse we step forward in frustration or anger or another emotion that wants to create chaos.

Some of you are thinking that you don't have the luxury of time to yourself to know how you feel. That is understandable. You have to contend with families, work, stress, busy schedules. But most of us at least have a little time in the car when we can turn off the radio and be still. We can find a few minutes in a week to be still without the distractions of our phones or computers or something else we may be using to avoid sitting still and getting honest with ourselves.

Some possibilities are found only in stillness.

It is not because things are difficult that we do not dare,
it is because we do not dare that things are difficult.
Seneca

SEPTEMBER 13
BE FABULOUS

The following quote reminds us not to shrink from being our best. Many of us can identify with playing small and shrinking so that others feel better. The reminder that when we do our best, we give others permission to do their best is powerful because the flip side of that is, when we don't do our best, we give others permission to not do their best. We aren't going to be excellent all the time, but when we shrink back in fear when we should step forward with truth (instead of lies to ourselves that keep us going in circles) we are likely not serving our clients, families or those around us.

Just as often as we can be afraid to be wrong we can also be afraid to be fabulously amazing!

What causes you to shrink?

Our deepest fear is not that we are inadequate. Our deepest fear is that we are powerful beyond measure. It is our light, not our darkness that most frightens us. We ask ourselves, who am I to be brilliant, gorgeous, talented, fabulous? Actually, who are you not to be? You are a child of God. Your playing small does not serve the world. There's nothing enlightened about shrinking so that other people won't feel insecure around you. We are all meant to shine, as children do. We were born to make manifest the glory of God that is within us. It's not just in some of us; it's in everyone. And as we let our own light shine, we unconsciously give other people permission to do the same. As we're liberated from our own fear, our presence automatically liberates others.

Marianne Williamson

SEPTEMBER 14
BE SHINING

We all want to be fabulously amazing, right? We want to use our skills and talents to fulfill purposes and reach potential, living life fully and abundantly while we are on this earth, right?

So why would we have difficulty with being fabulously amazing? One reason could be that at some point in our lives, someone didn't want us to be. They were insecure and felt that if your light was shining their light wasn't.

But that isn't true. My light can shine and yours can, too. If we turn our lights off, we are all eventually left in the darkness.

You may have had a family member or friend growing up who would put you down because they were jealous. Or you may have associates or friends now who do the same: when you move forward, they want to pull you back. When you expand in life, they want you to shrink so they feel better. But no amount of shrinking by you or anyone else will make them feel better in the long-run; they have to do that themselves.

We want to let others excel and have the spotlight and shine, but we don't want to hide our talents, potential or light under a basket in order for that to happen. We can use our light to make others' spotlight brighter—and illuminate everyone's possibilities.

We are each gifted in a unique and important way.
It is our privilege and our adventure to discover our own special light.
Evelyn Dunbar

SEPTEMBER 15
BE BRIGHT

J ust as we want others to allow our light to shine, we want to be conscious of encouraging others to shine and be their best.

If you catch yourself wanting someone to fail or you find you don't want the best for someone, you are likely jealous and want "their light turned off."

Some symptoms of wanting to turn others' lights off are biting words to or about them, not wanting them to succeed and not wanting them to be happy.

When you catch yourself doing this, change the thought and choose to desire the best for that person. Keep in mind you can not particularly like someone or not really enjoy their company, but you can still want goodness for them; you can be jealous but choose to desire good for them.

We often miss that. We think if we are jealous, we "can't" desire good things for someone. But it is actually the choice to want to see them succeed that could eliminate jealousy.

When we change our jealous thoughts to positive ones that build-up, we not only help another to shine, we brighten our own light.

How bright is your light?

We cannot hold a torch to light another's path
without brightening our own.
Ben Sweetland

SEPTEMBER 16
BE BRIGHTER

When we shrink back, we turn off our light. We brighten and dim our light not only with our actions but also with our thoughts and intentions.

Think of someone you know whose light shines. Now think of someone you know who doesn't seem to have any light left. What is the difference between them? Their actions are likely very different, but the difference between them starts internally, with their thoughts and intentions.

Our lights brighten when we want the best for ourselves and others and when we act on those positive thoughts and intentions. When we have our thoughts, words, intentions and actions all in line, we are not only moving toward our own goals, we are illuminating others' paths, too.

If you are not moving toward your goals with energy and excitement, take a step back and see what is not lined up. Are you saying you want five new clients but not taking action? Are you saying you want kinder interactions with someone but your intention is really to "win" or get your way?

When we are going in circles instead of moving toward a goal, we likely are out of sync with our thoughts, words, intentions or actions. And when we are going in circles there is a lie involved somewhere—usually to ourselves. Our light isn't shining so brightly and we are wondering why we aren't happy or getting where we want to be.

We all get off track, but the great thing is, we can usually get back on track with just a few changes in choices. If you need help, talk to your manager or someone you trust today because when we turn down our lights, we leave our possibilities in the dark

Thought is the sculptor who can create the person you want to be.
Henry David Thoreau

SEPTEMBER 17
BE THRIVING

"Your playing small does not serve the world. There is nothing enlightened about shrinking so that other people won't feel insecure around you." - Marianne Williamson

When you saw this quote in a previous message, did you have the thought, "Why would anyone play small?" Or were you someone who thought, "Wow, I didn't know anyone else did that, too!" We play small to make others feel good, but if you stop and think about it, when we play small, we are actually judging others to be not as good as us in some way. Not as cool, not as secure, not as smart...

If we feel that we need to shrink, we must feel bigger and better. From one perspective, shrinking seems kind, but from the other it seems judgmental: who are we to decide they aren't as "big" as we are?

When we shrink so others don't feel insecure, could it actually be that we feel insecure around them in some way? ...that we have a fear that needs addressing?

We think we are doing it to be kind and to build others up, but that doesn't seem authentic. If we shrink to try to somehow make others feel bigger, we start a cycle of smallness that is hard to break.

If the first-string running back pretends to be not as good to make the second-string guy feel better, how does the team do? Have you ever heard the expression that you play to the talent level you are playing? In tennis, golf or quilting, playing with people better than us makes us better.

In life, being around people better than us makes us better. You don't want to shrink; you want everyone to thrive.

Don't shrink yourself to build others up. We could all just end up small. Instead, be excellent and we all could end up there, too.

There is no passion to be found in playing small,
in settling for a life that is less than the one you are capable of living.
Nelson Mandela

SEPTEMBER 18
BE FEELING LIGHT

What goals and responsibilities have you been shrinking back from? Be honest with yourself about it; either say, "I don't really want that goal" and move it aside or take a step toward it today.

What responsibility are you shirking? What decisions are you putting off? There are decisions we don't want to make, including decisions about our own lives and happiness. We may be an avoider or we may be a blamer and want someone else to be responsible for us. If you struggle with that, make a decision to step forward and be personally responsible for your happiness instead of blaming others or trying to make others responsible for you and your happiness.

As heavy as being responsible for ourselves sounds, we likely feel a lot lighter when we actually do it.

Every man's happiness is his own responsibility.
Abraham Lincoln

SEPTEMBER 19
BE INTENTIONAL

We have been talking about being fabulously amazing and not playing small to make others feel more secure, but we also want to be aware of when we are faking being amazing. Yes, sometimes we have to push through fears and "fake it until we make it." But if we consistently act in fear, we could be bordering on arrogant instead of amazing.

We all know people who are cocky or arrogant (and we have all been either or both at some point). They seem confident, but really, they are likely using consistent cockiness to cover insecurity.

Stepping forward in arrogance could be the same as shrinking because it is stepping forward in fear. Maybe the difference is in the intention. If we want to belittle another person rather than raise him or her up, we probably have an insecurity that needs some attention. (That belittling behavior can become a signal for personal change instead of a normal behavior. We get to choose.)

There is a difference between cocky arrogance and fabulously amazing. If you want to succeed and want others not to, you may be dealing in insecurities. If you want to succeed and also want others to have success, you may still have insecurities you are dealing with, but you are stepping forward in "amazing" instead of in fear.

Look to help someone be amazing today and you will likely be, too.

When we seek to discover the best in others,
we somehow bring out the best in ourselves.
William Arthur Ward

SEPTEMBER 20
BE RESPECTING

W hen we want to shrink to help others feel better about themselves, we could be judging that person or persons to be "less than us" in some way—not as pretty, not as smart, not as capable, not as good—or else we wouldn't feel the need to play small. Consciously trying to play small may seem that we are being kind and helping the situation when, actually, we may not be acting as kind as we thought and are probably not helping anyone in the long run.

If someone is insecure or wants control, they are fearful in some way. If we play small, we shrink in fear so we are not helping so much as just bringing more fear into the relationship.

Playing small is fear, but being fabulous "you" and giving others the "stage" and support to be fabulous "them" is building up. We can step back and enjoy their light without trying to diminish our own by playing dumb or incompetent or unaccomplished.

There is a subtle difference between the two that likely begins with intention and awareness. We have all played small and will do it again, but we need to remember that when we intentionally shrink, we are judging that others can't shine on their own. And when we shrink, we are bringing fear into the situation instead of love and respect.

Know that everyone shines in their own way and we can use our light to illuminate everyone's possibilities.

The greatest good you can do for another is not just share your riches,
but reveal to them their own.
Benjamin Disraeli

SEPTEMBER 21

BE STILL

The moment we want to shrink in fear is often exactly when we should step forward in action. But as we said before, we want to step forward in something other than fear, anger or revenge. Those don't solve anything; they can create a false confidence but still leave the problem. We are human and we are going to have unproductive thoughts we would rather not have. The key is to process them to thoughts we want to act on before we take action. In other words, be still in our negative emotions and process them to ones we want to take action on before we act.

Be still in anger and act in grace and truth.

Be still in offense and act in mercy.

Be still in embarrassment and act in kindness.

We all have times we want to act in revenge or jealously—it is easy and sometimes "fun" to do because we get on a little power trip—but we have to decide if that is how we will choose to act or if we want to move to something more productive. We get bold and take action when we are angry or offended, but if the only times we can boldly step forward is when we are negatively fueled, we may need to rethink that—we could be hiding behind negative emotions to avoid the truth. That doesn't sound like a safe hiding place, does it? It doesn't mean we sit still and let wrongs be done, it means when we do act, we are acting in truth, not defensiveness or jealousy. One gets things accomplished and the other creates chaos.

For example, your manager asks about the results of the marketing money he or she gave you and you lash out rather than admit that you didn't spend it well… it is gone and you have nothing to show for it. You may have avoided embarrassment, but you still have the problem of not effectively marketing as well as not knowing how to properly plan and handle money. If you are hiding behind negative emotions, talk to your manager, counselor or friend today. Your possibilities may be looking for you.

The strangest and most fantastic fact about negative emotions
is that people actually worship them.
P.D. Ouspensky

SEPTEMBER 22
BE ILLUMINATING

When we play small for someone else, that relationship is based on something false. It all seems innocuous, but when we become aware we are doing it, why do we want to continue?

Yes, we want others to feel good about themselves, but if someone is going to be threatened by your success and happiness (success isn't necessarily about money), then they are probably not going to be happy until you are not. You and others will have to dance around their insecurities to make them "happy."

If we have to "play small" around someone, they likely aren't going to be happy until we "fail" and are unhappy. If we keep making decisions around that kind of person, we might just end up giving them what they want without intending to.

We want to stop shrinking around people who don't like us or don't like themselves, because we could start making decisions in other areas of our lives based on what pleases others instead of what is the right thing to do. It is hard and we will still shrink at times, but remember, shrinking doesn't shine our light, it dims it. And if we keep playing small, that relationship is based on their control; it is "fake" and is a hard habit to get out of.

Keep in mind humility and supportive kindness are important. Just as we want to be aware of when we play small for others to feel bigger, we want to be even more aware of when we play big so others feel small.

When we play small, we dim our light, but any time we intentionally want to make someone else feel small, we likely extinguish our light and a multitude of possibilities along with it.

Live today shining your light brightly with an intention for others to do the same.

We don't want fear in any form to shape our lives into something less than they are purposed to be.

Much of what people have lost has been due to an insistence on things being safe.
Charlie Russell

It costs so much to be a full human being that very few have the love
and courage to pay the price. One has to abandon altogether the search
for security and reach out to the risk of living with both arms.
Morris West

SEPTEMBER 23
BE NONCONFORMING

We are all unique. No two of us are the same—not even identical twins. We have different talents, skills and abilities. We have different natural personalities and perspectives.

So if we know we are different and are supposed to be, why do we spend so much time trying to fit into a mold and be like others? Is it to be "liked"?

We are told to "differentiate" ourselves, but when we do, we can be made to feel like we need to fit in rather than be who we are.

This week, be aware of when you are doing something to fit in instead of because you want to or because it is the right thing for you to do. They could be one and the same (the thing you are doing to "fit in" could also be the right thing to do), but being aware can help us spot where we are sacrificing who we are for who someone else wants us to be.

The hardest struggle of all is to be something
different from what the average man is.
Charles M. Schwab

SEPTEMBER 24
BE DISTINCTIVE

A reader shared: "Recently I have attended several conferences and at times I have had these feelings of 'I don't fit in.' I wasn't like others; for example, we had different values and different views of our businesses.

"After sulking for a few days I decided that I need to turn it around somehow—what is it that makes me different and how can I use and harness that? I haven't nailed it down yet, but I am moving in that direction."

Most great "advances" start with a problem. We rarely get to a new level without something making us uncomfortable enough to change. Not "fitting in" can be the exact problem we need to uncover the way we do fit. Being different can make us feel inadequate or "wrong" when actually it is probably very right. In other words, our uniqueness isn't a problem to be solved but more likely a possibility waiting to be uncovered.

What are your strengths?

What is it that makes you different?

How can you incorporate those into your business?

Always be a first-rate version of yourself,
instead of a second-rate version of somebody else.
Judy Garland

SEPTEMBER 25
BE UNIQUE

As unique as we are, there is something in us that wants to be the same. What a conflict. It is really difficult to continuously try to mirror others when we don't enjoy the reflection.

So maybe our real desire is not to be the same, but to be accepted as we are—flaws, quirks, mistakes and all. What if what we really want is for others to like our uniqueness? But here is the problem: if your uniqueness threatens me in some way, I am probably not going to like it. If your "different from me" makes you better or more likable than me, then I am not going to like you. (Well, not me. I am probably going to like it. "I" represents anyone in your life—and human nature).

If your "different" pushes you to the top in production, the former top producers may start to feel insecure about it and, instead of respecting you, find fault. If your different seems to get you more marketing assistance or friends, others may become jealous, and that jealousy may reveal itself as putting you down or snubbing you. If your "differents" are positive behaviors that bring success to you, there are those who will want to bring you down. Unhappy people sometimes have a problem with happy people.

And since few of us want to be taken down, snubbed or ridiculed, we can end up stepping back before we ever step forward to try. Sadly, there are moments or whole seasons in life that we would rather be liked and conform than use our unique gifts and characteristics and be ourselves.

That thinking can lead us to a life of mediocrity rather than excellence, because most of us would rather settle for mediocrity and "fit in" instead of to be excellent in our unique ways and stand out.

If we are always looking to fit in, we may end up hopelessly chasing other people's possibilities instead of simply uncovering our own.

The strongest force in the universe is a
human being living consistently with his identity.
Tony Robbins

SEPTEMBER 26
BE USING YOUR GIFTS

If we find we are having a hard time pushing through an obstacle or if we would rather blend in than utilize our purposeful talents and "stick out," we might need a little attitude adjustment. Attitude adjustments start with awareness.

There are so many reasons we could have a difficult time, but they all likely involve the past and the future. It can be hard to recall, but did anyone ever try to make you feel small for simply using the gifts and talents you have?

Whether you are a singer or the quarterback, some will applaud you while others may be jealous and will want you to stop using your talents and working for excellence. They want you to be like them. You might still sometimes find yourself wanting to shrink so others feel bigger around you.

Sometimes, the reason we aren't fruitful with a goal is not because we aren't equipped but because somehow we were made to feel wrong for working to be excellent. From the classroom to the workplace there are going to be those who want you to lower the grading curve instead of be excellent. Sadly, negative peer pressure doesn't go away at any certain age.

We can receive a message from others that lower production is better—you'll be liked more. Isn't that really saying, "I don't want to do the work to be better (or I don't have the ability), so I want you to be worse"?

Will you use your uniqueness to make a difference in your business and fulfill your purpose or will you put your gifts on a shelf and conform to others' ideas of what they want you to be?

There's nothing enlightened about shrinking
so that other people won't feel insecure around you.
Marianne Williamson

SEPTEMBER 27
BE A CONTRIBUTOR

When we find the thing that makes us different and better, we can also find ourselves wanting to hide it, shrink back and be the same again.

What if each of us has things in us we are supposed to bring forth to contribute to the world but we shrink back because we don't want to stick out or be a target or because we aren't perfect or "good enough"?

The thing that makes us different could be part of our purpose, but we won't explore it. We won't bring it forth. We won't let it shine because we are afraid of being judged or criticized.

If we won't let our talents or gifts see the light of day then instead of shining like those around us, we can end up living with a shadow over us. And think about it—we will likely still be a target, just a victim-kind of target instead of a victor-kind.

That is the long way to say that if we let what others think shape us instead of what is the right thing for us to do, we may miss our purpose and our possibilities.

What is the "different" in you that you can use to make a difference?

Accept who you are and revel in it.
Morrie Schwartz

SEPTEMBER 28
BE IRREPLACEABLE

We have heard it said: what makes you different makes you beautiful. And, of course, what makes us different can make us successful.

We spend time and energy trying to be like everyone else, yet it seems the moment we start to accept and utilize our "different" is the moment our possibilities come to life.

What is your "different"?

If you don't know and appreciate what differentiates you from others, stop and take the time to identify those characteristics. Think about: What are you passionate about? What would you like to be known for? Why do people do business with you? How would you like your clients to feel? What is a need that isn't being met for clients?

How can you incorporate these into your business? Once you have an answer to what makes you different, explore how you can utilize and express your uniqueness. Then test out your ideas. If you don't like the results, you don't have to stick with it; you can try something new.

Whether it is in action or attitude, identify the little ways you are different and celebrate them. More possibilities seem to show up when we accept and celebrate our different talents and passions rather than stifle them.

Enjoy and embrace your "different" instead of hiding it. You might find possibilities that had been hidden before.

To be nobody but yourself in a world doing its best to make you everybody else means to fight the hardest battle any human can ever fight and never stop fighting.
E.E. Cummings

In order to be irreplaceable one must always be different.
CoCo Chanel

SEPTEMBER 29
BE VALUABLE

While looking at what makes us different and ways to incorporate that into our work, a reader shared…

"When I think about what is unique about me, I think about it in terms of how I contribute.

"I think I am 'diplomatic.' I like very much seeing issues resolved rather than letting them hang between people and situations. This drives me to find ways to bring people together in a way that doesn't alienate or blame.

"This is significant to me because I didn't utilize this previously. I wanted to be like those around me—operating in drama and pointing fingers, blaming others. I finally discovered this 'passion' when I discovered the value in who I am. Somehow that made me feel okay to be different."

It takes energy to be different, but it might take more energy not to bring out what is within us. In other words, sometimes it is harder to stifle a passion than it is to utilize it and be different.

Don't be afraid to be different. You never know what possibilities may come of it.

The person born with a talent they are meant to use will
find their greatest happiness in using it.
Johann Wolfgang Von Goethe

SEPTEMBER 30
BE ENJOYING TODAY

In reflecting on what makes her different, a reader realized it is the lessons she learned from her experiences...

"I experienced, among other things, divorce and starting a career after sixteen years of not working outside the home. In choosing to do what I felt to be right instead of what is acceptable, I have come out on the other side of the experience much happier than I was before. The lesson that stands strong amid many is that being accountable and responsible for ourselves is empowering, and while it may go against our instincts, it really does 'make' us happy. I use that wisdom to help my clients: I am very straight with them about their situation, their choices and creating a plan that keeps them moving toward a financially independent future and not stuck in the past.

"If you sweep stuff under the rug or hold things in instead of processing them, you begin to build a huge tumor in your belly, and then you are going to explode. When a client (or friend or family member) wants to avoid, I do my best to not let them.

"We learn from the past, plan for the future and live today. I try to help my clients find their happy middle place...of enjoying today. I so enjoy empowering women and families to understand the responsibility of choices—that they can make them—and that independence is very gratifying."

This advisor takes to heart her philosophy of financially planning for the future and living (joyfully) in the present regardless of the situation, gender or circumstance. Many professionals have a guiding thought or principle that shapes their business. Can you put words to yours?

Happiness is not something you postpone for the future;
it is something you design for the present.
Jim Rohn

OCTOBER 1
BE A BUILDER

We all have times we wish we could take back. Unfortunately, we can't take a moment back, but we can do something to move our "brick" if we need to.

Every situation comes with a brick—and we use it to build either a wall or a bridge.

While we can't take the moments back, we can take action to move our brick.

If you are building a wall between you and another person, you can do your part to move your brick from the wall to the bridge.

For example, forgive, ask forgiveness, work to resolve the issue, seek to understand the other side, look for options.

Neither a wall nor a bridge will be built in a day, but each interaction and thought helps build one or the other.

Where do we want to place our bricks?

Whenever you're in conflict with someone,
there is one factor that can make the difference between damaging
your relationship and deepening it. That factor is attitude.
William James

OCTOBER 2
BE MOVING BRICKS

A reader wrote that she had a disagreement with a friend over the weekend. She sent a simple text with an apology and the relationship was restored.

She moved her brick from the wall to the bridge.

That was easy.

But sometimes moving bricks is not so easy. Sometimes the other person chooses to keep the brick. They want to stay mad or offended and put a wall up.

At that point it becomes a waiting game. While we are waiting, our job is to be patient and work to not grow bitter about the relationship while we are waiting on the other person to choose to communicate. I say work, because it is hard work to not grow bitter when someone is choosing to hold a grudge or stay angry with us.

Sadly, the relationship may not ever be restored, as the other person may choose to stay angry forever (that's not very fun for him or her—it is exhausting to stay angry). We can't do anything about them. But we can do much with ourselves. If we are doing our part (honestly doing our part in thought and word, no lying to ourselves) we can wait easier and pursue our possibilities instead of letting them pass us by.

Don't let a wall with a person create a wall with your possibilities.

We are all full of weakness and errors; let us
mutually pardon each other our follies.
Voltaire

He who cannot forgive breaks the bridge over
which he himself must pass.
George Herbert

OCTOBER 3
BE WELL-WISHING

When we have disagreements or difficulties in a relationship, whether it is with a client or a friend, hopefully we can resolve it quickly. But when we have reached out and the other party chooses not to reach back, we still want to do our part to be willing to communicate when they are. (We talked yesterday about how easy it is to become bitter in that situation.)

A good test to know if we are doing our part is this: if someone who has held a grudge or stayed silent or angry with us showed up today looking to heal the relationship with honest conversation and forgiveness, would we be willing to do the same?

Would you welcome him or her with open arms, be ready to discuss the problems, own your part and give forgiveness for theirs? Can you desire for them to be happy?

This doesn't mean that you must have all parts of your previous relationship restored. It simply means you are both being released more quickly from the possibility pursuing obstacles and anxieties that come with an unresolved, broken relationship.

Are you doing your part?

You will know that forgiveness has begun when you recall those
who hurt you and feel the power to wish them well.
Lewis B. Smedes

OCTOBER 4
BE LIGHT

For relationship problem resolution and prevention, gratitude is a great start.

Gratitude for our relationships can lead us to thoughts and behaviors that prevent problems, but when problems do arise, gratitude is a great tool to help us to be ready for restoration. If the relationship is not supposed to be restored, then gratitude is a perfect start to healing and a deterrent to bitterness.

If you have a strained or broken relationship, sit down and make a list of good moments you experienced because of the relationship. List how you are a better person because of it. What you learned and how you grew. You can express these thoughts to the other person or not; just the act of creating the lists helps us to focus on the positive and to become grateful and light rather than on the negative and become heavy and bitter. This doesn't mean we won't still have to process the problem, just that we will likely be kinder and more productive while doing so.

If we can't look at the positives from having experienced the relationship and be grateful for it, we want to ask ourselves if we had more "love" for self (pride) than for the other person and the relationship. Or if we have something to forgive ourselves for in the situation that we don't want to admit.

Whether the relationship problem is personal or professional, gratitude is always a good start to new possibilities.

Without deep humility, true forgiveness is impossible…
and will never happen.
Martha Kilpatrick

One forgives to the degree that one loves.
Francois de La Rochefoucauld

OCTOBER 5
BE FIRST

When we have a problem with someone and won't forgive, it could be we need to forgive ourselves first. When we hold a grudge against another, we might find the grudge is really with ourselves, but we don't want to admit it. The problem with that avoidance is that we don't heal and move on. Yes, we get to play the role of victim and deflect responsibility, but we also deflect peace, power and possibilities when we do.

If you don't own your part in the problem and be grateful you had your former client, then you will be uncomfortable to see them at social functions and you may let it damage your self-esteem—as well as your social life.

If you don't own your part and be grateful you had a friend or partner, then you could become angry and unhappy and want to make others unhappy, too.

If we won't forgive, we really make life somewhat miserable for everyone around us. And when that is happening, the first person to forgive is likely ourself.

1. List the other person's complaints and identify what is true.

2. Ask yourself what change in attitude or action will prevent this same situation in the future.

3. Ask: how can I be a better me and fulfill my roles and responsibilities in the future?

4. Forgive yourself and then the other people and move on instead of staying stuck.

If we won't forgive someone, the real someone we need to forgive first could be the person in the mirror. When we deflect responsibility, we deflect possibilities.

The offender never pardons.
George Herbert

OCTOBER 6
BE ENERGIZED

Like it or not, we can't separate out our physical and mental or our personal and professional lives. Our mental is affected by our physical and our professional is affected by our personal. And the opposite is true, too. The point is, as much as we may want to deny it, the health of our bodies can affect the health of our businesses. Our energy levels, attitudes and confidence can be affected by what we do with—and what we put into—our bodies.

If everything is working for you, then keep doing what you are doing. But if you don't feel strong and confident in your professional life, if you need a boost in your energy level or a change in how you master the time in your day, keep reading.

Little changes in the care and attention we give our bodies can make a bigger difference than we imagine in the productivity of our businesses. Today, pay attention to how much water you drink.

The Mayo Clinic website says: every system in your body depends on water. Lack of water can lead to dehydration. Even mild dehydration can drain your energy and make you tired. The fatigue you feel could be thwarted with drinking the right amount of water for your body. Consistent intake of adequate water has also been credited for weight-loss and good skin. (Bonus!)

1. Determine the "right" amount of water for your body.
2. If you have a hard time drinking water, fill a container each morning and have a goal of drinking it throughout the day.

The simple act of drinking the proper amount of water your body needs could give you a little boost in energy that could make a difference in your possibilities.

It sounds so elementary, but it's worth a reminder.
Live a balanced and healthful life in order to reach the top.
Jeff Beals

OCTOBER 7
BE AWAKE

Reader's Digest says that foods high on the glycemic index will help you fall asleep in half the time you normally do if eaten four hours before bedtime. Well, that's great for bedtime, but doesn't it stand to reason that if we want to be most productive and energized through our day, we avoid foods that make us fall asleep quicker?

We know our bodies best, so start paying attention to how you feel after you eat certain foods for lunch or snack. You will likely notice that carbs (bread, white rice, potatoes) and sugar will leave you sluggish and desiring a nap instead of calling a potential client.

We all love a sandwich and the cookie that comes with the sales meeting lunches, but if you want to get the most out of your work week, test out having dessert once a week instead of every day (or 1/2 the dessert instead of all of it) at lunch and see if you work through the afternoons easier and happier.

Possibilities are easier to pursue when we are awake for them.

The higher your energy level, the more efficient your body.
The more efficient your body, the better you feel and the more
you will use your talent to produce outstanding results.
Anthony Robbins

OCTOBER 8
BE SATISFIED

When it comes to fighting afternoon (or morning) weariness, it is not just the kind of food we eat, but also how much we eat, that affects our energy.

Yes, sugar, bread, and fried foods can seem to steal energy from our bodies rather than fuel them, but so can overeating any kind of food. I have no idea what happens in our bodies when we overeat, but something does that makes us lethargic instead of energized to take on the rest of the day.

A few tips for energy eating:

> Be aware while you eat. Chew your food instead of mindlessly putting things in your mouth. This can help us stop eating when we are satisfied instead of waiting until we hit "full."

> There is a difference between feeling satisfied and being overly full. The difference is a degree of miserable. When we are stuffed, we don't feel good. So why do we go from satisfied to miserable so easily? Well, it may not be all our fault. "They" say it takes twenty minutes for our brains to know we are full. So stop eating when you are satisfied. If you still want more, you can have it. That simple awareness can be the difference between spinning our wheels looking for something to do to waste time until we feel more awake and making calls to two clients and three potential clients.

> Leave something on your plate. Growing up, we either fought with siblings over food or were made to clean our plates. So we are likely conditioned to eat everything on our plate. But if you get in the habit of leaving a couple of bites, you might become more mindful of how you feel rather than automatically eating whatever is there.

Overeating is a form of self-anesthesia.
Norris Chumley

OCTOBER 9

BE DISCIPLINED

We all have different coping skills and ways to fool ourselves into making changes that are good for us. For example, if you don't eat a healthy diet—you avoid fruits, vegetables or anything that isn't processed—you can "trick" yourself into making changes.

Processed foods just aren't as good for us and our energy as food in its natural state. But if you tried to deprive yourself of your favorites, you probably wouldn't make a lasting change. So ease into changes you would like to make. Instead of taking something away, add something. Add a fruit or vegetable a day. Or if you are an over-achiever, go all out and add a fruit *and* a vegetable.

As your body starts to feel invigorated rather than sluggish, you may actually enjoy replacing some of the processed foods with more energizing choices.

There are not many of us who do not enjoy french fries, apple pie and easy-to-grab processed foods. But if we limit those things to an occasional treat rather than a normal part of our daily diet, we will likely find our new self-discipline gives as much of a boost to our possibilities as our extra energy to our bodies does.

Give your body good stuff today.

Self-respect is the fruit of discipline;
the sense of dignity grows with the ability to say no to oneself.
Abraham J. Heschel

OCTOBER 10

BE IN MOTION

A body that moves, keeps moving.

What we do most seems to multiply itself.

Since you likely sit or stand at a desk most of the day, you probably don't naturally move much during the day. Wherever you are on the moving scale, take it up half a point this weekend. Add something. It doesn't have to be much. Just move, stretch, or lift something. Try out a new class or just walk around the block.

You may already move enough, but if you don't, add a little extra movement to your life. Who knows, you could be adding possibilities, too.

The human body is a machine which winds its own springs.
Julien Offroy de la Mettrie

Take care of your body. It's the only place you have to live.
Jim Rohn

OCTOBER 11
BE MOVING

Self-discipline in our personal lives can affect our discipline and energy in our workdays.

Many studies and articles discuss the correlation between regular exercise and business success. A new study just came out that found jogging, swimming or lifting weights in a gym at least three times a week could increase your income up to nine percent. (Cleveland State University, *The Economic Times)*

There are so many reasons why this could be: regular exercise improves attitude and mental health, and increases energy and confidence, just to name a few. But what if it is as simple as recognizing that the self-discipline we use to get up and move our bodies (or to say no to the second piece of cake) is the same self-discipline we use to make that extra call or to control our emotions when problems arise?

We have talked about the concept of—if you use it, you don't lose it—that what we consistently use and exercise in our lives gains power in all areas of our lives. If we exercise the "self-discipline muscle," it gets stronger and more powerful. If we don't use it, it weakens, and self-control can slowly lose power in our lives.

I know it is a simplistic view, but possibilities don't have to be complicated. We don't have to exercise our bodies to be successful, but when you are looking for an extra boost in your life—or just for a day—make the choice to exercise your body in a way that works for you and see if it makes a difference in your possibilities.

The first and best victory is to conquer self.
Plato

OCTOBER 12
BE UNSTUCK

Our mind-body connection is like our car-key connection; most of us can't explain how it works, we just know it does. A reader shared this about how when her mind is not where she wants it to be, she can find a solution in a little movement of her body.

"A little movement activates chemicals, gets endorphins going and can shift negative adrenalin to positive. To get to positive feelings, a simple activity like a brief walk makes a difference. But a walk outside can be hindered by the location of the office or the weather.

"So If I get stuck or if something happens and I am angry or hurt, I get up and climb the stairs in our building. Walking down gets the blood flowing. But the walk back up is not so easy, and the chemicals produced naturally by my body—the endorphins that flow after the activity, combined with intentional thoughts like looking for the good in my situation or finding what I have learned from the experience—help shift where I am and how I choose to feel about things.

"It helps with problems like being tired, stuck in what to say or procrastinating a task. When I get back to my office, I walk straight to the phone and make the call without thinking.

"If shoes are a block to exercising, keep a pair of comfortable flats in a bag that looks professional (not a gym bag that draws attention in the middle of the day) and you can put them on once you are in the privacy of the stairwell."

How do you get unstuck and move through moments of procrastination, anger or anything else that keeps you from your possibilities?

Movement is a medicine for creating change in a person's physical,
emotional, and mental states.
Carol Welch

OCTOBER 13

BE WILLING TO CHANGE

If your daily routine is working for you, don't change it.

But if it isn't, change something. If you find yourself tired in the afternoons, change something and see if it helps. If you find you are lacking motivation, change something.

Remember, change doesn't have to be forever (and actually, it can be quite difficult to change patterns we have established, so don't worry that it is permanent just by trying it for a few days). It is not a tattoo. The change can be easily reversed. So test out a change and see if it makes a positive difference. If it doesn't, test out another one.

If you are having trouble identifying a productive change to make, talk to your manager, a friend or colleague.

Sometimes it is not the actual change to our routine that makes the difference in our possibilities, as much as simply the willingness to change anything at all.

The choice for change is all yours.

Being willing to change allows you to move from
a point of view to a viewing point—
a higher, more expansive place, from which you can see both sides.
Thomas Crum

OCTOBER 14
BE EXPLORING

If making a lasting change usually doesn't happen on the first attempt, why will we not try out a new diet or exercise behavior for a few days? What are we afraid of?

The first thing that comes to mind about being resistant to change is that we might have to give up something we like. But there are a couple more that come to mind that aren't as obvious.

We are afraid others will like the new behavior. When we try something out and don't like it, we can go back to the old behavior. But what if we test something out and others like it? Then there is a whole new "pressure" problem.

Others will like my new kind of behavior and I will be pressured to continue. Others will like my new slimmer figure and higher energy level, and I will be hassled to keep exercising. It is just better to not even try the things that I know I won't like anyway.

Another one is pride. Pride doesn't want to admit that what we are doing now isn't perfect. (Even if we already know we need to change.) "Why do I need to change anything?!" Pride can keep us from making changes. If pride is keeping you from making changes in your diet/exercise, is it keeping you from doing anything else that is good for you?

We don't have to change anything we don't want to. If we can identify a healthy change that would improve our lives and businesses and we are not willing to at least test it out for a few days, we want to know why not. Because the same issue that is holding you back could be holding back possibilities, too.

The reason men oppose progress is not that they hate progress,
but that they love inertia.
Elbert Hubbard

OCTOBER 15
BE DESTINED

If we think of situations that are hurtful, they often involve things like lies, half-truths and broken relationships.

Whenever there is physical or emotional separation—from something as simple as a judgmental thought to something as complicated as a break-up—there is pain. We can end up playing that situation over in our heads, taking us away from productive activities and distracting us from the people who are currently in our lives.

For example, we may replay a client loss in our thoughts so much that we end up avoiding seeking new clients or serving those we have because we lose confidence, or simply because we are spending our time thinking of the lost client.

It can be the same with personal relationships. We can be sad or angry that certain persons aren't in our lives any longer to the point we lose sight of the ones who are.

I heard someone say that if a person is no longer in your life, they are not part of your destiny. This may or may not be true, but it certainly gives us another perspective, doesn't it? Instead of concentrating on the broken relationship, we can focus on what we were supposed to learn from it, being grateful we experienced it for the time we did. Then we can move forward toward our purpose, believing that what we need will come   including, possibly, a chance with the same client or relationship again.

Own your part and forgive yourself as well as others before you attempt to move on. If you get new clients before you are ready, or a new relationship while you are still blaming someone in the old one, those new relationships may end up by the wayside when they didn't have to.

The idea that if someone isn't in our lives any longer, they aren't part of our destiny doesn't give us permission to not be accountable—we are still responsible for our situations and attitudes—it gives us permission to be released from guilt and pain and move forward toward our purpose.

You can clutch the past so tightly to your chest that it
leaves your arms too full to embrace the present.
Jan Glidewell

OCTOBER 16
BE GRACEFUL

Emotional separation rarely feels good. Just because we have parted ways with someone doesn't mean we have to feel an emotional separation. In other words, we don't have to be angry about their departure from our lives. When there is separation in our minds, we could be creating it.

The concept that if someone is no longer in our life they are not part of our destiny doesn't give us permission to be unkind or critical. It releases us to move on without constraints. But the problem is we won't be able to move on if we are still angry. If we choose unforgiveness, we could be creating the separation instead of fate. When we get over our negativity, we can be certain that person is not part of our destiny. Yet if it turns out they are, we want to be prepared for them to re-enter our lives in some way. Forgiveness and a positive attitude allow destiny to make the decision rather than our anger.

Sometimes that person is part of our journey, just not in the way we thought; we won't know until we clear out the anger and unforgiveness and get out of our own way. What if someone is part of our happiest destiny but we have let fear and resentment choose a different path for us?

Be ready for resolution; have good thoughts of the person. Forgive yourself and him or her for whatever you need to. They may be part of your destiny in some way, but everyone may have things to learn first.

People spend too much time finding other people to blame,
too much energy finding excuses for not being what they are capable of being,
and not enough energy putting themselves on the line,
growing out of the past, and getting on with their lives.
Michael Straczynski

OCTOBER 17
BE FORGETTING

A good thing to lose might be a bad memory.

Remembering our own or someone else's mistakes can keep all of us held back from our purpose. If we hold on to our own mistakes, we will likely spend more time in our emotional closet than we do contributing to the world in a positive way. If we hold on to others' mistakes, we hold them back, as well as feed our anger, superiority or victim mode. When we won't give mercy to another person and move on, we are forgetting our own mistakes. If we need to keep pointing out others' flaws, we need to check in with our insecurities.

Learn the lesson in the "failure" and move on. If we find we are holding on to and possibly enjoying the memory of someone else's shortcoming, we could have been not only looking for it, but also contributing to their "failure" in some way.

Of course, it is different if there is danger involved and, certainly, we need healthy *boundaries*, but for the most part, letting offenses go—our own and others—will allow us to spend time pursuing possibilities instead of reliving a bad memory.

The beautiful journey of today can only begin when we
learn to let go of yesterday.
Steve Maraboli

OCTOBER 18
BE MORE HAPPY

If we are unhappy in some way, maybe we are simply ungrateful.

When we focus on ourselves with a fearful perspective we are often unhappy. But when we refocus on ourselves and others with a grateful perspective, we will likely feel the positive effects immediately.

Gratitude could be the quickest and simplest way to change our happiness.

So for those situations where you are experiencing "emotional separation" from someone—whether you are upset with them or they with you—practice gratitude.

Think of the person or situation and make a list of five things to be grateful for around that situation. The first three will likely be pretty easy; it is the last two we have to dig for that may make a bigger difference. If five grateful items are easy, then make it ten. You want to list until finding more gets tough. And ponder this: if you can quickly and easily come up with five items for the list, it could be you have been creating a negative story around a neutral (or even positive) situation.

Each time you begin to let that situation have a negative power in your life, replace those negative "what if" thoughts with positive, grateful "what is" thoughts.

A person may not be in our lives any longer and may not be part of our future physically; but if we don't work to focus on the positives, this person may still be in our future emotionally—in a negative way.

We want to learn from the "bad" and focus on the "good" because otherwise we can get stuck in yesterday and miss our possibilities in this day.

As always, if you need help, get it. You have too much to do to waste time and energy on things that aren't serving you or your clients.

Cultivate the habit of being grateful for every good thing that comes to you, and to give thanks continuously. And because all things have contributed to your advancement, you should include all things in your gratitude.
Ralph Waldo Emerson

Some people grumble that roses have thorns; I am grateful that thorns have roses.
Alphonse Karr

OCTOBER 19
BE HAPPIEST

Did you make a grateful list around a difficult situation yesterday?

Do it again today by adding three more things.

If your difficult situation involves a business break-up,

> think of at least one thing you learned
>
> think of at least one thing you gained
>
> think of how the relationship benefited you
>
> think of times others were kind or helped you through a tough situation

If your difficult situation involves a personal break-up, think of things they did for you (even if it was that you had someone to blame besides yourself for your life not being as you wanted). Maybe they got you coffee; maybe they fixed something around the house. Perhaps they made you laugh one morning. Maybe they pumped your gas. Maybe they gave you the courage to do something you didn't think you could. Maybe they took care of certain tasks so you didn't have to.

Have you ever written a letter to someone but you didn't mail it? Write a letter of gratitude to the person you are struggling with and don't mail it. It could help you find a shift in your perspective.

When we focus on the positive, we tend to move more quickly through to the "other side" of a situation instead of staying stuck in it. It doesn't mean we take a Pollyanna perspective and ignore what needs addressing; focusing on the positive may allow us to have more productive interactions when we do address a problem.

If you want to stay where and as you are, you can, but if you have something holding you back from pursuing your positive possibilities, you have options. Try gratitude. If it doesn't work, get help. Your possibilities are waiting—maybe just on the other side of gratitude.

Gratitude unlocks the fullness of life. It turns what we have into enough, and more. It turns denial into acceptance, chaos into order, confusion into clarity. It can turn a meal into a feast, a house into a home, a stranger into a friend. Gratitude makes sense of our past, brings peace for today, and creates a vision for tomorrow.

Melody Beattie

OCTOBER 20

BE LETTING GO

What we focus on is what we give power to. If we focus on negatives, that is what we will experience. If we focus on positives, we will experience things in a positive light.

Now that you have listed items you are grateful for around an uncomfortable situation, will you be grateful you had the relationship rather than angry about it?

Someone may not be part of our destiny any longer, but we don't want to be in a one-sided relationship, where we are the only one still in it and not in a positive way.

If you are angry, you could be in a one-sided relationship. The other person has moved on and you are the only one in it (from the dry cleaner to a client to a friend).

Are you enjoying the relationship? Probably not, and as much as you might like to be angry, is it really making you happy?

Try being grateful you experienced the good parts instead of angry for something not being the way you want it to be.

If you kick a stone in anger, you'll hurt your own foot.
Korean Proverb

We must be willing to let go of the life we've planned,
so as to have the life that is waiting for us.
Joseph Campbell

OCTOBER 21
BE ADMITTING

If you still have trouble working through a situation, stop and think of times you have been unkind or "wrong" to others. Recalling those moments could help you be more forgiving of those times the person or people involved didn't behave how you would have liked.

If we are staying in anger, resentment or revenge mode, we may be forgetting the times we have wronged others or simply withheld kindness. When we recall our own shortcomings and contributions to a problem, we can much easier release others, including ourselves.

And if we really think about it, sometimes when we won't let go of something, the reason could be that we are actually angry at ourselves and don't want to admit it.

Be still and find out what you are really angry (fearful) about. It isn't always the other person.

Someone or some situation may not be "part of our destiny" anymore, but it doesn't mean they can't be viewed as a positive or neutral in our lives. We can view a past situation as negative (and be affected negatively) if we choose to, but if our negative perspectives are holding us back from being productive, happy and reaching our goals, we may want to work to choose something else.

…and when we do, we will likely find positive possibilities we couldn't see before.

The mental and physical space we create by letting go of things that belong in our past gives…us the option to fill the space with something new.
Susan Fay West

We need to learn to love the flawed, imperfect things that we create, and to forgive ourselves for creating them. Regret doesn't remind us that we did badly; it reminds us that we know we could do better.
Kathryn Schultz

OCTOBER 22
BE PRODUCING

Every so often it is good to check in with ourselves. So for a few days we are "checking in" to see where we want to make a change.

Action + Attitude = Outcome

Okay, so that is not always true, but it is a good reminder of our responsibility in situations.

It is so easy to get off track with our thoughts and attitudes. We all mess up. We are going to fall short. But we can use a past experience to help us know how we want to respond in the future. We still may not get it right, but we can, at the least, begin to spot our part in the problem.

If you need help processing a situation to get to a productive attitude, talk to a friend or counselor who can help you move through the "normal emotions" to get to the truth and the heart of the matter. The tiniest shift in attitude can make a big difference in how we feel, and the sooner we find that shift—a productive, truthful one—the quicker we will move through and move on to more possibilities.

We cannot change our past. We cannot change the fact that people will act in a certain way. We cannot change the inevitable. The only thing we can do is play on the one string we have, and that is our attitude. I am convinced that life is 10% what happens to me and 90% of how I react to it. And so it is with you...we are in charge of our Attitudes.

Charles R. Swindoll

OCTOBER 23
BE PERSEVERING

We don't pursue our possibilities without perseverance.

Dictionary.com says "perseverance" is the steady persistence in a course of action, a purpose, a state, etc. especially in spite of difficulties, obstacles or discouragement.

Many of us quit when things get tough in a particular area of our lives. Maybe you persevere in business but you give up in relationships. Or maybe you have no problem pushing through tough times in relationships, but you quit when you find out you are not naturally good at a task instead of learning it. Or maybe you push through in growing your business, but you shut down when conflict arises.

We are all learning as we go, and perseverance helps us to get to the other side—where the lesson is. As we stand on one side of a problem, we can't see the lesson and if we don't push through, we won't ever know it. We will keep going in circles with the same problem (it will just look different) until we persevere, push through and get to the other side where the wisdom/knowledge/lesson waits.

Every possibility comes with a "predicament" that we have to make choices about; otherwise it wouldn't be a possibility it would already be. Anything is possible…with perseverance.

Nothing in this world can take the place of persistence. Talent will not; nothing is more common than unsuccessful people with talent. Genius will not; unrewarded genius is almost a proverb. Education will not; the world is full of educated derelicts. Persistence and determination alone are omnipotent. The slogan "press on" has solved and always will solve the problems of the human race.

Calvin Coolidge

OCTOBER 24
BE THROUGH-OUT

As we persevere it is helpful to be aware if we are doing so with a positive intention or a negative one. It is quite easy to fall into a bad attitude when a problem develops.

If we persevere and push through an issue with a vengeful, hurtful or angry intention, those feelings may not go away when the problem is finished. Then we can end up with another problem that looks different but is fundamentally the same.

We want to pay attention because if we "win," those negative emotions become our model for getting what we want. We can get in a habit we don't know we are in, but since it is working for us, we don't care. If we don't get what we want, we can pout, cry, bully, take the victim role or punish people until we do. But that is likely not our most productive, healthy or happiness-producing tactic.

So what if we worked on persevering through an issue with the emotions we want once we get on the other side? In other words, if you want to be angry on the other side, be angry through it.

If you want to be vengeful on the other side of the problem, be vengeful through it. If you want to be "right," be right through it.

On the other hand, if you want to be balanced and have a productive relationship on the other side, work to be balanced and communicating through the problem. It doesn't mean we won't get off-track at times; it simply means we consciously work to get back on.

If we are through an issue and feel "unhappy," we probably want to step back and take a look at our intention, because we may have pushed through to the other side of the outward problem but still have an inward one and not know why.

Pushing through with an intention to hurt someone—whether it is belittling, taking something from them, or wanting them to suffer—may get us through to the other side with the outcome we desire, but it could keep us stuck...and suffering in our lives.

Persevere in a way that produces the fruit you want in your life.

When things go wrong, don't go with them.
Elvis Presley

OCTOBER 25
BE PEACE-MINDED

One good reason to persevere until we get to peace is that if we don't push through problems to the other side, they stay problems. And wouldn't we rather have resolution?

That sounds simplistic, but isn't it really that simple when you think about it? Our emotions can make a situation more complicated: fear of what others think, angst about the future, unforgiveness over the past, anger about *whatever*, pride that is offended, blaming instead of owning.

Really, if we managed the negative emotions instead of nurturing them (...Yikes! It is hard to believe that we might nurture entitlement instead of personal responsibility), wouldn't difficulties be so much easier to resolve? If we stay in a problem instead of moving through it, could it be that we are choosing to stay in negative emotions instead of focusing on a healthy long-term intention?

Sometimes the problem is the problem, but other times we are. Work to resolve unproductive emotions and the problem will likely take care of itself.

It's not that I'm so smart;
it's just that I stay with problems longer.
Albert Einstein

OCTOBER 26
BE A CAPTAIN

When we hear stories of achievement, rarely do they not include times of great difficulty and triumph. If a person is going to push through to achieve goals beyond their normal capacity, he or she is going to certainly face a time of crisis where there is a choice to quit or to continue.

It's okay to redirect your focus and try another way or to quit if you really don't want to do something. But if you really want "it," don't quit. "It" may not look like you wanted it to; you may have to completely change your plan, expectation or people involved, but if so, you will likely find the new way was the best way.

Because we are imperfect, we will have problems. This is not a life of smooth sailing. Sometimes there will be no wind; at other times there will be frightening storms, but eventually the storm ends and we have calm seas again. The storms help us learn, make adjustments and become "sailors." As much as we don't want to experience those storms, we must. Otherwise we won't go anywhere; we won't move forward.

And really, who would you rather sail with: a confident captain who has been through problems or a captain who has known only calm sailing?

Pursuing possibilities means we will sometimes have to experience stormy seas and persevere.

A ship is safe in harbor, but that's not what ships are for.
William G.T. Shedd

OCTOBER 27

BE RISING

Persevering involves believing even when outside circumstances point against achieving our goal.

Think of a time that you could not see how something was going to work out—then, not only did it work out, it worked out better than you ever imagined it could have.

We all remember times it seemed nothing could turn out well. Every outside circumstance pointed to "failure." Yet, somehow, things did work out. What was the difference in those times? Was it your actions, words, intention, attitude…a combination of those? Or something else?

Persevering means we believe possibilities will come even when we can't see any sign of them on the horizon.

You may encounter many defeats, but you must not be defeated.
In fact, it may be necessary to encounter the defeats, so you can know
who you are, what you can rise from, how you can still come out of it.
Maya Angelou

It always seems impossible until it's done.
Nelson Mandela

OCTOBER 28

BE BLISSFUL

Have you ever looked back on a chaotic or painful time in your life and realized how you became a better person through it? Most self-aware people would rather have personal growth and peace than personal comfort. If we keep moving through a difficult time, learning the lessons we are supposed to learn, we likely come out better on the other side—more contributing, productive and loving, and less entitled and fearful. But if we don't keep moving through and learning our personal lessons, we can be stuck in anger and become bitter.

Perseverance helps us move through, but we must be aware of how we are pushing through and with what kind of intention. Pushing through in anger rather than objectivity and truth may get us to the other side but will likely still leave us needing to push through ourselves. We have pushed through the obvious problem, but then we wonder why we aren't happy. We can get what we wanted, still be unhappy and not know why.

Before we get to the "stage" of perseverance, we will be in some level of suffering (we don't have to work to push through easy times, do we?). So we must work to leave that suffering behind as we push through. An intention of revenge will ultimately leave us unhappy (even if we get what we want). An intention of being "right" can leave us in victim mode, a place we can like so much (for the attention we get and how we get what we want) that we end up wanting to stay the victim instead of moving on to something healthier and more enjoyable for us and those around us.

If we are in a place of bitterness or resentment, then we are probably stuck in a "stage." And do you want to be stuck in a stage of joy, peace and abundance or stuck in a stage of "I deserve," and blame? It is your choice. The most joyful person you know had the opportunity to give in to anger rather than move through to more productive days and peaceful life.

To be most productive, we want to be aware of how and why we persevere. Our possibilities depend on it.

Things don't go wrong and break your heart so you can become bitter and give up. They happen to break you down and build you up so you can be all that you were intended to be.

Charles Jones

OCTOBER 29

BE HAPPY WITH YOURSELF

Have you ever quit something and then found yourself jealous of someone else who didn't quit? …Maybe a person who is achieving or experiencing what you would like to experience? If we are jealous, we could actually be angry at ourselves that we didn't "endure." It can be a natural reaction to wish we had something that another person has. To choose to work for what you want yourself is good, but to be jealous of that person who has "it" is not so good.

You have seen the quote by Joan Didion expressing that to be jealous is really to be dissatisfied with yourself. Instead of using energy being jealous, use it to push through and finish your goal. If you use your energy building what you want instead of trying to "take" it from someone else, not only will you likely reach your goal but you will also have a better chance of happiness.

Stop and see if you are jealous of anything or anyone. If you find you are jealous, look for where you are unhappy with yourself. You may find an area or situation you didn't push through. Maybe you wish you had persevered to finish a class, or pushed through fear to reach a goal or pushed through pride in a relationship. It is not too late. You can take the class, you can pursue the goal, you can push through pride when it shows up.

If we aren't willing to do the work necessary to be happy ourselves, then we really shouldn't be jealous of others who are. Keep in mind that real happiness isn't about material things; it comes from inside us. No one else can push through to do the work for us. Others can help (or hurt—be aware of who you listen to) and encourage us, but we are responsible for pushing through to our own happiness and possibilities.

If you are experiencing a jealousy of someone because you didn't persevere to achieve a goal, recognize your discontent with yourself and either let the jealousy go or do something about the goal today.

In the long run, we shape our lives, and we shape ourselves. The process never ends until we die. And the choices we make are ultimately our own responsibility.
Eleanor Roosevelt

The jealous are troublesome to others, but a torment to themselves.
William Penn

OCTOBER 30
BE PUSHING THROUGH

A big factor in our possibilities is perseverance. If we quit early we leave our possibilities unpursued. Quitting can leave us with a whole new set of issues—from self-esteem issues to resentment. Leaving or putting something on hold is okay if we have peace about it. If we don't have peace, however, we still have work to do—probably related to pushing through negative emotions. For example, pushing through fear to finish the task or pushing through anger and resentment because we quit too early. We can choose anger but it likely won't get us any closer to what we really want.

If you have tried to push through negative emotions but haven't been able to, then try doing something with an intention to help the person or persons you are cross with, even if it is only a helpful, kind thought that the person doesn't ever know about. If you choose to think a kind thought once, you can do it again and again, until you have pushed through the negative emotions. Then you can re-direct all the energy you spent being angry to beginning to work toward your goals—in the office, relationships, business.

Keep in mind that when we choose not to push through something—from negative emotions (we can actually nurture them because we want to stay angry) to a task (we keep looking for excuses)—we become a "victim" of ourselves, not of someone else or of circumstances. From an unresolved argument to a task left incomplete, we want to pay attention to what we are angry about and decide if we want to persevere to achieve something more productive or stay where we are.

It isn't easy, but it is important because the person we really end up helping is ourself. We all need help pushing through negative emotions and fears. If you need help, contact a friend, a coach, or therapist today. You have too much to contribute to be stuck in a place you could be pushing through.

If you want happiness for an hour, take a nap.
If you want happiness for a day, go fishing. If you want happiness for a year,
inherit a fortune. If you want happiness for a lifetime, help somebody.
Old Chinese Proverb

OCTOBER 31
BE A GOOD GATEKEEPER

Many people and many situations may want to block our possibilities—including ourselves.

In fact, we can be our biggest blocker of possibilities, because we can hold onto old words said and past situations, keeping ourselves stuck in a place that isn't productive. Yes, someone may have hurt us—even deeply—but we are the gatekeeper who decides what is going to get through, stay and influence us, or what is going to be deflected and dismissed.

We are the framer who reframes old, bad pictures and makes them new with a fresh perspective—when we choose to be.

Sometimes we want to hold onto old hurts so we have something or someone to blame. We can end up enjoying being "the victim" for attention or maybe so that we don't have to move forward or maybe because we can control others easier in this mode.

But keep in mind that when we choose not to move forward we are likely the one blocking our possibilities instead of the person or circumstance we are pointing to.

Pay attention to the possibilities you block and the ones you invite in. They could give you an understanding about your gatekeeping choices, the person you are becoming, and the life and business you are creating.

The best years of your life are the ones in which you decide your problems
are your own. You do not blame them on your mother, the ecology,
or the president. You realize that you control your own destiny.
Albert Ellis

NOVEMBER 1
BE WILLING

When we deny there is a problem, the problem doesn't go away. In fact, it could get worse.

If we deny there is a problem with the car, is the problem going to go away if we don't get it checked out?

If we are unwilling to face the problems of market conditions or our marketing/communication strategies, do they go away? Sometimes…but maybe not before our clients do.

If we deny emotional wounds do they just disappear?

Likely not. But their negative effects often do when we choose to own our part and forgive ourselves and others.

If we blame someone else for the things we don't like in our lives, do our lives get happier? Not until we take responsibility for our own choices in action and attitude instead of blaming another.

We can be unaware a problem exists, but the moment we know, we need to be willing to deal with it. Even if it is only hearing the other person out or exploring options, a simple active step is a beginning.

The attitude of being willing to consider a problem actually exists is a great first step in discovering a solution.

Self-acceptance comes from meeting life's challenges vigorously. Don't numb yourself to your trials and difficulties, nor build mental walls to exclude pain from your life. You will find peace not by trying to escape your problems, but by confronting them courageously. You will find peace not in denial, but in victory.
J. Donald Walters

NOVEMBER 2
BE TURNING IT AROUND

If we know denial often prolongs a problem, why would we use denial as a default setting?

I did not say that.

I didn't do that.

I don't do that.

My child didn't do that.

If we rush into defense mode without gathering facts and deny any wrongdoing before we know the truth, we likely have a default setting that isn't serving us.

There are many reasons we could be in that habit, but one is perfectionism.

The idea that we are supposed to be perfect is a lie. We are supposed to be amazing, engaged, contributing, informed and excellent but we cannot be perfect.

We are going to be these things most of the time, but we are also going to fall short and be wrong, unkind, self-centered, fearful, uninformed and mediocre. We are going to slip into gossip, laziness and procrastination. We are going to say something unkind and wonder why we just let that cross our lips.

When our behavior is less than excellent, if we can turn around, admit it and apologize, then we likely don't have a problem with denial. If we won't or don't, that could be a signal that we are in denial about a behavior or situation we would be better off facing.

There are times we can be in short-term, situational denial to cope with something. If you find yourself there, call a counselor. If you are just in a habit of denying there is any problem with your marketing plan, investment process or your style, then call a friend or your manager who can support you and hold you accountable as you identify and make changes to improve your business and relationships. When we have a habit of denial, we may deny ourselves of possibilities, too.

The worst lies are the lies we tell ourselves. We live in denial of what we do,
even what we think. We do this because we're afraid.
Richard Bach

NOVEMBER 3
BE SOLUTION-MINDED

What are you "in denial" about?

Ask a friend or your manager or someone you trust to tell you if there is a problem, situation or truth you are unaware of or choosing to ignore. In other words, what are you missing that would make your life, your business or a situation better?

Then begin the process of facing, solving or learning what you need to. You might start by reading a book on the subject, pondering it, taking action or calling in the necessary professional for help.

Sometimes we are only an arm's length away from our goals and need a little help seeing how we may be pushing them away.

Rather than denying problems, focus inventively, intentionally on what solutions might look or feel like. Our mind is meant to generate ideas that help us escape circumstantial traps, if we trust it to do so. Naturally, not all hunches are useful. But then you only need a single good idea to solve a problem.
Marsha Sinetar

NOVEMBER 4
BE OKAY

They say if you run from a bear, it will chase after you. But if you face it and "make yourself bigger" it will go away. (Please don't test that out—evidently it also depends on the species and the bear itself.) In most cases, our problems are like bears. If we try to run, our problem will chase after us.

Remember the expression, "If you resist, it will persist"? Avoiding may feel more subtle than resisting, but it is still as powerful in its squandering of possibilities.

There are events or moments in our lives that if we don't deal with them, can create wounds. Few of us want to admit we have wounds or that there was ever a problem we didn't handle well, but if we don't, we could be denying and running… and what we are running from is ever with us until we turn around, face it and deal with it. It is like a little shadow running along behind us. We feel its presence, but we avoid dealing with it until we have the courage to turn around and face it.

"It" can be as simple as an associate's comment that we are not good at our job. Or a negative belief we have of ourselves or a situation we would like to take back. Or it could be a wound we caused another. We may not get to go back and deal with the people who were originally involved, but we can deal with ourselves and our part in it.

If you find yourself not working toward your goals or not achieving them, stop and see if you have something you have been running from that you need to deal with. Own your part. Forgive others and yourself and move on toward your goal. If you need help with this call somebody—friend, counselor, clergyman. Sometimes it's nice to have company when you are facing something…whether it is a bear or a problem.

If I had a formula for bypassing trouble, I would not pass it round.
Trouble creates a capacity to handle it. I don't embrace trouble; that's as bad as
treating it as an enemy. But I do say meet it as a friend,
for you'll see a lot of it and had better be on speaking terms with it.
Oliver Wendell Holmes

The healthy and strong individual is the one who asks for help when he needs it.
Whether he's got an abscess on his knee or in his soul.
Rona Barrett

NOVEMBER 5
BE STEPPING OUT

Sometimes in order to deny responsibility we hide behind things.

We can hide behind our past, our money, our lack of money, our children, our job, our victimization, our busyness, our silence and much more.

Anything that we use to avoid engaging or to avoid responsibility is an excuse that may shift the current focus from us, but it likely won't help anyone in the long run. We may make it through a moment, but instead of moving toward goals and enjoying our lives, we will simply move from one hiding place to another.

We'll hide behind our past so that we don't have to step out and excel in our future. We will hide behind "what happened to me" so we don't have to be vulnerable.

We can hide behind something else so we don't have to accept responsibility for our emotions, our future, our actions or our lives. When we catch ourselves hiding behind something, we may be able to step out with just the awareness and desire to come out from behind whatever it is. But sometimes we need a little help from a friend, clergy or counselor.

Until we step out and face what needs facing we won't be joyfully working towards our goals and we will wonder why we are not happy—and why everyone else seems to have all the possibilities.

You must take personal responsibility. You cannot change the circumstances,
the seasons, or the wind, but you can change yourself.
That is something you have charge of.
Jim Rohn

NOVEMBER 6
BE EXCEPTIONAL

That's not my job.

That's not my problem.

It may not be our specific job, but isn't any help toward success for our employer ultimately part of our job? It may not be your job, but could you help out this time and then discuss the division of responsibilities for the next time? If you were in a store, hospital or restaurant and when you were in need, you received the response of, "That's not my job," wouldn't you be a little taken aback?

Yes, there needs to be a division of job responsibilities in order to be most efficient and productive, but when there is a need we can meet, should we be of service or deny it's our job?

There are some tasks we don't want to do because we don't like it, it is beneath us, we are prideful, we are afraid we will have to do it again, we feel like it should be someone else's job and they are shirking it. Instead of helping out, we deny responsibility for it.

There are so many reasons we want to avoid a problem or task and some are very valid. If it isn't your job, then have an honest, productive conversation about it so that you are helpful in finding a real solution to its assignment of responsibility.

The question to always ask ourselves is: are we being helpful or obstinate? If we aren't willing to discuss the issue and would rather avoid it, that could be a signal we are contributing to the problem rather than being a helpful part of a productive solution.

We are what we repeatedly do.
Excellence, then, is not an act, but a habit.
Aristotle

NOVEMBER 7
BE PAYING ATTENTION

When we are feeling heavy and restless, we may want to look at what we are denying. We could find a key to our peace.

Some things we deny:

…*Our gifts and talents.* We don't deny all of them, but many of us do deny at least a few because we are afraid to use them or because we don't want to be different and stand out.

…*Our hearts.* Our hearts are sometimes not pretty. In fact, there are times they are downright unattractive. When we deny those times, we can end up staying stuck in those moments. But when we recognize and confess them, we tend to move out of them quicker. When we feel heavy and unhappy, we can start with our hearts and see if what is inside matches up with our beliefs and intentions. If we get honest with ourselves—even if we don't like what we find— we will likely begin to feel lighter and happier as we clean out the old and work on the new.

…*Others the chance to grow and be better.* We all mess up. It is part of the journey and being human. We are supposed to learn from mess-ups and get better at our jobs and various roles. But we have a tendency to deny others the chance to utilize the lessons they need to grow and be better. We would often rather keep them stuck in old roles and old moments and old mistakes— particularly if we don't like the person. Let people grow into the best they can be (personally and professionally) and you will likely find you are growing too.

We want to pay attention to what we are denying because we could be denying possibilities, too.

The worst lies are the lies we tell ourselves. We live in denial of what we do,
even what we think. We do this because we're afraid.
Richard Bach

NOVEMBER 8

BE WILLING

Life is full of paradoxes. The idea that sometimes we have to lose to win is contradictory to our type-A thinking. We are programmed to win… to be right. But how many situations are escalated because we cross a line? Our ego can cause us to cross a line we really don't want to cross and pride deters us from going back to say, "here is where I was wrong." We tend to point fingers and say, "I did nothing wrong, I am the victim!" There are also situations that may not escalate, but we don't get peaceful resolution because we want to be right instead of resolve. For example, if two parties are seeking resolution—maybe it is a partnership trying to resolve an issue, maybe it is a dispute between client and customer --if both parties intention is to resolve it fairly, then they will. But if one party just wants to be right or get the most out of it they can or prove a point, then likely both parties lose. They may carry around the problem because they never resolved the real issue.

If a couple is in counseling and the intention is to restore and have a great relationship, then they likely will. But if the true intention of one person is to be right instead of have an amazing relationship, then they will go in circles. The one whose intention has shifted to wanting to be right will be able to say she tried to work it out, but did she really? And then instead of taking responsibility, there is more blame. Blame is a great tool to keep responsibility off us and on the other person. When we are willing to look at our part in a situation, we are truly seeking resolution instead of just to win. That willingness can be the difference between possibilities pursued and possibilities lost.

We don't have to be willing to resolve an issue, but we do want to be honest about our intention regarding it. It isn't easy, but it is freeing. Stop and ask what is truth? What is authentic? We aren't going to get it right all the time, but we can stop and rewind when we have something other than peace. Don't give up on a cause you believe to be right, but do work to take your ego out of it and make sure it is about what is right, not about you being right.

We don't want pride to make our decisions. Seek what is right rather than seek to be right. We will repeatedly mess up, we are human, but be willing to resolve and peace may not be far behind. Sometimes we have to "lose" the desire to be right in order to win peace, resolution and a joyful life.

Proud people breed sad sorrows for themselves.
Emily Bronte

NOVEMBER 9
BE POWERFUL

Do you have a need to yell? We all get to a point sometimes that our frustration, fear or insecurity level is so high that we begin to yell. But if we find ourselves yelling or belittling people often, then we might want to step back and examine ourselves. Right now, you may be thinking, why would I examine myself? The other person is the one with the problem or I wouldn't have to yell at them!

There lies part of the issue: we want to blame others rather than take responsibility for our part in a problem then work as a team to find a solution. Yelling is a good way to make someone else take all the blame.

That behavior often comes from insecurities. When we are confident, we don't need to use yelling and belittling as a communication practice. When we own our part in things, we can calmly discuss the situation, but when we need to blame because of our feelings of inadequacy, we start yelling to put up a wall in order to "defend" ourselves. We want to hide something.

We want to feel important and "powerful." But when we are a habitual yeller, we likely actually feel powerless, out of control and afraid; and we don't want anyone to see that. There is no real power and few possibilities in trying to push others down.

There are times that anger and raising our voices is appropriate. Used as a normal communication practice rather than an exception, it becomes de-energizing and de-motivating to others and may signal denial in ourselves.

...yelling doesn't make a thing any more possible.
Angie Sage

NOVEMBER 10
BE BIG

Think about the times you yell.

Are you frustrated? Then say, "I am frustrated about..." That is more productive than yelling in order to not have to admit your frustration and lack of control.

Are you afraid? Then try saying, "I am afraid..."

Our yelling doesn't allow for productive dialogue. It passes our fear on to others. Do we really want to walk around making someone else carry our fear around? Communication could help reduce the fear and unite people to work with you toward a goal.

Are you prideful? Then just say, "I am yelling because I need you to think I am important."

Are you just in a habit? Stop and tell yourself, "I don't know why I am yelling." Then begin to talk in a normal voice in a productive conversation rather than a one-sided rant. An attitude of seeking to understand can help.

If you need more help to change a behavior of yelling consider these:

> Make apologies to those you yell at. When you do, it will likely feel so freeing you will want to keep that behavior and throw out the other one.

> Ask those around you to kindly hold you accountable.

> Read a book on the subject or see a psychologist.

Don't be tied to any habitual unproductive behavior. There are many reasons we yell and sometimes it is appropriate, but habitual yelling with an intention to belittle says more about our personal problems than it does the problem at hand.

We all need to make it a habit to try something new and different. When we do, we may find new and different possibilities, too.

In a controversy, the instant we feel anger, we have already ceased striving for truth and have begun striving for ourselves.
Abraham J. Heschel

To belittle is to be little.
Unknown

NOVEMBER 11
BE CONFIDENT

When we find ourselves yelling, belittling or trying to control those around us with anger, then perhaps we are feeling out of control and insecure ourselves. Maybe we yell. Maybe we storm off. Maybe we get silent and won't communicate. Maybe we even shed some tears—tears can be used to control others, too.

We all have frustrating and emotional days and will end up losing our cool. That is going to happen; we are human. And there are times raising our voices is appropriate, but when yelling is habitual and we find ourselves wanting to tear down rather than build up, then we want to stop and ask ourselves why that is. Ask yourself, "What am I afraid of?"

We could be afraid or our anger could be just a habit. So when you find you are yelling or withdrawing, stop and decide who you want to be. If that is the person you want to be, then continue. But when we find we want to be someone else, we can stop right in the middle of the moment, de-escalate and choose our response rather than let it just happen to us.

Unfortunately, we will all have these behaviors at some point because we are human. Problems seem to arise when we use them consistently to control others because we do not know or will not choose another way.

I read in the book, *Bo's Cafe,* about a man who gave permission to his child to tell him when he was becoming angry. This may not be a good solution for everyone, but when we make changes we often need help and accountability to progress. So if there isn't someone you can feel safe with to help you identify those moments you are not acting in line with what you believe, then get help. There are a multitude of solutions and many people waiting to help you. Call a friend, therapist, clergy or coach today to help you move through any behavior you don't want to be stuck in.

All cruelty springs from weakness.
Seneca

NOVEMBER 12
BE RECOGNIZING

We have said before that it is likely not a good idea to make decisions when we are angry.

Steven Stosny says in *Psychology Today* that anger magnifies the negative aspects of a situation and gives these tips about dealing with your anger.

1. Recognize anger as a signal of vulnerability, that you feel devalued in some way.
2. When angry, think or do something that will make you feel more valuable, i.e., worthy of appreciation.
3. Don't trust your judgment when angry. Anger magnifies and amplifies only the negative aspects of an issue, distorting realistic appraisal.
4. Try to see the complexity of the issue. Anger requires narrow and rigid focus that ignores or oversimplifies context.
5. Strive to understand other people's perspectives. When angry, you assume the worst or outright demonize the object of your anger.
6. Don't justify your anger. Instead, consider whether it will help you act in your long-term best interest.
7. Know your physical and mental resources. Anger is more likely to occur when you are tired, hungry, sick, confused, anxious, preoccupied, distracted, or overwhelmed.
8. Focus on improving and repairing rather than blaming. It's hard to stay angry without blaming and it's harder to blame when you are focused on repairing and improving.
9. When angry, remember your deepest values. Anger is about devaluing others, which is probably inconsistent with your deepest values.
10. Know that your temporary state of anger has prepared you to fight when you really need to learn more, solve a problem, or, if it involves a loved one, be more compassionate.

The more we learn to deal with unproductive emotions, the more productive possibilities we will find.

Temper tantrums, however fun they may be to throw,
rarely solve whatever problem is causing them.
Lemony Snicket

NOVEMBER 13
BE BUILDING

What we are yelling about is usually not what we are angry about. We often have a fear we are not aware of or not sharing with the person we are yelling at that is the source of our anger.

If you are a habitual yeller, make a list of the times you find yourself yelling the most and determine what you are afraid of. Work on resolving the fear and the yelling could begin to take care of itself. Sometimes just acknowledging your fear and insecurities makes a difference.

If we are trying to make a dinner reservation and we are yelling at the hostess, we are tearing down the very person who is building our evening for us. If we are trying to build a business and we are consistently yelling at the people who are there to help us build it, we are tearing down the people who are the foundation and trying to build the business, too.

If we are trying to build a family and we are always yelling at the people in it, we are likely tearing down the very heart of what we are trying to nurture.

We owe it to those around us to learn to communicate in a productive, solution-seeking manner rather than trying to tear down what we say we are working to build.

When we begin to build with—and build up—others, we will likely find ourselves building a strong foundation for ourselves, too.

Anger is one letter short of danger.
Unknown

NOVEMBER 14
BE UNRESISTANT

You have heard it said that—if you resist, it will persist—a small phrase that is a big reminder about the stuff we don't want to be happening in our lives and calls attention to our responsibility in the problem.

So often we think we are just innocent bystanders in an issue—if not all-out victims—when we do have some responsibility, if only in our attitude.

We may not like a situation, but as the words express, if we keep fighting it instead of surrendering, seeking to understand, being objective, taking responsibility or one of many other productive approaches, "it" will keep happening in our lives.

Now, I am not saying that we are to become a doormat or that we don't stand up for what we believe in. I am saying if something is not working for you in your life, take a step back and look at your attitude. Are you avoiding? Are you blaming? Are you angry or bitter or just frustrated? We may feel that we have no option, but we likely do—even if it is only an internal shift in attitude.

If you need help surrendering something or knowing what to do with a problem, contact your manager, team member or counselor today. If there is a way to move through a pesky, persistent problem and on to new possibilities, we want to explore it.

This may shock you, but I believe the single most significant decision I can make on a day-to-day basis is my choice of attitude. It is more important than my past, my education, my bankroll, my successes or failures, fame or pain, what other people think of me or say about me, my circumstances, or my position. Attitude is that "single string" that keeps me going or cripples my progress. It alone fuels my fire or assaults my hope. When my attitudes are right, there's no barrier too high, no valley too deep, no dream too extreme, no challenge too great for me.

Charles Swindoll

NOVEMBER 15
BE COOL

This week someone asked, "What do I need to work on? What do I need to change?"

This person had a friend who was struggling with an issue, and while she could see her friend's problem, her friend couldn't.

This made her realize there were likely issues in her own behavior or attitude that she couldn't identify, just like her friend.

How cool is she that (1) she not only realized there were probably issues in her own life she couldn't see and (2) that she initiated asking what they were!

We don't want to spend our time going in circles, stuck in old problems when we could be moving forward toward what we want.

Consider asking someone you trust to help you identify an attitude or action in your life that could be keeping you stuck in a place you would rather not be.

Not wanting to know our part in the problem could be part of our problem.

Our dilemma is that we hate change and love it at the same time;
what we really want is for things to remain the same but get better.
Sydney J. Harris

NOVEMBER 16
BE READY TO ACT

Resisting something can take many forms—for example, avoidance. Sometimes we avoid because we are resisting the truth.

How many times do we avoid something because we don't want to deal with it or we are afraid to know the answer or we think we already know the outcome? Then when we do finally face it, we find out we should have addressed it sooner. What we avoid is often either not as bad as we thought or wouldn't have been if we had just faced it rather than avoided it.

We miss deadlines because we don't want to deal with something or make a decision. We destroy relationships because we avoid conflict. We miss opportunities because we want to avoid rejection.

If we look at avoidance as fear, we can stop and ask ourselves, "What am I afraid of?"

There are times that we are supposed to be still and wait instead of taking action. But we know the difference between being still in peace and avoiding in fear and want to be ready to act when the time comes.

Acting on something we have been avoiding gives us energy, momentum and creativity.

What have you been avoiding? How can you begin to face it today?

You can avoid reality, but you cannot avoid
the consequences of avoiding reality.
Ayn Rand

NOVEMBER 17
BE NOT AFRAID

Avoiding steals possibilities.

There is waiting for the right time and there is avoiding. We know the difference.

To help myself move through things I want to avoid, I use the thought, "Love doesn't avoid."

When we are avoiding, we can stop and ask, "What am I afraid of?"

We don't have to act right then, but knowing the truth of why we are avoiding helps us begin to turn that fear around.

A common activity people may avoid is marketing/business-building. There are so many reasons we avoid it, but likely, one common issue—fear.

> I'm not good enough.

> What if they ask me something I don't know?

> What if they say no?

> Why would they want to do business with me?

> They probably already have someone they work with.

We are often afraid of not being good enough or not perfect. Well, none of us is perfect. In fact, our mistakes are probably what have made us better.

If you are not growing your business and would like to, make a list of what you are afraid of and turn those fears around either with action or attitude. If you need help, talk to your manager, coach or someone else who wants to see you reach out to the people who may need your services. Other people's possibilities could depend on it.

Criticism is something we can avoid easily by saying nothing,
doing nothing, and being nothing.
Aristotle

NOVEMBER 18
BE STRONGER

You have heard it said that a large number of things we fear don't happen. We spend time and energy being anxious about something until we face it—going in circles rather than moving toward our goal. Then when we face it, we either find it wasn't the monster we imagined it to be or we deal with the monster that it is. Avoiding creates more anxiety than facing something.

Avoiding the truth could be as big a possibility deterrent as there is.

Why do we want to avoid the truth? Because we are afraid we will get in trouble or lose something: respect, a person, a job. Or we are afraid we will have to do something we don't want to. Or to avoid confrontation.

We think if we avoid it, it will go away. Or if we don't do anything, no one else will notice the problem either, or maybe it will get better.

Sometimes things do get better without us taking action, but rarely without us at least taking notice. If nothing else, we have to work to acknowledge the truth ourselves.

Think of it like a journey and the truth takes us down the right road, but lies to others or ourselves automatically put us on a road heading away from what we really want.

Before long, we can wind up a long way from where we wanted to be and will either have to create a new map to get to our goal or make a whole new goal.

Since we don't have a satellite view of our life map, it is harder to see how avoiding the truth expends unnecessary energy by taking us over mountains and around water and through deserts, when we could easily be on a straight path. We could use our energy to love and serve those around us instead of negotiating self-created obstacles.

We don't want to waste time, energy or possibilities on lies to ourselves.

Being strong does not mean avoiding the truth.
It means accepting it, learning about it, and dealing with it head-on.
Unknown

NOVEMBER 19
BE UN-AVOIDING

Waiting for the right timing is good. Avoiding because we don't want to deal with something is often not so good.

When we are uncomfortable, in pain, or upset—physically or emotionally—that is a good sign there is a problem.

We often ignore or avoid the little things hoping they go away or resolve themselves. But when they don't, they turn into big things that if we had just taken care of when they first occurred, they would have been much easier to deal with.

We know our bodies and we know our relationships. There are times we are going to miss a signal, but more often than not we know when something needs tending to. We just avoid dealing with it and then we wonder what happened!

When we ignore signals and symptoms because of avoidance, we are usually just going to have a bigger "mess" to clean up later.

When we avoid, we can end up letting life happen to us. And when we do that, our possibilities seem to happen for everyone else but us.

If this is not the right time to deal with something, at least admit to yourself there is a problem and you want a solution. Sometimes that helps the solution find you.

The difficult problems in life always start off being simple.
Great affairs always start off being small.
Lao Tzu

NOVEMBER 20
BE A CAPTIVE THINKER

We tend to think our thoughts don't matter as much as our words and actions. But not only do thoughts drive our words and actions, but our thoughts also highly affect our peace, attitude and outcomes.

If we want to honor the people around us, we need to honor them with our thoughts, too. Not every thought that pops into our heads is going to be positive or kind or true. But the thoughts we allow to stay can be.

As we become more aware of our thoughts, we will notice non-honoring thoughts and when we do, we can consciously change them or work to process them—if we choose to. It is the "choosing to" part that is hard because sometimes we would rather hold a grudge than let it go.

Have you ever noticed what kind of possibilities show up when we hold a grudge?

I don't know for sure, but it seems they aren't as positive as the ones that show up when we let something go and desire the best for those around us.

One cannot think crooked and walk straight.
Unknown

NOVEMBER 21

BE SELF-HONORING

If we step back and look around us, we see people who astound us with how beautifully they use their skills and talents and love. Yet if we asked one of those wonderfully astounding people if they were exceptional, they would likely say no. There might even be times they would "shrink back" a little and start to tell you their flaws and ways they fall short.

Many of us see beauty and talent in others but have a tendency to find flaws in ourselves.

As we work on honoring those around us, we want to honor ourselves, too. Set boundaries, praise yourself, do things that are important to you, pamper yourself on occasion, be kind to your body, feed your spirit, know your purpose, ask for help, value your contributions.

Honoring those around us while ignoring our own needs for nourishment and encouragement will likely not be productive in the long run. If we are going to care for our clients and families and do our jobs well, we have to become aware of the balancing act involved in honoring ourselves, too.

Self-honor (self-respect) is in no way selfish.
Before I can give to others, I must have something to give.
Only by first creating my own self-esteem and happiness,
do I possess the resources to contribute anything meaningful to others.
Jonathan Lockwood Huie

NOVEMBER 22
BE BALANCED

Yesterday we remembered to honor ourselves.

We know how to honor others but have difficulty actually doing it because we get tired or aggravated and want to take care of ourselves... and yet still, we can forget to intentionally honor ourselves.

A beautiful woman shared the following story:

"My marriage was breaking up and we decided to go to counseling through the divorce so we could understand how we got to this point. Because of the actions of my husband, it would have been easy to only blame him for the crisis the marriage was experiencing. The world says we can blame the other person for everything but I too, was to blame for the breakdown in our marriage. One of the many things I learned is that when someone hurts you, do not hurt them back. Period. Even if society says to hurt them back. Just take care of yourself... the rest will fall into place. So whenever I had a desire to do or think something unkind of him, I chose instead to do or think something kind for myself. I can always feel good that I didn't ever choose to be ugly through any of it. There is peace in that.

"It has been a long, painful journey but I am a much better person now. In fact, if God gave me a choice to go back and not have to endure that pain or to go through it and be the person I am now, I would choose the pain in order to be who I am now. I am such a better person."

She was an awesome person before, but now she is so much happier and even more wonderful. In fact, she and her husband ended up not divorcing and are happier than they ever have been. Instead of dishonoring another person, we can choose to honor ourselves. And with that choice we are somehow honoring the other person, too. If we all choose to honor others more, even when the world says we have a "right" not to, we may be happier people with ourselves and others. When we find we want to dishonor and "get back at" a spouse, associate or manager, we will probably be better off in the long run if we are honest and solution-seeking rather than prideful and disagreeable. Instead of doing something in revenge to them, what if you did something supportive, educational or "growing" for yourself?

You might find you have fewer problems with others and more positive possibilities for yourself when you do.

Every thought is a seed. If you plant crab apples, don't count on harvesting Golden Delicious.
Bill Meyer

NOVEMBER 23
BE REALLY LISTENING

Another way to honor others is to listen. Really listen and hear what they are not saying as loudly as what they are.

Stop what you are doing, look them in the eye and listen.

Instead of interrupting, giving excuses or defending yourself, listen with intent to understand and then respond with something like, "I can see how you might think that. Thank you for pointing that out. This is how I was seeing it." or "I didn't know you felt this way, what can I do to…?" or "Thank you for sharing that with me, how can we…?" And continue with a conversation that allows you both to express how you feel, how you would like the situation to improve and agree on options for change.

We don't have to be offended. We can choose to honor the other person by simply allowing them to express how they feel and hearing it. Maybe the "biggest honor" we can be given is someone caring enough to tell us the truth. We want to be able to receive it.

We don't have to agree with their words, but the simple act of giving ourselves to the relationship, rather than avoiding, honors everyone.

Man's inability to communicate is a result of his
failure to listen effectively.
Carl Rogers

NOVEMBER 24
BE MAKING A DIFFERENCE

We can have a hard time celebrating ourselves.

If you have a hard time celebrating yourself, stop and ask yourself why that is. Do you shrink back at the thought? Do you not feel good enough to celebrate yourself?

There is no one who does not fall short, again and again. And when we do, we need to ask forgiveness where we can and make changes in our lives and businesses that will prevent a situation from arising again.

We tend to think the other guy didn't make as many mistakes as we did. But successful business people (and parents and friends) will tell you they have made mistakes and still do.

Wouldn't it be wonderful if we could learn all our lessons the easy way? But sometimes our most impactful lessons come from our own most painful mistakes.

The lessons we pass on to others are often the ones we learned the hard way. We are likely more passionate, as well as more forgiving about the mistakes and experiences we lived instead of read about. That doesn't mean we can't learn from others (and it is wise to read and learn), that just means the thing each of us individually is to teach others could come from our own experience.

The point is, we can't let our shame or pain keep us from making a difference with what we have learned.

Keep moving forward toward your purpose and celebrate where you are even if sometimes it is hard to celebrate how you got there.

When you make a mistake, don't look back at it long. Take the reason of the thing into your mind and then look forward. Mistakes are lessons of wisdom. The past cannot be changed. The future is yet in your power.
Hugh White

If you have made mistakes, even serious ones, there is always another chance for you. What we call failure is not the falling down but the staying down.
Mary Pickford

NOVEMBER 25
BE A TEAM PLAYER

We don't get anywhere great without some help.

Have you identified your "team"?

Your team is those people who have pushed, pulled, or carried you to where you are. They have supported you, believed in you and believed for you when you couldn't do it for yourself. They have cheered you on, straightened you out and maybe leaned on you, too.

Celebrate them today.

If you know who they are, call, email, send a note or walk down the hall.

If you haven't yet identified your team, take the time to do so and contact them if you can to say thanks.

Our team changes. The people who were in our lives five years ago may not be today, but remember them gratefully, too. They were part of your journey that carried you to this moment and your present possibilities.

Make it a habit to tell people thank you.
To express your appreciation, sincerely and without the expectation
of anything in return. Truly appreciate those around you,
and you'll soon find many others around you.
Truly appreciate life, and you'll find that you have more of it.
Ralph Marston

NOVEMBER 26
BE ENGAGED

Celebrations are ways to honor and mark something or someone as special. It tends to make us appreciative and leans us toward living in the present moment and being engaged in it. To truly celebrate, we have to stop and experience the feeling in our heads before it will be expressed in our lives.

Today, celebrate differences instead of attacking them. If your associates have a different approach and personality than you, why not let them enjoy it? We have all experienced, at some point in our lives, the effects of someone being unkind because we are different from them.

We dress differently or talk differently. Our clothes are better or not as nice. We have a different personality or a different approach to doing business. Yet, often in business, we struggle to see the value in a person who does things differently from us. If they are getting results and not doing anything wrong, why does it bother us? Are we jealous? Afraid?

When we stop and "celebrate" the difference, it can enhance our own productivity. When the person who is different begins talking in a meeting, do you shut down? Perhaps you cut him or her off? That pride can keep you from hearing a good idea or learning something new.

Different doesn't equal wrong. But there is a caution: we shouldn't use the idea of celebrating differences as an excuse to behave poorly or be unproductive. There is nothing to celebrate about poor, unkind or lazy behavior, but there is still much to celebrate about the person.

We don't have to throw a neighborhood party to extol each other's differences, but we can stop and experience the benefits of celebrating. Who knows, when we stop putting down the other person, we may not only notice them flourishing, but ourselves, too.

Share our similarities, celebrate our differences.
M. Scott Peck

NOVEMBER 27
BE CONSISTENT

What is one thing you can do throughout the year to keep the feeling of community, gratitude and wellbeing that Thanksgiving brings?

A few ideas:

Write three notes of thanks a week.

Deliver one compliant "goodie" to a client each month: a cookie, lunch, coffee, visit.

Make the phone call just to say thanks.

You can't keep the activities of Thanksgiving going all year, but you can keep the spirit. Cultivate more gratitude.

Feeling grateful or appreciative of someone or something in your life actually attracts more of the things that you appreciate and value into your life.
Christiane Northrup, MD

NOVEMBER 28
BE CHOOSING GRATITUDE

Happiness promotes possibilities. And while happiness is a choice, we can sometimes use a little help getting there.

Robert Emmons and Michael McCullough report: "Grateful people report higher levels of positive emotions, life satisfaction, vitality, optimism and lower levels of depression and stress. The disposition toward gratitude appears to enhance pleasant feeling states more than it diminishes unpleasant emotions. Grateful people do not deny or ignore the negative aspects of life."

Gratitude is powerful no matter how it is delivered. And while the receiver of the thankfulness benefits, it is the person giving the gratitude who benefits the most. It is often what we give (good or bad) more than what we receive that makes the most impact in our lives and our possibilities.

As the researchers point out, when you are grateful you don't avoid or ignore problems, you just don't have as much "space" for negative emotions and, therefore, the problems simply don't seem as difficult. In fact, when you are experiencing high levels of gratitude, you may actually feel like facing things you have avoided.

The holidays, while wonderful, can be stressful, and there is no doubt your business day can be stressful. To help decrease stress levels and increase optimism and energy, try gratitude.

For the next week, make a decision to start your day in a grateful way—something that works for you. Consider making a decision to intentionally give gratitude at least one more time in your day and feel the change in your life.

Choose gratitude. It will make the happy choice for you.

In our daily lives, we must see that it is not happiness that makes us grateful, but the gratefulness that makes us happy.
Albert Clarke

NOVEMBER 29

BE SINCERE

The negative emotions we face in little ways every day affect our businesses if we choose to let them. Remember the subtle forms of fear—jealousy unforgiveness, revenge—and all the insecurities that come with them? One way to greatly reduce, if not completely eliminate, those little productivity robbers is gratitude.

When we practice gratitude, it doesn't mean we are not tenaciously determined and highly motivated; we are just as motivated and determined, maybe even more so. Gratitude may help us to sustain what we are building.

One reader observed that he "liked the idea that sincere gratitude is a business practice, rather than a passing thought. We all know that it is far easier to maintain the relationships that we have than it is to get new business. Additionally, if thanks and gratitude are passed on only when all of the other businesses do the same (i.e. Thanksgiving, Christmas), its value is diminished."

When we practice gratitude only through the holidays, its powerfully positive effects are diminished in our lives and businesses.

When you say thank you, mean it. Look the person holding the door or your coffee in the eye and say "thank you" with genuine gratitude for the kindness or the cup of coffee you are about to receive.

Tell your family/friends some form of thank you every day. An email, note, hug, make their favorite cookie, etc.

Tell your clients, associates, managers, or firm leaders how you appreciate what they do for you on a personal and/or corporate level. You may not have met your company's leaders but you may appreciate how they guide the firm through difficult times or decisions they made to position the firm well. Or perhaps how respected the company you work for is in the community because of their leadership.

Gratitude is not just in the words. It is a genuine internal appreciation for the person and/or act. The big smile you give the coffee guy and the grateful hug to your family member with sincere appreciation can convey as much as the words.

A full heart overflows into lives—in both business and personal relationships. What are you filling your heart with?

As we express our gratitude, we must never forget that the highest appreciation is not to utter words, but to live by them.
John F. Kennedy

NOVEMBER 30
BE EVER-SEEKING

Another idea to make gratitude a way of living is to write one note a week to someone you do not know.

Maybe the mayor put sidewalks down in your neighborhood and it has increased a feeling of community and promoted walking. Tell him.

Maybe you saw that a young golfer reported herself when she realized she had turned in the wrong score and she lost the tournament but she gained your admiration. Tell her.

Maybe you read that someone was doing something unique for others. Encourage them.

Maybe you saw an act of simple kindness or sportsmanship on television or in your town. Honor that behavior with a simple note.

When you begin to look for ways to appreciate others, you will be amazed at how much good there is in a day. The newspaper and Internet offer a multitude of possibilities for appreciation.

With all the bad news in the world, it can be easy to become discouraged and a little depressed. Discouragement and the blues are not big promoters of possibilities, so the more we deter them the better. Writing a note a week to someone you don't know makes you search for good news in the midst of the more prevalent bad. This small task will be a catalyst helping you celebrate the good rather than focusing on the bad in other areas of your life. Seeking good in the midst of misfortune is a key component of seeing possibilities others can't.

Keep a list of the acts you have acknowledged with your weekly notes. It will serve as encouragement and a reminder of good when you need a lift.

Giving appreciation without receiving anything and without expecting anything back brings a whole new world of possibilities to your life.

Give cheerfully and freely. It is the energy behind the giving that matters so do not give grudgingly. The law of cause and effect guarantees that you shall receive plenty for what you give.
David Cameron Gikandi

DECEMBER 1
BE CAREFUL

Whoever said, "Sticks and stones may break my bones, but words can never hurt me," lied to us. Words hurt! ...And words can heal. Words have the power to build up and tear down...businesses, relationships, people, *possibilities*.

Be aware of your words today. Is what you are saying true or is it your perspective? If the words are your perspective, try, "My opinion is that Bill needs more discipline." Rather than making your opinion truth as we often do when we blurt out in disgust—"Bill has no discipline." That negative off-the-cuff comment can skew a person's view of you or someone else. We can stifle possibilities by not tending to our words.

Let's say your boss made a comment about you without thinking, such as, "Susan doesn't want to do that." From that moment forward, others will think you do not want to participate in that activity and may not include you or promote you if it involves that particular work.

Or what if you made a mistake under pressure one day and you have worked hard to learn from that mistake? You are a whiz now in that area that relates to your job as well as the job you want to be promoted to. But a co-worker doesn't know this and makes comments such as, "He can't do that." Those comments said in passing (and ignorance) damage your ability to be promoted. A more honest comment might be, "I once heard him make a mistake. I am sure he has corrected that problem since he has done so well in this position, but you could talk with him about it before promoting him."

We don't want to be the person who holds anyone back—including ourselves. Little changes in our word choices make a big difference in our lives—in our attitudes, actions, thought patterns and how we are viewed by others.

When you use your words more deliberately, you will experience less drama and more time to be productive. You will find people respect you more and you may experience higher levels of self-esteem and self-discipline as well as more enjoyable relationships and personal peace.

Pay special attention to your words today and be aware of when you aren't being truthful or constructive with your words.

Handle them carefully, for words have more power than atom bombs.
Pearl Strachan

DECEMBER 2
BE WORDY

Learn to use your words. How many times have you heard a teacher or guardian say these five words to a two year old? And how many times have you wanted to say the same thing to a forty year old?

It is quite easy to get into a habit of hiding our hurt because of pride. When we do that, we can end up acting out our hurt feelings through non-verbal signals, snide remarks or sarcasm. When we must resort to biting remarks, eye-rolls or "running away" to communicate how we feel, it is time to take a self-imposed time-out. Sadly, many of us get so used to this form of communicating that we can begin to think it is effective.

Sometimes we even choose to mask those remarks with humor. We think our humor is hiding our real feelings of frustration, anger, resentment, or a number of other negative emotions, but it's not. We may want the other person to feel small, but we really end up hurting ourselves more.

The next time you are upset, stop and use your words to express how you feel, even if it is just to yourself.

My feelings are hurt.

I am frustrated.

I am embarrassed.

I am angry.

I am afraid.

You will find yourself feeling better—maybe just a little, but a little is better than nothing. Remember when we get to the truth, we get to peace. If we are going in circles with something, we are still lying to ourselves. Honesty to self cultivates positive possibilities. Avoidance, blame and not using your words crush them.

The next time you catch yourself using sarcasm or eye-rolls or biting remarks to express how you feel, stop, rewind and start over. "I am sorry. What I really wanted to say is..."

Use your words.
Unknown

DECEMBER 3
BE EXPRESSIVE

In consistent pursuit of your possibilities, you need to give special attention to words. Words create chaos, harmony or somewhere in between, depending on how they are used. There are many words to pay special attention to, but two words you should attach red flags to are "Always" and "Never."

Very few things are absolutes, so unless you are talking about taxes, death or breathing, you might want to reconsider your use of these two words.

"You are always late." Whether that is true or not, it is not the most productive way to begin a discussion about punctuality and your expectations. And it is probably not true. He was probably on time at least once.

"You never help me." Again, not the best approach to open a discussion about your needs and expectations. There might have been one time she helped you spell a word or answer a phone.

The words are so common for us that we often do not hear ourselves say them, but the other person does. Even if they don't hear the word in their conscious mind, they hear it in their subconscious mind and defensive emotions come right out, often sabotaging your purpose.

We lose credibility when we let resentment or revenge take over the conversation. Expressing what we need and want is important. Learning how to effectively say it may be the most important.

When we use "always" and "never" the other person remembers the one time they did help or the one time they were on time and may not hear what you have to say at all. Not only do you lose credibility, you may not get your issue resolved.

The next time you hear yourself use the words "always" or "never" with a negative intention, stop and correct yourself immediately. You will have a more productive conversation and the other person will probably appreciate your honest attempt to resolve the issue that is bothering you.

Always and never are two words you should always remember never to use.
Wendell Johnson

DECEMBER 4
BE UNDERSTANDING

Have you ever said the words, "I will never..."?

Our words reveal things about us we may not be fully aware of, particularly judgments.

When we say, "I will never (fill in the blank with an action)," we are actually being judgmental. It can be the same with "I don't understand..."

Sometimes we are really saying, "I don't understand that. Will you explain it to me"? But other times we are saying, *"How could you do that?"*

For instance, if you think to yourself, "I don't understand how someone lets herself gain weight like that." Get ready because one day, you probably will.

Or "I don't understand how someone can be so disorganized." Write it down because one day you will.

Parents particularly relate to this. After years of saying: "I will never yell at my child" or "I don't understand how they let their child behave that way," parents often find themselves living a similar experience they were judgmental about just a few years prior.

We don't have to change our words or behaviors, but learning more about ourselves, how we feel and believe, helps us to be more productive and peaceful in our work and our relationships. Being aware of what we don't want in our lives, as well as what we do, is important and helpful for us to be deliberate in our actions—big and small. Judging others just makes the other person feel bad and makes you feel worse about yourself when you experience the same thing some time later.

Instead of judging, ask yourself, "How can I help?" Or maybe just write a mental sticky note that you want to be watchful of that situation in your life and handle it differently when it arises. Perhaps even read articles or books on the subject so you can be prepared with your choice of action if that situation comes up in your life or the life of someone close to you. Be careful. The action we judge others for today we could be judging ourselves for tomorrow.

Any fool can criticize, condemn, and complain,
but it takes character and self control to be understanding and forgiving.
Dale Carnegie

DECEMBER 5
BE ATTENTIVE

We have the power to construct or destruct with our words. We all have frustrating situations in our work and personal lives. We do not need to carry those problems with us or blow off steam by speaking badly about our spouse or co-worker to everyone around us. That can contribute to the problem. But we do need to process the situation. For that, we need a friend who will not hold us to our words two weeks later.

In the "processing" process, we say things we don't want to be a normal in our life. Meaning, we are frustrated about a situation and need to process it in order to get it out, readjust our attitude and move on. Obviously, unless we like drama, we don't want that uncomfortable situation and those emotions to be a normal part of our life. Processing means we are speaking not to complain but to move on.

So in processing and searching for solutions, you are probably going to say words about someone that are not "building up" words. Find a friend that can understand the purpose of processing and not keep you in that uncomfortable spot later.

For example, after you have processed the problem, dealt with it and moved on, some people will say, "Why are you having lunch with Olivia? I thought you didn't like her." Rather than, "I am so glad you are having lunch with Olivia! You have worked through your disagreement and are really enjoying each other!"

Your processing friend should be someone who lets you move forward toward the life you want, not keep you in the distressing situation you were in.

And remember, sustainable solutions start with us, not the other person. Some change is needed in our attitude, actions, intentions or words. A good processing friend is one that helps you find the needed change and helps you get in sync toward your goal of a flourishing business and happy life.

Be attentive to the words you say and who you say them to. We want to use them to work toward healing. ✍❤

Whatever words we utter should be chosen with care,
for people will hear them and be influenced by them for good or evil.
Gautama Siddharta

DECEMBER 6

BE OF GOOD CHEER

As you rush around in overflowing malls gift-shopping for your family and friends and handling end-of-the-year requests for clients while still maintaining your daily duties, things can get a little edgy. The simple act of placing "joyfully" in your lexicon will lift your energy and maybe even the mood of someone around you.

When someone asks, "How are you?" You might think, "Busy!" But if you think or say, "Joyfully busy," you instill an awareness to be joyful regardless of the person who took your parking space or the sales clerk who isn't helpful. Your attitude makes all the difference. You can either be joyful or miserable; it is your choice. And when you change your attitude, you may find your circumstances change: the sales associate is more helpful, a parking space shows up.

When you want to say, "I am busy, stressed or overwhelmed," add joyfully. I am joyfully busy (reminds you that you have friends and family to be with) I am joyfully stressed (reminds you that you have a car that works so you can be in the parking lot getting what you need rather than sitting on the side of the road) I am joyfully overwhelmed (acknowledges the stress you feel in your job and personal life, but helps you be grateful and see a little light at the end of the tunnel). When you use "joyfully" to describe your life, you almost can't help but be joyful!

Positive words start positive possibilities. Help create the experiences you want in this season and through the coming year with your words and attitude.

You can create the energy to turn your dreams into reality
by knowing what to say when you talk to yourself.
Shad Helmstetter

DECEMBER 7
BE UN-OFFENDED

We have power over the words we speak and we also have power to decide what words we will receive. We cannot control the words of another, but we can control whether or not we will choose to be offended by them.

We have all said things that hurt another person's feelings. When we do, we usually want to correct that by rewinding and clearing up a misunderstanding, talking the problem through or apologizing. So shouldn't we be willing to return that courtesy when someone offends us?

We all have different "thresholds of offended" based on our past experiences, beliefs about ourselves and how entitled we feel. But there are times we simply want to create drama. Sometimes we don't like a person and seek to validate that dislike. There are times we are needy and, sadly, other times we may just want to play the victim and get pity.

We choose whether to be offended. If we choose to feel slighted, we must next choose to forgive and happily move on or to hold a grudge. We are happier, more productive people when we will choose not to be easily offended, and to let it go when we find we are.

Pay attention to your "threshold of offended" today and the words you are offended by. It will be an interesting way to discover new things about yourself.

When you are offended at any man's fault,
turn to yourself and study your own failings.
Then you will forget your anger.
Epictetus

DECEMBER 8
BE UNDISTURBED

Yesterday you were going to take note of the words that offended you throughout the day. Of course, we can be offended by crude behavior or jokes, and it is important to set boundaries or remove yourself from a situation you don't want to be in. You do not have to be around behavior you feel is inappropriate. The words we want to examine are the ones we feel are personal.

Usually when we get offended, there is a level of truth to it. Either because the comment is true in some way or we simply believe it is true in some aspect. For example:If you are woman who is six feet tall and someone says to you, "You are short." That statement doesn't offend you because you know it isn't true. If someone says, "You are tall," that is probably a neutral statement to you. But if someone says, "You are too tall," this comment reinforces that you believe you are too tall and you will probably take offense.

The same is true with "You are loud" or "You are bossy." 1. If you don't feel you are loud or bossy, you won't be offended. 2. If you know you are loud or bossy and are okay with it, the words won't bother you.3. But if you haven't owned it and you don't want to be loud, bossy or impatient, then you will probably take offense. Taking offense or "being sensitive" to something separates us from others emotionally and maybe even physically. And somewhere along the way, we lose a little confidence.

Separation and insecurities rob us of possibilities. So if you are offended, stop and ask yourself: Why am I hurt by those words? Then:

1. Examine the truth in it. 2. Own it. 3. And choose to do something—or nothing—about it. The words and the actual issue will continue to be a problem in your life until you do. There are too many positive possibilities to pursue in relationships, business opportunities and service for you to hold yourself back by grudges and offenses.

I'm not offended by dumb blonde jokes because I know that I'm not dumb.
I also know I'm not blonde.
Dolly Parton

DECEMBER 9
BE MERRY

In response to yesterday's quote, a reader emailed that she has always loved how Dolly seems to know what is important to take seriously, what should be taken as a source of amusement and how to take things seriously in an amusing way.

That about sums it up. We are more productive and happier people with more confidence and courage to explore possibilities when we don't easily take offense. Address what needs to be addressed—either with yourself or with another. And let go of what doesn't.

Sometimes our taking offense is valid and should be addressed; at other times we simply want to take offense. The problem with that is when we look for drama or to play the victim we miss positive possibilities that are right in front of our eyes. The best way to change your perspective is to stop and think of a time you have done a similar act. Most of us have done or said something similar to what we are taking offense with, such as dismissing someone's idea in a meeting or avoiding a person or forgetting to return a call. Recalling a time you have acted in a similar way will help you give grace rather than hold a grudge.

Look for good. When you happen to stumble upon the "bad," deal with it and move on. There is always a good way out of a bad feeling.

Promise yourself: To be so strong that nothing can disturb your peace of mind.
To give so much time to the improvement of yourself that you have no time to
criticize others. To be too large for worry, too noble for anger,
too strong for fear and too happy to permit the presence of trouble.
Excerpt from The Optimist's Creed

DECEMBER 10
BE A STARTER

At a time of year that is a celebration of joy with a spirit of new beginnings, light and love in the air, it can be difficult to reconcile the events happening around us that do not fit with that idea and feeling—difficulties and even tragedies that make no sense to us and leave us feeling helpless. Today, make a little difference for someone else by helping. Help someone somewhere in some way today. There are people around you that may need an extra bit of understanding, kindness and encouragement.

We know our difficulties but can't really know other people's struggles. As the old story goes, if we all put our troubles in a pile and could pick anyone else's, we would choose to take our own back. The point is that our troubles are not as tough as we think they are after we see what others are going through, and no matter how cheerful someone is choosing to be, that person has pains, too.

This is the perfect time of year to let care be expressed. In the midst of the hectic schedules and the wonderful social events, stop. Be present in the moment and silently ask yourself the question: Who needs help here? Who needs encouragement or a kind word or simply to be acknowledged?

Remember, everyone does…

The person who is aloof is likely just shy and afraid.

The person who is being a tyrant is likely just insecure.

The person who is happy-go-lucky and "always" in a good mood has problems, too.

Look for ways to give kindness today. No matter how you choose to help another—from giving a smile to giving a gift to giving respect, it will make a difference—for you, the other person and likely a multitude of people you can never know as that same gift of encouragement is passed on. It can start with you.

What are you going to start today?

Be kind, for everyone you meet is fighting a hard battle.
Plato

DECEMBER 11
BE PEACEFUL

Unfortunately, there is usually some form of "messy" in our lives somewhere. You get sideways with a client, your sisters aren't getting along and you are in the middle, you made a mistake and there is a problem with a client's account. When there is chaos, there is opportunity for learning and growth. To see that opportunity, it helps to be calm inside and have a sense of peace. That peace doesn't just show up; we must cultivate it within us.

Many of us wonder if personal accord is possible. It is, but it often means going against "the herd" to get it. The little things we do to cultivate peace in our lives will help us pursue the possibilities that are ever before us. When we win our internal "battles," the external ones don't seem so big. One way is: Don't say anything *about* someone you wouldn't say *to* them. Certainly, there will be times we slip or we will need to process bigger issues out loud with someone. But the more we work to manage what we think and say, the more peace we will have. This isn't easy because people like to gossip, and if you are no longer participating in bashing the usual "bashee," you might be shunned by the group. Since we all want to be accepted, that shunning can be hard to take. But if you had to choose, which would you want—peace or to be part of a group whose bond comes from talking about others? Find a group that enjoys talking about possibilities more than they enjoy talking about others.

This is helpful because we could start seeing the good in others rather than looking for the bad. It is quite exhausting to be continually looking for negative behaviors to substantiate how you feel about someone. When we do something to hurt another, we end up hurting ourselves. In unknown ways, we help ourselves out when we do the right thing regarding others.

There are always going to be times we slip up or when our words of processing turn into words of criticism, but being consistent in our endeavors for personal peace will be the key. Practicing personal peace habits is similar to physical exercise: the more we do it, the better we feel, the more confident we become and the stronger we are. These qualities are helpful to have when we are living to make a difference and pursue every possibility presented to us.

One man cannot hold another man down in
the ditch without remaining down in the ditch with him.
Booker T. Washington

DECEMBER 12
BE THINKING

Another way to cultivate personal peace is to believe the best of others. Have you ever seen an associate do something or heard them say words that were irritating to you and you judged this behavior as rude, unintelligent or wrong? If so, did you speak with the person about it to understand their side, or do you continue to think negative thoughts of him or her?

Those negative thoughts spill out into your interactions with that person directly and indirectly. Those thoughts can also elevate you in your mind to where you believe you are better than that person when, actually, your negative thoughts are pulling you down to the level you are imagining that associate to be.

If you don't have peace, one reason could be negative thoughts and views you hold of others. We can judge an act to be inappropriate or wrong without judging the person to be. We can also help our peace by having an attitude of helpfulness (How can I help this person?) rather than one of criticism (Can you believe her?).

If it isn't possible to talk with the person about your thoughts of him or her, do your best to replace the negative ones with neutral ones. Ask yourself: Why do I care? How did their actions affect me? If someone were frustrated with you, would you want her to seek to understand your side or to continue to think negative thoughts of you? If it is possible to talk with them but just not good timing yet, wait for the good time because timing is a key component of fruitful interactions.

Thinking well of people frees us up to think positive thoughts and not waste our energy on gossip—even if it is only internal gossip with ourselves. Don't waste a minute of your mind-space and energy on the negative. Remember, what we dwell on is what we become.

A favorite message from The Last Lecture is to assume the best of people and that if you wait long enough, people will surprise and impress you. Our personal peace is more important than grudges or negative thoughts and mindsets. Positive possibilities thrive with positive perspectives. Look to help another with loving correction rather than hurt with harboring judgment or jealousy.

When we judge or criticize another person, it says nothing about that person;
it merely says something about our own need to be critical.
Unknown

DECEMBER 13
BE FORGIVING

...of yourself and others. Personal peace might not be possible without forgiveness, particularly of yourself. If you still haven't forgiven yourself or another, this is a great time to do so. If you need help, get it. Life is too short to spend the time you could be using to explore possibilities in a wasteful way such as emotionally beating up yourself or another.

When we forgive others and ourselves, we also get a step closer to eliminating perfectionism. We are not perfect and cannot expect to be. We are going to mess up—say the wrong thing, do the wrong thing, believe the wrong thing. To expect otherwise is setting everyone up for failure. No matter how many excellent choices we make in a week, we seem to dwell on the two poor choices we made. Forgive yourself, make amends if necessary and move on.

One thing to keep in mind is the importance of responsibility in the forgiveness process, fully looking for and accepting your part in the problem. If you don't, you will likely repeat the issue and not know why.

When we seek the truth, we are seeking possibilities. And when we get to the truth, peace probably isn't too far behind.

To forgive is to set a prisoner free and discover the prisoner was you.
Unknown

DECEMBER 14
BE OF POSSIBILITIES

As wonderful as the Christmas season is, we often have so many expectations that we can easily lose sight of the simple wonders around us. We are thanking clients, maneuvering crowded stores and trying to meet others' expectations of holiday experiences while also addressing the fears the holidays sometimes bring. So these are a few simple reminders to let us experience all the joy and gratitude we can...

1. Remember we are not responsible for someone else's happiness and no one else is responsible for ours. We want to give and receive kindness, laughter, love, and the gifts that each of us brings to a relationship, but ultimately we are responsible for our own happiness. If we look to someone else to fix our happiness—or our aloneness or our relationships—we will be disappointed because we are the only person who can do that. Others can help, but ultimately we have to make the better choices in thought and action. (For instance, when we are needy, we need to reach out to an appropriate person rather than withdraw or whine.)

2. Remind yourself of the attitude you want and the purpose of the holidays. When someone asks how you are and you are stressed out, respond "gratefully busy" or "joyfully stressed." We can be honest and still use our words to either lift us up or bring us down.

3. Send gratitude notes or phone calls. Make a point of letting your words, actions and intentions overflow with genuine gratitude. When you do, they will automatically be accompanied by love and kindness and all the good this season represents.

It is easy to lose sight of the wonderfulness of the season because of the pressure it puts on us. Love your way through it and you will experience possibilities in a whole new way. If you need professional help to get through the holidays, get it. From a decorator to a clergyman to a therapist, there are people who want you to experience new possibilities you didn't know were possible.

How we perceive a situation and how we react to it is the basis of our stress. If you focus on the negative in any situation, you can expect high stress levels. However, if you try and see the good in the situation, your stress levels will greatly diminish.

Catherine Pulsifer

DECEMBER 15
BE ENJOYING

The holidays can bring out the best as well as the not-so-good.

The expectation for a "perfect" day can exhaust us, and we find ourselves controlling rather than enjoying. Expectations of our community and family can leave us feeling lonely rather than fulfilled.

Expect the best, but as always, if something unpleasant or hurtful occurs, first, look at your part in it. Second, look for the lesson (hint: the lesson will not involve negative things such as "I learned to never talk to her again!")

Third, rewind and start over, correct your words or intention in some way. Ask for or give forgiveness.

And, always, be grateful. Gratitude is the easiest way to change our happiness, our attitude and, somehow, a situation.

Remember, we choose our responses, attitudes, thoughts and intentions. Make them grateful ones and your holiday will be, too.

Gratitude unlocks the fullness of life. It turns what we have into enough, and more. It turns denial into acceptance, chaos to order, confusion to clarity. It can turn a meal into a feast, a house into a home, a stranger into a friend. Gratitude makes sense of our past, brings peace for today, and creates a vision for tomorrow.
Melody Beattie

Life is 10% what happens to you and 90% your reaction to it.
Charles Swindoll

DECEMBER 16
BE UNSTRESSED

Are you waking up excited about the day and Christmas or Hanukkah or are you stressed about your schedule and the drama that can accompany this time of year? We work on schedules and pay so much attention to our "to do" lists that we can forget the emotional difficulties that could be contributing to stress.

Do you have anything you dread this time of year?

Seeing a certain relative. Not being with family. Being with family. Wanting something in your life that isn't here yet. Wishing things were different

If we are dreading something, then likely we have experienced this situation in the past—more than once. In fact, the dreading may have become a habit or default setting. So what if we turned it around? What if you consciously said—I am going to embrace this situation rather than feel sorry for myself or anxious about it.

In other words, we could be producing the anxiety ourselves and, if so, we can also work to eliminate it. We may not be able to completely dispel it, but awareness is a solid start.

For example, we want to be with people we love, but we need to love them enough to not make them feel guilty if they aren't with us. To make someone feel bad that they are not with us rather than allowing them to fully enjoy where they are is selfish, isn't it? Or another example: We may wish a situation were different, but instead of fighting it, what if we accepted it for what it is and allow ourselves to look for joy instead of experience dread?

Decide this year to enjoy where you are and not play into any part of a pity or victim mentality. If you catch yourself wanting to blame and wanting anyone to feel bad rather than feel joyful, pay attention to that signal and decide how you want the holidays to be for you and others. We are responsible for our happiness, and the tiniest shifts can turn a moment from dread to joy.

If you need help, get it, because drama permeates everything and you have too much to accomplish and enjoy to be spending time in a habit of dread. When we let go of how we want something to be and allow it to become what it is supposed to, possibilities show up we haven't seen before.

What screws us up most in life is the picture in our head of how it is supposed to be.
Unknown

DECEMBER 17

BE CALM

Have you ever noticed the less we like to see the truth, the more of a drama person we are? (In life or just a situation.)

In a recent conversation with a reader about drama, the reader wisely said that drama is anger and sadness. And sadly, we often want to stay there rather than seek another way.

Merriam Webster's defines a drama queen as:

A person given to often excessively emotional performances or reactions.

When you see persons (or yourself) putting on an emotional performance with tears, yelling or anger, stop to consider what they are angry and sad about. And really get to the truth of the drama, not just the way they want you to see the problem. (Particularly get to the truth if you are the one you see being the drama queen or king.)

There can be many truths, but remember, what we appear to be mad about is rarely what we are really angry about. Many times we are angry about "symptoms" in a situation and don't want to get to the source—we would rather just be angry—but once we get to the truth, peace begins.

We may be choosing to be a drama person because

1. We want to control the person or situation.
2. We don't like the choices we have made and don't want to admit it.
3. We want others to see our suffering (but don't care about others' suffering).
4. We don't want to take responsibility or admit the truth and would rather blame.
5. We are angry, jealous or insecure and pride won't let us admit it.
6. We don't know there is another way to handle a situation.
7. We like being the victim and take things as a personal attack to support victimhood.
8. We like the power we perceive drama gives us. We are seeking attention.

We may choose drama for many reasons. These are just some ideas to make us all think about our own interactions and choices. When we choose drama, we often want to be angry and avoid the truth. A good standard to deter energy-wasting drama is to seek the truth. When we seek the truth, we may find we are drama-free and possibilities-rich.

To see your drama clearly is to be liberated from it.
Ken S. Keyes, Jr.

DECEMBER 18
BE JOYFUL

...and drama-less. A reader shared this story of what is possible when we become aware of our attitude habits and begin to choose our attitude instead.

"Anger and sadness are habits. I know this because I spent my life sad and angry—it was a habit.

"It was the way I had been taught to feel and the way I had felt for so long. My go-to emotions were fear and sadness. I was always injured and hurt by something or someone and had a habit of being the victim.

"It wasn't until I started to closely observe the habits of happy people that I began to understand that I could make a habit out of being happy, I could react to everything with a feeling of joy and understanding. My greatest teacher was a co-worker who knew everyone she met by name, remembered important things about their family, pets and hobbies, and greeted everyone with pure enthusiasm when she encountered them. I started to emulate her and it forever changed me."

This reader realized she didn't want to live a life of drama—full of anger and sadness—anymore. She wanted something different, so she built different habits.

We all make mistakes. We can easily get caught up in an old habit of gossip, fear, judgment or pride even when we know better. Forgive yourself, forgive the people you feel hurt by and move on.

Each moment is a new opportunity to rewind and create the habits and lives we want.

Attitudes are nothing more than habits of thoughts, and habits can be acquired.
An action repeated becomes an attitude realized.
Paul Meyer

DECEMBER 19
BE SOLUTION-FOCUSED

When we find ourselves in the middle of a drama situation, we can work to change it if we choose to and are prepared. Sometimes we are completely ill-prepared and find ourselves sitting with our mouth agape, confused about what is happening; we might become angry in return and when it is over, wish we had behaved differently.

Be prepared with how you want to react when drama hits. Some ideas are:

1. Stop and assess how you feel, then say it.

   I am confused, can we start over?

   I am frustrated.

   I am embarrassed.

   I am angry and working through it.

2. Ask yourself, "Is it true?"

   If it is, agree with them and say "Yes." or "That could be true."

   If it isn't true, calmly say "That isn't true." or "I don't know yet, but will let you know when I do."

   If they want to get to the truth, they will work with you to get there. If they just want to be angry or distort the truth, then likely nothing you say will make a difference.

3. De-escalate your voice. Stay calm. Watch your body language (eye-rolling, dismissive gestures). Stay focused on the other person's words, not their emotions.

4. Focus on a solution instead of the problem.

There are times that drama is control or bullying dressed in tears, withdrawal or yelling. There are other times people just need to get things out. We can all fall into drama behavior occasionally; we just want to make sure it isn't a habit.

When on the receiving end, we want to be prepared to calmly and kindly handle the situation rather than respond in kind. The more we handle today, the less we carry into our tomorrows.

If you don't manage your emotions, then your emotions will manage you.
Doc Childre and Deborah Rozman

DECEMBER 20
BE UNATTACHED

A woman I met on a plane relayed that in handling disputes, she will bring two people into her office at separate times and they will have two completely different versions of the same conflict. She said they lived the same experience, but their attachment to their individual perspectives was so powerful, that initially they couldn't see anything but their own story.

Our perspectives are all different, based on our wounds, fears and desires. And often, when in a conflict, we leave out our own part in the problem. Rarely do we add, "I did this and wished I had responded differently," or "I contributed to the problem this way." Most of the time we only blame and say, "He or she did…"

There are others who may be able to contribute their views on the problem, but often they have come into the issue in the middle of the story and fill in the gaps with their own version, based on what they want to believe or on their own personal past experiences.

Our different perspectives, as well as allowing our brains to fill in the gaps rather than seek the truth, are perfect ingredients for drama. Throw in using emotions rather than truth to form opinions and the perfect storm begins.

1. What is the truth?
2. What part did you play in the problem?
3. What was your intention?
4. What is your intention?

Is your intention to work this out or to be right? Are you choosing to be offended? Is your intention to work it out or hurt the other person? Are you allowing pride, anger or unforgiveness to make your choices for you? That is not a productive choice, and while it may be satisfying in the short-term, it is not in the long-term. Are you making assumptions around the situation or asking questions to seek the truth?

Be honest with yourself and less attached to your perspective and you will be able to work through problems quicker and easier with less drama and more possibilities

There are three truths: my truth, your truth and the truth.
Chinese Proverb

DECEMBER 21
BE HABIT-FORMING

The reader who changed her habits thus, changing her life from one of drama to one of productivity and joy, continued her story...

"I rarely purchase gossip magazines but a headline about losing weight caught my eye and I bought it at the checkout line like they want you to do. I got home and in five minutes realized there was nothing about weight loss but a lot about drama. So I tossed it on the counter and was horrified to later find my eight-year-old daughter interestedly flipping through the magazine.

"I was disturbed because I do not want her to find drama attractive.

"I am trying to teach her that when her feelings are hurt, she is going to say, "That hurt my feelings" and walk away or utilize another solution-oriented behavior instead of revenge or insults.

"Drama is a habit. What's her habit going to be? When kids start to socialize, they start to cultivate drama, and they are learning it from us. I want to give her something else, something good for her foundation.

"I didn't want children because I have suffered from depression and, since it is hereditary, was afraid of passing it on. But then I realized depression isn't just genetics, that it has so much to do with habits, too.

"I want to give her something else. Something great."

If you have seen yourself living sad and angry and you don't want to be there anymore, it may just be a bad habit that needs changing. As this reader did, making simple changes to your attitude and actions may make the difference. If you need help, get it.

Drama takes energy you could be using to create something great in your business and in your home. What are you creating? What are you teaching your kids to create?

Habits are safer than rules; you don't have to watch them.
And you don't have to keep them, either. They keep you.
Frank Crane

DECEMBER 22
BE DRAMA-LESS

I hate you.

You ruined my life.

I'll never be able to...

It's all your fault.

You did this.

These are just a few drama phrases you may hear, out of your own mouth or someone else's. When you hear them out of your own mouth, stop and ask yourself, "What is the truth?" The truth is: You may not like your friend or family member much right now, but you probably won't hate them forever. And if you did, you would be choosing to. A more productive response would be, "I am really angry with you right now, but I still love you." Or "I am angry and fearful right now; I need to process this."

In most cases, no one ruined your life. They may have caused you pain or difficulties you don't think you should have to endure, but they haven't ruined anything except what you feel you deserve. We are the ones who will choose whether we let something ruin our lives. As painful as experiences in life are, we decide how we let them affect us, whether we will expand, learn and grow or contract and be angry. We can either be bitter or better; it's our choice. A more productive statement might be: "I am angry and hurting. I am not willing to work through this yet. I don't want to forgive you yet."

"It's your fault.... You did this." It is not all the other person's fault. Remember, if we are adults we all have a part in something, and if we don't own our part, we will likely keep living that issue and not know why. Owning our part is a good idea for moving forward. And contrary to what we think, when we own our part, we feel better. Blaming statements don't get us very far; when we find ourselves saying them frequently, we need to examine our intentions and our willingness to be accountable.

There are many painful things in life, and our choices in action and reaction, thought, word and intention either move us toward healing or toward more pain.

Our words are the overflow of what is in our hearts. So when you hear yourself speaking drama words, stop and make a change. The best place to start is in thought and intention. Examine your intentions and thoughts and see if they are moving toward healing and forgiveness or if they involve anger, blame, resentment, and deserving something—from the corner office to being happy.

When we get to a point that we choose to stay with anger rather than move to forgiveness, we need to realize that *we* could be responsible for our pain, not the person we are blaming. Make healing choices and be happy.

Make the choice to leave old wounds in the old year and have a new beginning for the New Year. If you need help from a counselor, coach, clergyman or therapist, get it. Drama is a good habit for all of us to leave behind.

A little rudeness and disrespect can elevate a meaningless
interaction to a battle of wills and add drama to an otherwise dull day.
Bill Watterson

DECEMBER 23
BE JOYOUS

If we are going to leave drama behind and take a new habit into the New Year with us, leaving entitlement behind and picking up truth is a good start.

When we hear ourselves say "I deserve..." or in a conversation with another "you deserve..." we may want to examine our beliefs. "Deserve" can be an innocuous word or it can signal entitlement—that you think you are entitled to something: new car, being married, promotion, an easy life, what you want, how you want it.

"Deserve" can also be used to signal unforgiveness and unkindness as in, "You deserve to be miserable," or "You got what you deserved!"

If we all got what we "deserved," over the long-term we would likely be left with nothing (remember none of us is perfect), so we may be better served to be grateful for what we have as we move toward what we want.

Feeling entitled can leave us with a self-serving, self-pitying, self-centered, selfish attitude. While that sounds normal, it doesn't make us happy. If we view our jobs, relationships and marriages as privileges rather than entitlements we will likely be more nurturing, caring and grateful toward them rather than run the risk of becoming complacent in them.

Don't get me wrong; joys, successes and wonders are available for us all, but we can miss them or lose them when we begin to take them for granted instead of taking care of them.

Entitlement makes us feel more important than someone else. It brings a false sense of our importance, can get in the way of our happiness and is a good start to drama. Begin today to leave it in the old year. Choose to feel grateful rather than entitled and feel joy start to fill the space that anger and frustration once did.

Whatever joy there is in the world arises from wishing for others' happiness.
Whatever suffering there is in the world
Arises from wishing for your own happiness.
Shantideva

There is no man so good that if he placed all his actions and thought under the
scrutiny of the laws, he would not deserve hanging ten times in his life.
Michel de Montaigne

DECEMBER 24
BE CURIOUS

We can be angry with people and still love them. We can disagree with someone and still communicate with them.

But when drama comes into the picture, if we disagree with someone, we stop talking to that person. Drama can be dispelled if we will seek to understand the other person with the intention of truth and understanding.

We can disagree with someone and still respect and be kind to him or her. We aren't going to agree with everyone. And while disagreeing can bring healthy conversation and growth, more often than not, we let disagreement bring anger and frustration. Don't let pride and fear keep you in anger.

When we disagree, we can say, "I don't agree with that because..." and move on. More often than not, when we disagree with someone, we shut them down and don't want to get to the truth.

Part of life is lesson-learning and, as much as we would like to avoid it, many lessons come in the form of disagreements. While it is affirming and comforting to be in conversation with people who think as we do, it can be interesting to learn new perspectives from those who don't. Just because something is our opinion doesn't mean it is right, so it is good to listen to opposing views with curiosity for growth.

Keep in mind that when we want to hold a grudge or get emotional in the discussion, there is something else going on. Until we dig far enough to locate the source of that "something else" we will continue to invite drama in and keep peace and possibilities out.

Discuss with curiosity and seeking to understand rather than judgment or anger and you never know what wonders will follow.

When I disagree with a rational man, I let reality be our final arbiter; if I am right, he will learn; if I am wrong, I will; one of us will win, but both will profit.
Ayn Rand

DECEMBER 25
BE BELIEVING

We see "Believe" signs everywhere this time of year. And when we see the word, we either get a little spark of excitement for what is possible or we get a little cynical, thinking that believing doesn't work because our dreams haven't come true. Our businesses aren't where we want them to be; we have broken relationships; we feel unappreciated and unsupported. Things are messy and we don't know how we got here.

We need to be reminded that possibilities are more prevalent when we believe in the positive than when we don't. Sports teams who believe they will win seem to have a stronger chance than those who don't. People who believe there is good in the world seem to see more of it than those who don't.

As we prepare for a new year and focus on new goals or previous ones we haven't been serious about, we need to know what we believe. Do we believe we can do it or not? Every one of us has areas in our lives we have confidence in and those we are beginning to doubt. We can have attained goals in our business lives and still wondering why we haven't in our personal lives. Or we can be living our desires in our personal lives and still struggling in areas of our businesses.

Are you meeting your professional goals but feel unsuccessful in relationships? Are you satisfied with your personal life but feel inadequate in areas of your business? First, remember there will always be problems and difficulties because we are imperfect beings. But just because there will be problems doesn't mean we should just forget our goals, dreams and desires. Don't give up on what you know in your heart is possible.

Believe that broken relationships can be restored. Believe that you can forgive yourself and others. Believe that you can achieve your professional goals. Believe that you are good enough.

What do you really want? It is time to refocus and believe again for our goals and dreams that have been slow in coming. Look at the facts, make changes in action where they need to be made and believe again in positive possibilities. Once you know what you want, the first step to getting it is to believe it is possible.

It is not the mountain we conquer but ourselves.
Edmund Hillary

DECEMBER 26
BE ANTICIPATING

Believe something(s) wonderful will happen today.

Believe that someone who has intentionally not talked to you in months or years will contact you.

That you will meet your production goal.

That you will get the rock star parking spot.

That the misunderstanding will be resolved.

Maybe you will find the perfect gift.

Wonderful can even be as simple as you forgot to buy cream but you have just enough for your coffee in the morning.

As you are expecting wonderful, remember that others may be, too. So when it is in your power to give some wonderful today, do.

Send the donation to the food bank that may be overflowing with people who are cold and without work.

Praise the person you are hard on.

Give forgiveness to the person you don't want to forgive.

Wonderful doesn't have to be big. It just has to be received and recognized.

Recognize the wonderful things and people and blessings in your life by being grateful and giving gratitude in a multitude of ways—from "paying it forward" to praising to just being complete in the moment and feeling the abundance.

Recognizing the wonderful in our lives helps us see the possibilities, too.

There are only two ways to live your life. One is as though nothing is a miracle.
The other is as though everything is a miracle.
Albert Einstein

DECEMBER 27
BE DIRECTIONAL

Our feelings are real and active in our lives. They strongly contribute to our actions and our levels of joy or pain. While they are real and wonderful and remind us we are alive, they are somewhat like a racehorse: they are powerful and beautiful when controlled, but just as powerfully dangerous when they throw their rider and run around the track out of control.

When we have an awareness of reality and a desire to seek truth, our emotions can be great fun. They are gauges of what we believe and signals for changes we need to make in our lives. But when we lose sight of seeking the truth and let our fear, anger or jealousy dictate our actions and thoughts, then our emotions can be damaging to ourselves and others. We lose sight of our finish-line goal and run around without an intentional purpose except maybe to create chaos and hurt others.

Our feelings can be deceptive. We can feel fat and actually be unhealthily thin.

We can feel unattractive and actually be super-model material.

We can feel unintelligent and have a PhD.

We can feel "right" in our anger, grudge or resentment and be wrong.

Letting fear and negative emotions guide our lives rather than truth and choosing forgiveness can leave us like that racehorse running wildly around the track without guidance and purpose. The result can lead us and others to get off-track instead of to where we want to go.

We are all going to say and do things because of our feelings that we want to take back. We are going to let fear make decisions for us we wish we could take back because we are imperfect—we are wonderfully imperfect people.

When we realize we are letting negative emotions rather than truth and kindness make decisions for us, the sooner we rein in those emotions and let our finish-line goal be our direction, the less time, energy and love we waste.

What are you believing about yourself and others today?

Positive and negative are directions. Which direction do you choose?
Unknown

DECEMBER 28
BE GIFTING

You are taking care of clients and family and have likely been in a rush these last few weeks. You may be a little weary. You might be beating yourself up for not having cards mailed or gifts purchased or not having contacted enough clients or been good enough somewhere about something.

Today, take care of you and give yourself a gift. A gift of time or of relaxation. Maybe the gift of appreciating yourself or learning to receive and ask for help. Perhaps just the gift of a nap.

Contributing to others is where we find our greatest joy. In order to contribute well over time, we must take care of ourselves and give attention to our needs.

The ultimate lesson all of us have to learn is unconditional love,
which includes not only others but ourselves as well.
Elisabeth Kubler-Ross

DECEMBER 29
BE FULL

We as a society have many accepted norms. As we close out a year and look to leave some habits behind, we'll examine a few over the next few days—not to judge them right or wrong, but to know if we want society's norms to be concepts that shape our thinking or if we want to explore new ones.

For example: More is better. The world has the idea that bigger is better—and sometimes it is—but sometimes it is just bigger. If you have a large family, a large vehicle is likely better so you can all travel together. But if you live alone, a super large house or van might be better or it might just be bigger.

Remember our elders saying, "You can have it if you will eat it." Maybe that is a better motto for us to think about: we can have it if we will love it and appreciate it rather than just going by the idea that bigger is better and super-sizing everything we purchase out of habit. The portions served at restaurants are big, but normally not better for us. Can I and do I really want to eat it all? Sometimes yes, sometimes no. 4000 clients is more, but maybe not better for you overall. Can you effectively service 4000 clients by yourself? Maybe you can or maybe you want to scale down or possibly build a team.

People who live in countries where homes or cars normally are not as spacious usually come to the conclusion they don't need as much as they thought they did to live joyfully. Too much "stuff" can actually weigh us down rather than lift us up. What is "too much" is relative and varies at different times of our lives. Six-hundred pairs of shoes might be just right for you right now, but in five years, that number could feel like a few too many.

What do I need in order to be excellent at my job and roles? What do I need to feel full? What will I use? What do I need in order to make a difference for others—to use my gifts and talents and live joyfully?

When something starts to pull you down rather than enhance your life, that could be a signal you need a change—either in action or just attitude. It could be you want to downsize or it could be you just need to fall in love again with what you have. Sometimes more is better and sometimes not. The point is to make decisions based on what truly enhances our lives and businesses and, for that, awareness is a good first step.

The road to excess leads to the palace of wisdom...
for we never know what is enough until we know what is more than enough.
William Blake

DECEMBER 30
BE VALUING

Multi-tasking has widely been accepted as a special talent. People take pride in being able to do several tasks at one time. The problem with that is that we likely don't do any of those tasks very well, except maybe the ones that don't matter. We can check off our list as accomplished, but were the tasks really done?

If we are sharpening our pencil, reading something on the computer screen and writing a memo to someone in our office while we are talking on the phone, most likely the only thing that will be done well is the pencil sharpened. And even that might not be the case.

The person on the other end of the phone can tell if they have our attention or not; even if we fill in the gaps of what we miss in the conversation correctly, they will still feel unimportant. Possibly the person you are writing instructions to may eventually be frustrated because they need clarification they aren't getting and unless you were writing down your coffee order, you will likely have to take time later to give instructions again after you get done with your call.

A reader shared that when she would do another task while her child was trying to tell her about her day at school, her child would say, "Mom, stop and look at me."

There are going to be times that we must do more than one thing, but the more we can stop and "see" people—from clients to co-workers—the stronger and more satisfying our relationships will be.

When we give focus to a task, we are more likely to accomplish it well. Test-out focused work for one day. You will probably find you get more done in a less stressed, more satisfying and time-efficient way.

A weakness of all human beings is trying to do too many things at once.
Henry Ford

DECEMBER 31
BE BEAUTIFUL

Something else we may want to examine is our concept of beauty. Our culture says that beauty is symmetrical, shiny and "perfect." But that can be exhausting because we aren't perfect people. We are physically and emotionally flawed and to pretend otherwise can wear us out.

I am not saying that the art, people and things our society says are beautiful are not beautiful. I am saying that what if some of the things we think aren't beautiful really are beautiful, too? Like the grandmother who is wrinkled and weary but gets up with a smile to feed her three grandchildren she is raising. Or the really crabby client we haven't taken the time to seek to understand.

What if beauty is found in the truth, or in taking the time to stop and "see" people or things? What if beauty is experienced in the time and heart given to something?

Often in our busy work schedules and our hectic lives, we miss the beauty around us because we don't take the time to get to the truth or to really see someone or to appreciate the effort and passion given to a project—we are too busy for that. But since beauty gives us a little boost of happy and good energy, taking the time to notice it might be less of a luxury and more of a good daily practice than we think.

Today, take the time to see past the obvious and look for the beauty. You will likely find new and beautiful possibilities.

In every man's heart there is a secret nerve
that answers to the vibrations of beauty.
Christopher Morley

Everything has beauty, but not everyone sees it.
Confucius

CPSIA information can be obtained at www.ICGtesting.com
Printed in the USA
BVOW08s0146111013

333430BV00001BA/1/P

9 780989 169455